*Stay or Leave*

*Discover What You're Best At (audio cassette)*

*Discover What You're Best At (computer software)*

# DISCOVER WHAT YOU'RE BEST AT

NEWLY REVISED and Updated for the 1990s

## The National Career Aptitude System and Career Directory

## BARRY and LINDA GALE

A FIRESIDE BOOK
Published by Simon & Schuster
New York    London    Toronto    Sydney    Tokyo    Singapore

**Fireside**

Rockefeller Center
1230 Avenue of the Americas
New York, New York 10020

FIRESIDE and colophon are registered trademarks
of Simon & Schuster Inc.

Designed by Irving Perkins and Assoc.
Manufactured in the United States of America

9   10   8

Library of Congress Cataloging in Publication Data

Gale, Barry
Discover what you're best at: the national career aptitude system and career directory/Barry and Linda Gale.—
Newly rev. ed.
p.   cm.
"A Fireside book."
1. Occupational aptitude tests.   2. Occupations.   3. Vocational guidance.   I. Gale, Linda.   II. Title
HF5381.7.G34   1990
331.7′02—dc20                                                                                          90-9756
CIP

ISBN 0-671-69589-4

*Dedicated to:*
*Valerie, Adam, and Scott.*
*You've done it in the past,*
*You're doing it now.*
*The future is yours.*

# Contents

# Preface

Since 1982, when the first edition of *Discover What You're Best At* was published, hundreds of thousands of people have benefited from the National Career Aptitude System, and many of these readers have written to us to report on their success. Whenever possible, we have tried to incorporate their suggestions as we continue to test and retest the efficiency of the system. The new revised edition of *Discover What You're Best At* thus builds on the success of the first edition, but its basic intention remains unchanged. The book goes beyond all other career books that merely identify your *interests:* instead our system actually helps you to discover your *abilities.* It is unique because it contains a self-administered and self-scored career-aptitude evaluation system designed to help you identify your career strengths, set realistic career goals, and familiarize yourself with over a thousand different careers. *Discover What You're Best At* contains an objective, time-and-money-saving system that will make you more effective in selecting the right career or job.

Over the last twenty years we have traveled about 75,000 miles each year to lecture, to explain the National Career Aptitude System (NCAS), and to administer the test for the thousands of clients who have used our career-selection program. We subscribe to the philosophy that you must know what you are capable of doing before you know where you are going with your career, lest you end up going nowhere at all. We believe that knowledge of your aptitudes is the single most important factor in selecting your career.

And most people are not aware of their aptitudes, their worth or true potentials. Some place unfair limits on their capabilities as they continuously replay a mental tape that says, "I'm probably not good enough." Others, just as unrealistic, think they can accomplish everything just because they say they want to. This book will rectify both of these problems.

The NCAS is based on principles similar to those endorsed by state and national vocational-guidance associations, as well as other aptitude and screening tests used by schools, business, industry, and professional licensing examiners. It goes farther than those systems, however, by being a much more complete career guide: as well as the tests, we have incorporated scoring techniques that actually point you to a specific group or cluster of careers, along with a detailed description of each career in those clusters.

In preparing the new edition we are grateful to the many people from all over the country who have written to suggest that their relatively unknown job title be added to the Career Directory and Career Clusters. During the decade of the eighties new technologies have emerged and spawned new job titles. We have added as many as possible, and you now have access to an expanded Career Directory that contains more than 1,100 career descriptions.

As times change, requirements for entrance to certain jobs also change. For example in the past a bachelor's degree in library science was sufficient for most library positions. Today nearly all librarians need a graduate degree. Such changes in educational requirements are reflected in this revised and updated edition.

The adage "If it ain't broke, don't fix it" certainly applies to the six aptitude tests and scoring system. Based upon more than 300,000 satisfied readers and clients, only minor adjustments and slight fine-tuning were needed to bring you this invaluable tool for the nineties. One of these adjustments was to raise the upper limit of the highest scores so that no matter how great your abilities in a specific area, you can always obtain a precise and accurate measurement.

Whether you are contemplating entering the job market for the first time or considering a career or job change, *Discover What You're Best At* should help you focus on a career that is right for you—one that will be every bit as fulfilling and rewarding as you deserve.

We wish you much success.

*—Barry and Linda Gale*

# THE NATIONAL CAREER APTITUDE SYSTEM

## WHY THE NCAS IS FOR YOU

We know you're reading this book because you're concerned about your future: you want to find the *right* job, and you know that it must happen by careful choice, not haphazardly by chance.

Perhaps you've recently completed your formal education and now are seeking your first or second job. All too often we find that young adults make these initial selections on a wing and a prayer and with little understanding of their potential. Well, this book will remedy that.

Perhaps you're reentering the work force after several years as a homemaker. You need to translate your worthy experiences into salable skills needed in today's marketplace. Knowledge of your strengths and capabilities will direct you toward a career that is right for you.

Perhaps you're contemplating a job change because your current position inhibits your personal growth, limits your ability to do your best, or does not provide sufficient recognition or rewards.

Perhaps you're one of the five out of six who finds yourself in your job by accident. That's right, not by thorough career planning but by accident. You somehow stumbled into it. And now you know you're in the wrong job.

Whatever your present situation, you know that the decision you're about to make is too important to leave to luck, a whim, or what your best friend thinks you should do. You'll find a professional system in this book that really *works;* one that will give you a new, decisive, and exciting way to clearly view yourself, to determine your career strengths and to set appropriate goals. You'll have a much better sense of which job options are available to you and which careers are apt to be the most satisfying and rewarding. After using our system you will be well on the way to making one of the best decisions of your life—choosing the career that is most likely to guarantee your success. We want to help you *select* a career rather than settle for one.

## YOUR VALUE SYSTEM DETERMINES YOUR JOB SATISFACTION

To help you identify what is currently important to you, here's a list of commonly held job-related values. As you look them over, you'll discover that you instinctively feel some are more important than others for your overall job satisfaction.

Accumulating large amounts of money

Being in an environment that involves frequent change

Being involved in work that contributes to the advancement of moral standards I feel are important

Belonging to an organization or group

Creatively coming up with new ideas

Having day-to-day contact with the public

Having the independence to decide for myself what needs to be done

Helping other people directly

Performing a job that requires physical strength and stamina

Performing similar tasks each day

Receiving considerable recognition for my work

Setting my own time schedule

Taking extended vacations

Taking risks as part of my work

Traveling much of my working time

Working as a member of a team

Working primarily by myself

Working primarily for myself

Working where I can pursue the leisure activities I enjoy most

Working where my abilities are pitted against those of others

Working where there is an adequate salary and considerable security

Working with definite deadlines

Whatever career satisfaction means to you, the National Career Aptitude System (NCAS) is designed to help you find success by putting you on the right job track. Think of this book as a unique career system, one that will help you *Discover What You're Best At.*

## DO NEW TECHNOLOGIES CREATE NEW JOBS?

Neuropharmacologist, Biomedical-Engineering Technician, Laser-Beam Color-Scanner, Cardiovascular Perfusionist, Electro-Optics Physicist.

These job titles describe occupations that have emerged or may emerge as a result of changing technologies. Will many of us engage in new occupations in the near future, or is the change more subtle than that?

The introduction of a new technology is often accompanied by predictions of major changes in the workplace. In the past decade microcomputers were said to herald a new occupation: word processor. Yet as it turned out, word-processing software became a new tool for secretaries and other professionals. Lasers were expected to create a multitude of laser-technician jobs, but for the most part they simply became tools for welders, surgeons, and others.

Certainly some new occupations have arisen, but more often than not new technologies result in new tools for existing jobs. Virtually every occupation is changing, and what is critical is the adaptation to new skill requirements among all workers. Looking back over the past eight years since *Discover What You're Best At* was first published, most workers have seen changes in their jobs that resulted from technology. For example the job of researcher has changed from processing scant data in a cumbersome way—punch cards and mainframes—to processing reams of data with nearly immediate turnaround on a microcomputer. The task is no longer finding a little information on a subject; it is sifting through too much information to pull out what is pertinent.

Other people have seen the impact of new technology on managing retail inventory, diagnosing malfunctions in an auto engine, and improving methods of quality control, to name just a few examples. Although we can see technology's impact upon our work, our job title remains the same.

The primary lesson is that the work of the future will involve the continued acquisition of new skills. The question is what types of skills will these be?

Let's briefly look at the nature of skills needed in the emerging economy. Academic or technical skills immediately come to mind. While it is true that economists, engineers, physicians, and astronomers need much specialized training, basic literacy and numerical facility are now needed almost everywhere. Yet academic skills are only some of the skills needed. Personal-management skills are also vital today. Tardiness, absenteeism, or lack of basic grooming are handicaps in any job. Freedom from substance abuse as well as personal integrity and honesty, are rated as critical qualifications by nearly all employers. In many companies and organizations, retrenching has eliminated many layers of supervision and raised the value of personal initiative, responsibility, and creativity. The self-starter within an organization is desired more than ever before. But we do not work alone.

Teamwork skills are vital. Teamwork requires high levels of communication, coordination, and cooperation. Think about it and you'll most likely agree: Recent high school and college graduates are least prepared in this area. Our schools grade on individual performance. At work today you are graded in large part on your team's success.

## APTITUDES VS. INTERESTS

The NCAS is a complete program for evaluating your job potential and for using that evaluation to point yourself toward the career in which you will be most likely to succeed. Now, of course there are plenty of books and tests geared toward career planning. Some probe your personality; others evaluate your general intelligence; still others examine your attitudes and values; some survey your interests. A confusing array to be sure.

When we first mention career tests at our seminars, we usually hear, "A career test? Oh, I took one of those and it told me to be a forest ranger because I *like* to work outdoors," or "That sounds like the one I took years ago. It told me to be a psychiatrist because I *liked* to work with people."

It's possible that you have had a similar experience. Well, what you most likely had was a *career-interest inventory* and not a *career-aptitude test.* They are commonly confused.

The NCAS measures your *aptitudes*—what you are capable of doing now and what you will be able to do in the future if given the opportunity to learn. It is *very* different from an interest inventory, which samples what you think you might *like* to do. An interest inventory tends to deal only with the present, too—what you think you might enjoy *now*—and it can't possibly predict whether your interests will stay the same or change as your life experience broadens. So don't choose your career just on the basis of your present interests; they will most likely change.

Another weakness of interest inventories is that they're very subjective, based upon your own image of yourself. This self-perception is often inaccurate and will tend to limit your knowledge of yourself to only those characteristics you want to discover and perceive. But most important, we think, is the fact that interest inventories don't assess your actual ability to learn or perform certain tasks. Unfortunately your interest in a subject doesn't necessarily indicate that you could have a successful career in it. The mere fact that you are interested in something doesn't mean that you will be good at it, much less successful.

Now, our aptitude-testing system not only evaluates how much knowledge you have and the present status of your abilities, it also predicts the career areas in which you are most likely to develop and succeed in the future. And while no aptitude test can tell you what you *must* be, we believe that if you know what your strengths are, you can find advantageous ways to use them; and when you understand your weaknesses you can avoid being trapped by them. Decisions based on this awareness will help you go beyond your present horizon; choices derived from self-understanding will help you realize more nearly your full potential.

Ross, a high school senior who was taking this test when we met him, is a good case in point. During a break in the testing session he approached us to talk about his desire to be a mechanical engineer. As we chatted, it was obvious that he had a pretty good idea of what mechanical engineers do, and he sounded really confident about his ability to handle the courses leading to an engineering degree. We were impressed. But were we in for a surprise! Of the forty-three mechanically oriented questions, Ross answered only four correctly. He ranked near the bottom of the national norm. Another poor showing in the numerical section resulted in a similar low ranking. Obviously these were *not* the results you'd expect of a future mechanical engineer. Later a conversation with his father, a mechanical engineer, revealed that he had expected his son to be

a "chip off the old block" and for years had let his wishes be known. Ross, wanting to please his father, verbalized his father's wishful thinking as if it were his own. After seeing the results of the test and engaging in some further counseling, Ross decided to switch to business, for which his aptitudes were much stronger. We saw him recently, and he is doing well in his studies.

But you can see how Ross might not have fared so well if he had simply followed his expressed interests in selecting a college major.

Of course in planning your career you should consider your personality traits, attitudes, interests, and so on. But the most crucial area is still that of your *aptitudes*. You'll have to discover what you're best at before you can proceed, and that is what this book is going to help you to do.

## HOW WILL YOU BENEFIT

- *Save time:* You can save precious years, in fact, if you use this system to determine your aptitudes before you choose your college program or seek employment by trial and error.
- *Save money:* You may save thousands of dollars by using the NCAS to guide you in selecting the right college or technical-school program. And for the price of this book you will have information otherwise not available to you without an expensive evaluation at a career-testing center and hours of counseling.
- *Understand your strengths:* The NCAS will help you identify and measure your career potential objectively and will show you the areas in which your abilities can best be developed. It will help you discover your capacity for learning new skills and help you realize what you are capable of achieving
- *And your weaknesses:* You will understand your weaknesses so that you will not fall victim to them.
- *Gain encouragement:* The NCAS can supply you with information that may encourage you to change your job and pursue a career in a different direction from the one you now follow, or it may suggest that you continue with your current pursuits. A high-school secretary who took our test says, "My test just affirmed what I felt my directions were going to be. I have thought for a long time I would do well as a guidance counselor. By having something valid saying I am good in what I feel I want, I now have the courage to go ahead in what I want to do. I'm so glad

I took this test. I feel very good about the results." She went on to take night courses at a local college to complete her degree as a counselor.

- *Be able to set appropriate goals:* Preparing for your future means setting appropriate career goals. While it may be true that you want to "do your own thing," you should first find out *what your own thing is.* An employment agency counselor from White Plains, New York, Dianne Kleinmann, asked that her son Paul be tested in his last year of high school. Paul, a bright young man, didn't have any career direction at that time. His testing results indicated considerable strength in business. Several months later we received this note from Ms. Kleinmann: "Your test, and its results and suggestions probably did more to give Paul a career direction than any other influence! Can't wait for my next child to be tested." By the way we recently learned that Paul was an honor student at Northeastern University School of Business Administration and now is an executive salesperson at IBM.

- *Be guided in selecting a career:* Once you know your aptitudes, the Career Clusters will provide you with a realistic base from which you can make an intelligent choice of careers or course of study. A clinical counselor, Carla Adams, from Michigan, writes, "I am much impressed with your test and the system you have developed. Your aptitude approach in assessing career goals and potential is certainly effective. I see many who have grandiose notions of what their career should be, but have no special driving force other than that they heard a certain career was currently providing well-paying employment. Your testing system could alleviate a lot of future disappointment, open new areas of thought, and help me to do my job better."

- *Be opened to new areas:* The Career Clusters and the Career Directory will suggest many opportunities you may not have known exist or realize are within your reach.

## HOW DOES IT WORK?

The NCAS is based on a professionally devised battery of self-administered and self-scored career-aptitude tests that has been in use for the past twenty years. The tests measure your strengths and indicate your weaknesses in the areas of understanding *business* situations, *clerical* speed and accuracy, *logical* reasoning, *mechanical* reasoning, *numerical* concepts and understanding personal and *social* situations. After taking the tests you will score yourself, then use our charts on pages 82–85 to condense what you have learned about yourself into your own Career Cluster (more about Career Clusters on page 81). Once you know your Cluster, you will be able to go through the lists of careers for which your aptitudes are most suited and choose from among those that are most appropriate for your ambition and level, or prospective level, of education.

Now, before we go on, a few words about tests. We know how much anxiety even the word *test* can produce. You may have had negative experiences with tests up to this point and possibly scored low as a result. We hope you'll regard this test as simply an effective device to learn about yourself by gathering, evaluating, and measuring a relatively large amount of information in a rather short period of time. These measurements, when compared with the results of the thousands of others who have taken the test, will give you a benchmark for comparison and help determine your relative strengths and weaknesses. The NCAS is structured to measure your career potentials. It will provide you with a maximum of information about your abilities with an absolute minimum of stress. Sure, it is a test; but you're doing this for yourself, and you can choose the time and place to take the test—whatever is comfortable for you.

## A FEW WORDS OF CAUTION

The NCAS is a pretty comprehensive program, but naturally it's not going to do *everything* for you. It won't tell you how to prepare your résumé or what to wear to an interview, nor does it discuss the myths surrounding the job-hunting process. There are plenty of good books available on those subjects. The NCAS is also not designed to put you in touch with your feelings, nor to help you delve into your past experiences.

Obviously no test—not an I.Q., aptitude, interest, achievement, or special-abilities test—should be rigidly interpreted and taken as the unqualified solution. Tests are tools and not end-alls. The NCAS is not an infallible predictor, nor can it promise a solution to all career problems. Its prime function is to provide an invaluable tool for discovering what you're best at and in what areas you will likely *continue* to do well. The NCAS does that very effectively.

But no matter how high your test scores, success

in your career will also depend upon your drive, personality, ability to make contacts, motivation, and education. The NCAS is a fundamental program for heading you in the right direction, but you'll have to take it from there. For example Barbara, a recent widow who took the test, did well on several segments but scored at a truly superior level in the numerical section. Did that mean she could run out and immediately become a statistician or astronomer? Not likely. In her case she needed to overcome some personal hardships having to do with the death of her husband and to further her education before she would be able to find the job best suited to her abilities. But she knew, after taking the tests, what her focus should be.

By the same token, aptitude tests do not tell you that if your scores are low in certain areas, it will be impossible to achieve success if you decide on an occupation requiring those skills. But the costs to you in terms of time and stress will likely be *much* greater, and you may not achieve the success you could have had if you had focused on your strengths.

The battery of aptitude tests in this book, when used in conjunction with the Career Clusters and the extensive Career Directory, will provide you with the most important information you'll need to plan for the right career.

## TIPS FOR BECOMING A SKILLFUL TEST TAKER

Relax. Remember, this is something you are doing for yourself. This is a positive step in selecting a career, and it is designed to help you, not to cause you an undue amount of anxiety. Don't jam the test into your busy schedule, taking it on your lunch break or while you wait in the doctor's office. Set aside two and a half hours, preferably on a nonbusiness day and at the time of day you usually feel most alert.

As you prepare to take the test, follow these suggestions to avoid irritating distractions and delays:

- Have on hand a few sharpened pencils, erasers, and plenty of scratch paper for figuring problems.
- Make sure you have a wristwatch or stopwatch handy to time yourself during the six sections of the test.
- Ask members of your household to refrain from unnecessary noise while you take the test.

- Take the telephone receiver off the hook.
- Sit facing a blank wall, not a window; it's usually less distracting.

## ABOUT THE TEST ITSELF

- *Time limits:* We have often been asked, "Why are the tests timed? Isn't it what I can do, rather than how long it takes me?" Of course it is important to identify your strengths and weaknesses. But it is equally important for you to be conscious of how your results compare with those of others. For this reason we have set a time limit on each test to provide a standard for comparison. If you take an hour instead of ten minutes to solve certain problems, then you may have more correct answers but you won't derive a realistic assessment of your abilities. And in almost all work situations you won't have an hour to solve a ten-minute problem. So be aware of the time as you work, but don't go too fast. Speeding through the questions can cause you to make too many careless mistakes.

  You probably won't finish all the questions on each of the six tests within the time limit. Don't worry about it. Some test takers will finish some sections, and a few will finish all of them, but don't panic if you don't get through all the questions before the time has expired. You are taking the test to determine what your strengths are, and you certainly aren't expected to excel in every area!
- *Take the whole test:* The NCAS test comes in six parts, and you should do all six sections. You should work on each test for the full time allotted before moving on to the next. Even if one of the six sections seems difficult, stay with it for the full time allowed and just do your best. Even though you may think you don't need certain aptitudes for the careers you have in mind, it's essential that you learn your weaknesses as well as your strengths so that you will end up with the correct Career Cluster. So do take the whole test. You just might be pleasantly surprised with the results!
- *To guess or not to guess:* The tests are all multiple-choice—often called "multiple-guess" by people who take tests frequently. Therefore to guess or not to guess can be a pretty important decision. Here is the best procedure. If you read a question and haven't the *faintest* idea what the correct answer might be, please do *not* close your eyes and choose blindly. Just skip that

question and come back to it if you have time. On the other hand, sometimes you *will* understand the question but be uncertain about the answer. Survey the four possible answers and see if you can eliminate two of them. If you can, then select one of the two remaining answers even if you just close your eyes and choose. This process of selective guessing will give a more accurate picture of your aptitudes. When you get to the scoring section of the book, you will find a Score Correction Table, in which your scores will be adjusted to allow for guessing. The Score Correction Factor does not penalize you if you have guessed prudently, as we have suggested. But if you have guessed wildly, you will lose several extra points, and we *urge* you to leave blank any questions for which you have absolutely no idea what the correct answer is.

Often you will find that incorrect answers will have some elements of truth in them but are not correct in all respects. Here's an example:

Which of the following is farthest west?

a) Boston, MA   b) Atlanta, GA
c) Topeka, KS   d) Denver, AZ

The correct answer is *c*. Although Denver, *Colorado* is farther west, *d* is not correct because Denver is not in Arizona.

The correct answer must be totally correct; it may not have any incorrect segments.

Also, in multiple-choice questions you are to choose the *best* response from the four that are given. At times you might feel that if you could make up a fifth answer, it would be a better choice than any of those presented. This may be true. However, your task is to select the answer that is best from those given.

• *Don't make it more difficult:* You will avoid unnecessary errors if you read the questions carefully so that you understand all the information given. Then you can determine precisely what is asked for. If you are reasonably sure you have found the correct answer fairly quickly, don't dig deeper and deeper into a problem looking for meanings that were probably never intended. This may lead to answers never intended. Of course, you should examine each question thoroughly, but don't make it harder than it is.

• *Now, relax:* If you are one of those people who gets the test jitters, then breathe deeply before you begin. Keep calm. Some people find it relieves tension to stretch as much as they can, tense the muscles in their arms and legs, then suddenly relax them. A little nervousness is natural, and it may even be helpful—in keeping you alert and on the ball.

• *Use the special answer sheets:* These are provided on pages 169–170. You can remove them from the book by cutting along the dotted lines.

Here's a brief checklist on test taking for your review before starting the test:

• Choose a time and place that are best for you.
• Avoid distractions.
• Watch time limits, but don't panic over them.
• Take the whole test.
• Guess, if you can eliminate two choices.
• Don't overanalyze any question.
• The correct answer must be totally correct; it may not have incorrect segments.
• Relax—you're doing this for *you.*
• Use the answer sheets provided.

We urge you to use the NCAS as we have suggested. Of course you are free to take the tests however you wish, but if you do not adhere closely to the testing and scoring instructions, then your results may not reflect your true potentials.

Good luck!

# THE
# TESTS

# BUSINESS TEST

Discover if you have the aptitudes for business—to coordinate, delegate, manage, negotiate, organize, persuade, sell, and supervise. Can you make good business decisions?

**Directions:** Read the directions carefully, then work quickly and accurately on the test. Answer as many of the 58 questions as you can within the time limit. Use the answer sheet provided on page 169.

**Time Limit: 30 minutes**

1. When it is necessary for you to reprimand one of your employees, you should do so . . .

    a) only in writing on official company stationery.
    b) in private.
    c) during a coffee break.
    d) with an apology first, then the reprimand.

2. You are an honest person and have been selected as a mayoral candidate in a city that has a long-standing reputation for corruption. Which of the following should you do?

    a) Promise the voters that if you are elected you will conduct a complete, sweeping reform. Everyone in the present administration who is even suspected of being corrupt will lose his or her job.
    b) Determine through polls, surveys, and other proven techniques those corrupt areas which affect and concern most people and promise to try to reform them.
    c) During the campaign, try to avoid the issue of corruption so that those now profiting from it will vote for you and help finance your campaign.
    d) Avoid this political issue completely because corruption is too "hot" an issue and will most likely continue no matter what you do.

3. Which of the following attributes is most desirable for a secretary?

    a) fairness
    b) self-respect
    c) sense of humor
    d) accuracy

4. You are informed that your superior will soon make an on-the-spot check of the project on which you and your subordinates are now working. Would it be appropriate for you to . . .

    a) influence your people to work faster than usual?
    b) go to your superior and ask why you are being picked on?
    c) forget about it?
    d) briefly mention it to your people?

5. The competencies required to fulfill the tasks of a job vary with the level of the job. The standards necessary for a manager should be greater than those expected of subordinates with regard to . . .

   a) skill in one aspect of the work.
   b) speed.
   c) ability to instruct others.
   d) punctuality.

6. A new suburban neighborhood consists of twenty-six one-family houses. The price of each house is within the range of $85,000 to $95,000. On the last lot a more elaborate house is built and sells at a fair market price of $155,000. The effect of this last home will be to . . .

   a) raise the market value of the other twenty-five houses.
   b) stabilize the market value of the less expensive houses.
   c) influence the owners in the majority of houses to add more rooms onto their homes.
   d) lower the market value of the other twenty-five houses.

7. You are a typewriter manufacturer's sales representative, and your sales manager gives you the name of a retail dealer who has been approached many times before but has not bought any of your company's machines. Your sales manager informs you that if you can obtain the minimum initial order, you will receive double commission and extra paid vacation days. In the past, the dealer has admitted that your line of typewriters is superior to others on the market but that they also cost considerably more. During your sales presentation, which of the following should you emphasize most?

   a) all the faults of your competitors' machines
   b) the reasons that your machines are worth the extra cost
   c) that you and your family really need the double commission
   d) that other dealers who sell your line of typewriters will soon put this dealer out of business if he doesn't carry your line

8. Which of the following contains only items that are usually considered fixed monthly charges?

   a) interest, taxes, insurance, rent
   b) interest, taxes, power cost, labor for repairs
   c) insurance, painting, amortization, power cost
   d) insurance, taxes, replacement parts, travel cost

9. Which of the following industries is *least* affected by the ups and downs of the business cycle?

   a) food-processing industry
   b) construction industry
   c) automobile-manufacturing industry
   d) travel industry

10. The exchange of viewpoints at a conference is most valuable for solving problems that . . .

    a) are impossible to solve.
    b) necessitate a swift and decisive solution.
    c) are unusual and complicated.
    d) are simple and familiar to the participants.

11. Companies that wish to motivate their employees should consider rewards rather than penalties chiefly because . . .

    a) no one likes to deal out penalties.
    b) rewards frequently result in earnest cooperation.
    c) penalties usually have much effect on long-term behavior.
    d) penalties are never serious enough to amount to much.

12. If a co-worker in the factory is having frequent accidents, it is in all probability because that person is *not* . . .

    a) lucky enough to escape misfortune.
    b) confident enough on the job.
    c) paying enough attention to safe work habits.
    d) physically strong enough to do the job.

13. You own a retail shoe store. While attempting to sell to a customer a more expensive pair of shoes, you would *not* . . .

    a) suggest that this pair of shoes would most likely last longer, thus lowering the ultimate cost.
    b) emphasize that the style of this pair of shoes lends itself to many different outfits and occasions.
    c) degrade your own less expensive shoes.
    d) mention that this expensive shoe is worn by a select group in town and will certainly be admired.

14. As an applicant for a management position, you should be somewhat cautious if the available position is . . .

    a) due to an advancement.
    b) due to a resignation.
    c) newly created.
    d) just what you've wanted.

15. Sales managers should keep the personnel turnover at a reasonable rate. If you were a sales manager, which of the following causes of turnover of sales personnel would be reason for your greatest concern?

    a) promotion to a higher position
    b) illness or physical disability
    c) inadequate supervision
    d) retirement

16. When selecting one of your employees for a supervisory role, you should place the greatest significance on the applicant's . . .

    a) intellectual capacity and formal education completed.
    b) ability to perform the work that will be supervised.
    c) knowledge of the work and potential for leadership.
    d) sincerity and loyalty to the company.

17. A file clerk under your supervision reports that the information you now want is missing and guesses that it has been removed from the file drawer and is currently being used by some other department. To ensure that this situation does not recur, you should . . .

    a) not allow other departments to borrow your files.
    b) have your file clerk inform you of all materials borrowed by the other departments.
    c) set a limit on the number of items that can be borrowed from your files.
    d) have an out-of-file card filled out and inserted for each item as it is borrowed.

18. Your supervisor has asked for periodic, clear, and thorough reports on the progress you are making in meeting your objectives. You should present . . .

    a) oral reports; it is easier for your supervisor to relay your oral reports up the chain of command.
    b) oral reports; they require less time and effort to prepare.
    c) written reports; they provide permanent records which can be referred to later.
    d) written reports; they create less time for discussion.

19. A business conference can be used as a training technique. It will be *least* effective when . . .

    a) the agenda avoids problem areas.
    b) each of the participants is an expert in the problem to be discussed.
    c) each of the participants is most articulate.
    d) each of the participants has a different point of view.

20. As a life-insurance salesperson you should have information about a prospective client before you can recommend a particular policy. Which of the following is the *least* important factor that you should consider?

    a) the present financial situation of the prospective client
    b) the expected future financial earning capacity of the prospective client
    c) how many years the prospective client expects to live in your sales district
    d) the kinds of insurance and other investments the prospective client now owns

21. Which of the following characteristics would apply *least* to entrepreneurs? Entrepreneurs are usually . . .

    a) the firstborn child in their family.
    b) excellent managers.
    c) moderate risk takers.
    d) adept at maximizing their ability as "doers."

22. For years, advertising firms have used famous people to promote products. To be most effective in persuading the public to purchase a particular product, what characteristics should the famous person have?

    a) credibility, attractiveness, a position of power or prestige
    b) attractiveness, wealth, a good command of today's "in" sayings
    c) forcefulness, attractiveness, height
    d) credibility, a big smile, a melodious voice

23. You are a sales representative for an advertising agency and have clearly explained to your prospective client how your services would benefit his company. Now which of the following questions should you ask to close this business deal?

    a) "Would you like our company to represent you? Yes or No?"
    b) "I should think three daily advertisements on radio would be about right to start with, don't you?"
    c) "Why don't you give me a call sometime, when you think we could help you?"
    d) "Don't you think we do a great job?"

24. Initially, which of the following specific activities would beginning, inexperienced accountants most frequently be performing?

    a) preparing comparative financial statements
    b) checking petty-cash vouchers
    c) interpreting financial reports
    d) using billing machines

25. Independent companies can improve their sales records by controlling certain selling activities. One common method of control is to assign salespeople to specific sales territories. Which of the following improvements would *not* take place when sales territories are established?

    a) an improvement in customer relations
    b) a reduction in sales expenses by eliminating duplication of effort
    c) an attainment of a more thorough coverage of your market
    d) a creation of more buying power in the sales territory

26. A customer in your restaurant requests a particular brand of wine that you do not stock. It would be best for you to . . .

    a) tell the customer to bring that particular wine from home from now on.
    b) inform the customer that you do not have that brand but you have others that are of equal flavor, body, and bouquet which you would like to serve.
    c) ignore the customer's request for that specific brand and proceed to serve a comparable one, since it is hard to tell the difference.
    d) tell the customer that only cheap restaurants serve that particular brand and you wouldn't stock it.

27. It is your very first day at work in a chemical plant and you are assigned to work with an experienced technician. At one point during the day, you realize that the technician is about to violate a basic safety rule. The best thing for you to do is . . .

   a) turn your back so that you will be unable to witness the violation.
   b) say nothing until the rule is actually broken, then mention it.
   c) call it to the technician's attention without delay.
   d) say nothing now, but discuss it during coffee break with other workers.

28. Your position requires you to submit a number of forms and reports once each week. The most advisable system for fulfilling this task is to . . .

   a) schedule a definite period of time each day, or on a weekly basis, for the completion of these reports.
   b) complete the forms whenever you have spare time.
   c) delegate this task to one of your subordinates.
   d) abbreviate your answers and refer your supervisor to last week's forms.

29. Most industrial psychologists would say that it is generally undesirable for middle-management employees to become aware of changes in company policy through the informal grapevine because . . .

   a) it shows that someone involved in upper-level decision-making has leaked information and cannot be trusted.
   b) it shows that the decision-making body does trust middle management.
   c) it distorts and exaggerates the information out of proportion.
   d) it duplicates the work of the formal information dissemination procedures.

30. Which of the following characteristics would *least* likely apply to sales executives? The sales executive . . .

   a) is mentally superior to the majority of his subordinates, but is not surrounded exclusively by less capable people.
   b) readily accepts responsibility.
   c) has the ability to teach and motivate others.
   d) is often moody and inconsistent in order to keep the sales force alert and attentive.

31. In your attempt to deal satisfactorily with a complaint that is imagined rather than real, the complaint should be considered . . .

   a) just as important as a real grievance.
   b) trivial, since it has no real basis.
   c) indicative of a labor union's attempt to initiate unrest within the company.
   d) when you get around to it. There is little need to rush, since it is not real anyway.

32. Usually the price of a two-pound can of pineapple slices is less than that of two one-pound cans because . . .
    a) on larger cans the company can do more advertising.
    b) a lower grade of pineapple is used in larger cans.
    c) customs officials do not tax large cans that come from Hawaii.
    d) packaging costs are not relative to the amount of pineapple in the can.

33. You are an office manager, and one of your nine clerks, Alice, has voiced a complaint. Her complaint is that her co-worker, Bob, has a much easier work load and far less complicated assignments than any of the other clerks. Which of the following actions would be most appropriate?
    a) Schedule a meeting of your nine clerical workers and discuss this problem.
    b) Explore the basis of Alice's complaint.
    c) Politely explain that Bob's work load is none of her business.
    d) Reduce Alice's work load and give some to Bob.

34. As a department-store manager should you encourage or discourage your employees from making suggestions for increasing the sales and efficiency of the store?
    a) Discourage; employees may take offense at your asking them to do something extra.
    b) Encourage; employees will find fault with one another's work and may produce rival factions, which will lead to competition and efficiency.
    c) Encourage; employees may develop pride and added interest in their tasks, which will improve overall efficiency.
    d) Discourage; employees will think less of you, for it will seem that you do not know how to manage the store.

35. As manager of a supermarket, you should assign tasks to a new employee that . . .
    a) give the widest exposure to all facets of the supermarket.
    b) isolate this worker to ensure a minimum amount of distraction.
    c) will be the most interesting in order to promote an interest in the food industry.
    d) offer the best chance to attain concrete results.

36. The primary reason for a senior department supervisor to delegate authority to a junior supervisor is to . . .
    a) see if the junior can find new or better ways to get things done.
    b) provide an opportunity for the junior to "sink or swim."
    c) make the senior's job easier.
    d) release the senior for more important duties.

37. In order to have your employees willing to follow new standardized procedures, you should be prepared to . . .
    a) explain the advantages of the new procedures.
    b) do part of the work yourself until the employees learn the new procedures.
    c) give the employees extra time off if they save time by using the new procedures.
    d) deal with a labor strike.

38. From management's point of view, the most desirable quality in a newly hired office clerk is . . .

   a) the absence of outside hobbies or interests.
   b) the ability to sufficiently perform the assigned duties.
   c) the eagerness to ask questions about all aspects of the business.
   d) the ability to organize other people for a worthy cause.

39. A new office worker is told by a more experienced employee that he is making a few serious errors in his work. The best reason for him to heed this advice is that the experienced employee . . .

   a) will not offer advice again, unless it is taken the first time.
   b) has had more experience on the job and probably knows what should be done.
   c) will become an enemy unless the advice is taken.
   d) will probably become a supervisor quite soon.

40. The more highly specialized your work becomes, usually the . . .

   a) more geographic mobility you have.
   b) more protection you have from unemployment.
   c) larger the city you will live in.
   d) more travel you must do for the company.

41. You are an optician whose eye-care center features a large selection of fashion eyewear for the whole family. One of your customers is purchasing her first pair of prescription glasses, and you would also like to sell her a pair of prescription sunglasses. In attempting to make this additional sale, you should say . . .

   a) "You should get sunglasses, too."
   b) "Do you need sunglasses?"
   c) "While you're here, let's take a look at frames that make attractive sunglasses."
   d) "You will need sunglasses this summer, and it would be silly for you to look anywhere else, for we have the best selection in town."

42. Which of the following characteristics would apply *least* to entrepreneurs? Entrepreneurs . . .

   a) prefer tasks involving some objective risks.
   b) work harder when influenced by a financial reward.
   c) tend to think ahead.
   d) work harder at tasks that require mental manipulation.

43. Personnel workers should have good interview techniques. The more capable ones regard the interview process as . . .

   a) a warm, friendly, wandering conversation.
   b) a warm, friendly conversation guided by a definite purpose.
   c) a rather rigid, purposeful discussion.
   d) a rather rigid procedure which clearly separates the interviewer from the interviewee and is systematized to evoke all the information needed.

**44.** You are a front-desk clerk at a downtown hotel. You are talking with one of the guests, who has obviously misunderstood what you have said. At this point it is best for you to say . . .

    a) "I'm sorry I didn't make it clear."
    b) "You are wrong about that."
    c) "I think you misunderstood me."
    d) "Excuse me, but I think you are somewhat confused about that."

**45.** The members of the board of directors of the Candle Golf Club in Nevada realize that the association's profits have fallen dramatically over the past few years. They call a general-membership meeting and cooperatively decide to initiate three possible solutions. First, they decide to raise the club dues by 20 percent. Secondly, they decide to obtain a limited gaming license so they can make extra money during special club events. Their third solution is to conduct a membership drive and to charge only an initial $385 for all newly enrolled families. The three plans were initiated, and the club's accounting book showed a profit for the first time in the past four years.

On the basis of the above information, which of the following is most likely true?

    a) The membership drive netted only two families, because many families cancelled their membership when the dues increase was announced.
    b) These actions prompted a complete audit of the club's financial records, and it was found that the accountant and a member of the board of directors had been systematically investing the club's funds in stocks that had depreciated.
    c) The community felt that $385 was a small fee for membership in this club, so many rushed to enroll.
    d) In the fifth year of these new policies, the club had to close because of lack of funds.

**46.** A department administrator should realize that it is usually best *not* to . . .

    a) assign specific responsibilities to immediate subordinates.
    b) delegate authority wherever responsibilities have been assigned.
    c) make a subordinate responsible to more than one administrator.
    d) check the progress of delegated assignments.

**47.** You have decided to begin a mail-order business from your home. Which of the following procedures would you use?

    a) Select a product that is widely sold in retail stores so that your prospective customers will be familiar with it.
    b) Have a post-office box number as part of your address so you will not be bothered by crank phone calls from customers who find your telephone number in the telephone book.
    c) Try to minimize expenses by avoiding mailing labels that have "Return Postage Guaranteed" printed on them.
    d) Offer a money-back guarantee on everything you sell, for it promotes confidence in your product.

**48.** You are the head of a large departmental office. Your attitude toward grievances should be to . . .

    a) pay little attention to them.
    b) attend to grievances and make the necessary adjustments to alleviate all of them.
    c) maintain strict discipline and that will eliminate nearly all grievances.
    d) know which grievances occur most frequently and attempt to prevent them from occurring.

**49.** You are the sales manager of a stockbrokerage firm, and a customer has complained that one of your salespeople has been inattentive and unable to help with a financial problem. You then investigate the situation, talk with your salesperson at length, and determine that the customer's complaint is a by-product of overanxiety about finances. Of the following, your most appropriate option is to . . .

    a) refer the customer back to the salesperson.
    b) handle this customer yourself.
    c) refer the customer to another salesperson.
    d) refer the customer to another stockbrokerage firm.

**50.** As a good manager you certainly foster initiative in your staff, but you realize that at times it can be counterproductive. The greatest detriment occurs when the staff member . . .

    a) wastes time and energy in an unprofitable activity.
    b) does things differently from what you would have done.
    c) acts superior to the other workers.
    d) makes errors in judgment.

**51.** Your supervisor insists on explaining the procedure for doing a job which you know how to do very well. You should listen attentively because . . .

    a) you can still do the job your own way after the supervisor leaves.
    b) you may catch the supervisor in an error and thus prove to yourself that you know more.
    c) your attentiveness might impress the supervisor.
    d) it will be your job to perform the task the way the supervisor wants it done.

**52.** Which of the following is the *least* sensible cash and finance practice for a small retailer?

    a) Maintain a close personal relationship with your local banker.
    b) Make checks out to "cash" and assign them to various expense accounts.
    c) Establish, in advance, a line of credit at your bank.
    d) Deposit each day's cash receipts in the bank.

**53.** Certain factors can promote a higher level of employee performance. Select the one most frequently suggested by industrial psychologists.

    a) recognition of a job well done
    b) job security after a certain amount of time on the job
    c) close supervision by a manager
    d) a full package of money-related employee benefits

**54.** The most significant reason for a company to establish definite work schedules for its employees is that . . .

 a) it clears the relationship between the administration and the subordinates.
 b) the workers are more satisfied when a routine is created.
 c) it lessens the chance that an important task will be inadvertently overlooked.
 d) it helps the bookkeeper compute the payroll.

**55.** If a committee of employees is to meet with an administrative officer for the specific purpose of improving relations and dealing with grievances, it would be best if the meetings were held . . .

 a) whenever the need becomes apparent.
 b) whenever requested by the employee committee.
 c) upon the consideration of the administrative officer.
 d) at regularly scheduled times.

**56.** As a member of a corporate policy-making committee you generally make your best contributions to the committee when you . . .

 a) abandon your own point of view and accept the view of others.
 b) overcome other committee members' resistance to your ideas.
 c) persuade the other committee members to accept your major ideas but back off on minor points.
 d) combine your ideas with the ideas of the other committee members.

**57.** There are very few tools for measuring average amounts of work accomplished by an employee. Considerable emphasis is usually placed on the fallible judgment of other people to construct these standards of measurement. These time standards are set either by experienced workers or by a time-study industrial engineer. Once these time standards are set . . .

 a) they can be used to schedule production.
 b) they cannot be changed.
 c) they cannot be used to estimate the cost of sales.
 d) they can eliminate the need for supervisory personnel.

**58.** Many business careers have become extremely specialized. The narrow scope of these jobs frequently leads to boredom and a lack of excitement. In order to counteract some of these negative effects of specialization, many large corporations use *job enlargement* as a device to improve employee motivation and efficiency. Which of the following is *least* likely to be an example of beneficial *job enlargement?*

 a) adding more complexity to the tasks performed on a job
 b) increasing the time spent at a task and adding a number of similar tasks.
 c) involving employees more in the decision-making processes
 d) training employees to handle more than one job and utilizing a system of rotation

# CLERICAL TEST

Discover if you can work rapidly and precisely with minute details. Can you find comparisons? Can you decode materials? Find misspelled words? Memorize on the spot? File or research information quickly?

**Directions:** Read the directions carefully, then work quickly and accurately. Try to answer as many of the 78 questions as you can within the time limit. Precise timing on this test is a must! Take the full 22 minutes, but not any longer. Use the answer sheet provided on page 169.

**Time Limit: 22 minutes**

In the first 10 questions, select the name that is *exactly* the same as the given name.

1. Given: Kenneth H. MacDougall, Co.

    a) Kenneth MacDougall, Co.
    b) Keneth H. MacDougall, Co.
    c) Kenneth H. MacDougall, Co.
    d) Kenneth H. MacDougal, Co.

2. Given: Hartmann Theatre Supply Co.

    a) Hartmann Theatre Supply Co.
    b) Hartman Theater Supply Co.
    c) Hartmann Theater Supply Co.
    d) Harteman Theatre Supply Co

3. Given: Connecticut Sanitation Service, Co.

    a) Connecticut Sanitary Service, Co.
    b) Connecticut Sanitation Services, Co.
    c) Connecticut Sanitation Service, Inc.
    d) Connecticut Sanitation Service, Co.

4. Given: Whisconier Greenhouse, Gardens, & Nursery

    a) Whisconier Greenhouses, Garden, & Nursery
    b) Whisconer Greenhouse, Gardens, & Nursery
    c) Whisconier Greenhouse, Gardens, & Nursery
    d) Whisconier Greenhouse, Gardens, & Nurserys

5. Given: Mademoiselle Maxine's Beauty Shoppe

    a) Mademoiselle Maxine's Beauty Shop
    b)   Mademoiselle Maxine's Beauty Shoppe
    c) Mademoiselle Maxine Beauty Shoppe
    d)   Madamoiselle Maxine's Beauty Shoppe

6. Given: Stephen Tannielli Jr. Associates

   a) Steven Tannielli Jr. Associates
   b) Stephen Tannielli Jr. Associates
   c) Stephen Tannielli Sr. Associates
   d) Stephen Tannielli Jr. Association

7. Given: Brookfield Automotive Car Center

   a) Brookfield Automotive Car Center
   b) Brookfield Automotive Car Centre
   c) Brookefield Automotive Car Center
   d) Brookfield Automotive Care Center

8. Given: Perreault Industrial Printing, Ltd.

   a) Perreault Industrial Printers, Ltd.
   b) Perreault Industrial Printers, Inc.
   c) Perreault Industrial Printing, Ltd.
   d) Perreaull Industrial Printing, Ltd.

9. Given: The Tecumseh Audio-Visual Equipment Co., Inc.

   a) The Tecumpseh Audio-Visual Equipment Co., Inc.
   b) The Tecumseh Audio-Visual Equiptment Co., Inc.
   c) The Tecumseh Audio-Visual Equipment Company
   d) The Tecumseh Audio-Visual Equipment Co., Inc.

10. Given: Selectric Motors Sales and Service, Inc.

   a) Selectronic Motors Sales and Service, Inc.
   b) Selectric Motor Sales and Service, Inc.
   c) Selectric Motors Service and Sales, Inc.
   d) Selectric Motors Sales and Service, Inc.

In the next 8 questions, select the number that is *exactly* the same as the given number.

11. Given: 37207

   a) 37027
   b) 37207
   c) 73207
   d) 37007

12. Given: 9 6 4 6 3 1

   a) 9 1 6 3 4 6
   b) 9 6 4 6 3 1
   c) 9 6 1 4 6 3
   d) 9 6 4 6 1 3

13. Given: 7442259

   a) 7442259
   b) 7422459
   c) 7445229
   d) 7224459

14. Given: 9969669

   a) 9996669
   b) 9969669
   c) 9969969
   d) 9669669

15. Given: 3 8 6 3 3 8 2 6 3

   a) 3 6 8 3 3 8 2 6 3
   b)    3 8 6 3 8 8 2 6 3
   c) 3 8 6 3 3 8 2 6 3
   d)    3 8 6 3 3 8 6 2 3

16. Given: 890213089

   a) 890321089
   b)    890231089
   c) 809213809
   d)    890213089

17. Given: 9648270253162948

   a) 9648720253612948
   b) 9648270253162948
   c) 9648270253612498
   d) 9648270235612498

18. Given: 8838638886368433688633

   a) 8838638866368433688633
   b)    8838638886638433688633
   c) 8836838886368843368633
   d)    8838638886368433688633

For the next 8 questions, select the name that would come first if filed alpha-betically: last name first, then first name if necessary, then middle initial if necessary.

19. a) Walter W. Mensen
    b) Jay P. Menkin
    c) Robert B. Mennings
    d) Scott L. Mennison

20. a) Adam R. Galen
    b) Bernice N. Gale
    c) Charles P. Gable
    d) Darlene S. Gable

21. a) Melanie A. Roberts
    b) Marsha J. Roberts
    c) Juan T. Roberto
    d) Alice A. Roberts

22. a) Stephen C. Gleason
    b) Steven B. Gleason
    c) Phyllis F. Gleason
    d) Pauline G. Gleason

23. a) John D. Smith
    b) Marshall T. Smythe
    c) John A. Smith
    d) Helen W. Smithey

24. a) Alfred R. Simon
    b) Valerie Simone
    c) James Simon
    d) Anne C. Simon

25. a) Diane B. Brown
    b) Dianna K. Brown
    c) Dena J. Brown
    d) Dianne A. Browne

26. a) Rose F. Torielli
    b) Randy W. Toriello
    c) Rosa T. Torielli
    d) Regina B. Toriello

In each of the following 16 groups of words find the one misspelled word.

27. a) abilaty
    b) achievement
    c) adept
    d) aptitude

28. a) casualty
    b) disappoint
    c) wheather
    d) government

29. a) benefit
    b) opportunity
    c) employment
    d) salery

30. a) hinge
    b) athority
    c) succeed
    d) chorus

31. a) technique
    b) restaurant
    c) safety
    d) similer

32. a) apropriate
    b) synonymous
    c) rhubarb
    d) cemetery

33. a) physicist
    b) secratary
    c) lithographer
    d) librarian

34. a) dietitian
    b) counselor
    c) veternarian
    d) upholsterer

35. a) nineteenth
    b) ninety
    c) nineth
    d) nineteen

36. a) oblique
    b) meticulous
    c) prognosis
    d) allowence

37. a) supersonnic
    b) connoisseur
    c) psychology
    d) dilemma

38. a) stubornly
    b) adroitly
    c) sufficiently
    d) subversively

39. a) vehement
    b) verbatim
    c) visinity
    d) vivacious

40. a) counterfit
    b) monetary
    c) revenue
    d) financial

41. a) misapprehension
    b) misunderstanding
    c) misconseption
    d) miscalculation

42. a) unconquerable
    b) invincsible
    c) unsurmountable
    d) irresistible

In each of the next 12 sets, select the one that is different from the other three.

43. a) Laura A. Gallo
       28 Scarboro Avenue
       Newport, RI 02840

    b) Laura A. Gallo
       28 Scarboro Avenue
       Newport, RI 02840

    c) Laura A. Gallo
       28 Scarboro Avenue
       Newport, VA 02840

    d) Laura A. Gallo
       28 Scarboro Avenue
       Newport, RI 02840

44. a) Carole Mason
16907 N. Main St.
Palos Verdes, CA 90274

b) Carol Mason
16907 N. Main St.
Palos Verdes, CA 90274

c) Carol Mason
16907 N. Main St.
Palos Verdes, CA 90274

d) Carol Mason
16907 N. Main St.
Palos Verdes, CA 90274

45. a) Peter Pinto Associates, Inc.
Capital National Bank Bldg.
111 E. 17th St.
Lummi Island, WA 98263

b) Peter Pinto Associates, Inc.
Capital National Bunk Bldg.
111 E. 17th St.
Lummi Island, Wa 98263

c) Peter Pinto Associates, Inc.
Capital National Bank Bldg.
111 E. 17th St.
Lummi Island, WA 98263

d) Peter Pinto Associates, Inc.
Capital National Bank Bldg.
111 E. 17th St.
Lummi Island, WA 98263

46. a) Callicoon Center Bakery
10132 12th St. NW
Huntsville Station
Albuquerque, NM 87112

b) Callicoon Center Bakery
10132 12th St. NW
Huntsville Station
Albuquerque, NE 87112

c) Callicoon Center Bakery
10132 12th St. NW
Huntsville Station
Albuquerque, NM 87112

d) Callicoon Center Bakery
10132 12th St. NW
Huntsville Station
Albuquerque, NM 87112

47. a) Phillip G. Fillmore
Philadelphia College
8392 Saint Austin's Place
Philadelphia, PA 19113

b) Phillip G. Fillmore
Philadelphia College
8392 Saint Austins Place
Philadelphia, PA 19113

c) Phillip G. Fillmore
Philadelphia College
8392 Saint Austin's Place
Philadelphia, PA 19113

d) Phillip G. Fillmore
Philadelphia College
8392 Saint Austin's Place
Philadelphia, PA 19113

48. a) Steven J. Armakian
10302 N. Wisconsin Avenue
Apartment 27B
Baltimore, MD 21227

b) Steven J. Armakian
10302 N. Wisconsin Avenue
Apartment 27B
Baltimore, MD 21227

c) Steven J. Armakian
10302 N. Wisconsin Avenue
Apartment 27B
Baltimore, MD 21227

d) Steven J. Armakian
10302 N. Wisconsin Avenue
Apartment 27B
Baltimore, MD 22127

49. a) Armando Weybosset
67852 Netherland Terrace
Route 34
Mansfield, OH 44902

b) Armand O. Weybosset
67852 Netherland Terrace
Route 34
Mansfield, OH 44902

c) Armand O. Weybosset
67852 Netherland Terrace
Route 34
Mansfield, OH 44902

d) Armand O. Weybosset
67852 Netherland Terrace
Route 34
Mansfield, OH 44902

**50.**  a)  Maximilian S. Weatherby, Jr.
Drawer 742
92451 McQuay Rd. SW
Sessums, Mississippi 38668

b)  Maximilian S. Weatherby, Jr.
Drawer 742
92451 McQuay Rd. SW
Sessums, Mississippi 38668

c)  Maximilian S. Weatherby, Jr.
Drawer 742
92451 McQuay Rd SW
Sessums, Mississippi 38668

d)  Maximilian S. Weatherby, Jr.
Drawer 742
92451 McQuay Rd. SW
Sessums, Mississippi 38668

**51.**  a)  Campbell Wynnewood
Pacific Cooperative Bank
49753 Glen Heather Drive
S. Morgantown, WV 25426

b)  Campbell Wynnewood
Pacific Cooperative Bank
49753 Glen Heather Drive
S. Morgantown, WV 25426

c)  Campbell Wynnewood
Pacific Cooperative Bank
49753 Glen Heather Drive
S. Morgantown, WV 25426

d)  Campbell Wynnewood
Pacific Cooperative Bank
49753 Glen Heather Drive
S. Morgantown, WV 24526

**52.**  a)  Barbara J. McCormick, Ph.D.
69961 Mt. Pleasant Road
c/o The Queen's College
Queensboro, NY 10306

b)  Barbara J. McCormick, Ph.D.
69961 Mt. Pleasant Road
c/o The Queen's College
Queenboro, NY 10306

c)  Barbara J. McCormick, Ph.D.
69961 Mt. Pleasant Road
c/o The Queen's College
Queensboro, NY 10306

d)  Barbara J. McCormick, Ph.D.
69961 Mt. Pleasant Road
c/o The Queen's College
Queensboro, NY 10306

**53.**  a)  Evelyn Marlowe
5465 West Chippewa
c/o Veterans Administration
Johnstown, PA 15906

b)  Evelyn Marlowe
5765 West Chippewa
c/o Veterans Administration
Johnstown, PA 15906

c)  Evelyn Marlowe
5465 West Chippewa
c/o Veterans Administration
Johnstown, PA 15906

d)  Evelyn Marlowe
5465 West Chippewa
c/o Veterans Administration
Johnstown, PA 15906

**54.**  a)  Dr. Martha Chipman
University Towers
16-298 Wood Acres Lane
Los Angeles, CA 90016

b)  Dr. Marhta Chipman
University Towers
16-298 Wood Acres Lane
Los Angeles, CA 90016

c)  Dr. Martha Chipman
University Towers
16-298 Wood Acres Lane
Los Angeles, CA 90016

d)  Dr. Martha Chipman
University Towers
16-298 Wood Acres Lane
Los Angeles, CA 90016

For the next 10 questions, select the answer that fulfills all the requirements stated.

**55.** Select the one that contains both an E and a 5.

    a) 6, 3, A, R, K, 4, 5
    b) j, 9, 5, B, C, P, F
    c) 1, 3, E, 8, J, 5, z
    d) A, E, 4, f, 7, 9, 2

**56.** Select the one that contains both a 2 and an M.

    a) W, 4, S, 2, 8, 5, C, N
    b) P, J, M, 4, R, 6, 7, H
    c) 6, G, 2, V, 7, 8, N, D
    d) L, M, 4, O, B, K, 2, W

**57.** Select the one that contains *two* E's.

    a) P, U, E, R, T, O, R, I, C, O
    b) L, I, T, T, L, E, R, O, C, K
    c) P, E, R, T, H, A M, B, O, Y
    d) N, E, W, O, R, L, E, A, N, S

**58.** Select the one that contains a T, an S, a 3, an 8.

    a) 2 T 8 1 7 S A Z 3 D F 5
    b) S T A R 4 6 8 P U 9 N 2
    c) 9 8 6 7 C U R T 2 S 4 0
    d) 1 R 3 T 5 P 7 M O S 6 9

**59.** Select the one that contains an F, a 6, an L.

    a) 5 9 E K 4 6 8 A F W T
    b) 3 F C L 2 3 8 6 Q E
    c) E A F 7 1 0 3 L 9 5 3
    d) P L 8 6 R A V 2 4 8 M

**60.** Select the one that contains a 9, a 4, a D, an N.

    a) 2, 4, 8, 6, A, B, M, T, D, 0, 9, H, R
    b) P, B, 9, 3, D, 8, 2, 4, J, M, B, P, 6
    c) E, M, 8, 7, 6, 9, B, D, 2, 1, N, 6, 4
    d) 6, 9, F, H, D, R, S, 3, 7, N, 3, 5, 7

**61.** Select the one that contains *three* E's and *two* N's.

    a) T E E N A G E G I R L
    b) M A C H I N E M A D E
    c) P U T T O N G R E E N
    d) N O N E O F T H E S E

**62.** Select the one that contains *three* I's and *two* N's.

    a) M O U N T A I N V I E W
    b) I N D I A N A P O L I S
    c) S I L V E R S P R I N G
    d) W E S T V I R G I N I A

63. Select the one that contains *two* 9's, one B, one 7, and one G.

   a) 9 8 7 S T U 6 B D 0 4 6 9 C 1 2
   b) 5 7 8 9 G A 4 9 C B 1 3 6 2 8
   c) B A D R 7 7 9 C 6 4 6 8 B G
   d) 2 9 1 B 6 6 E F 7 W A B G

64. Select the one that contains *two* eights, one R, and one six.

   a) 9 J 8 6 P D 9 T 8 U R 4
   b) E 6 G 9 V 8 2 8 P M Q B
   c) 8 T H 6 L P R O R 9 6 S
   d) C R 4 8 N Z 8 L 3 9 9 R

Questions 65 and 66 refer to the information given below.

The cost of a display advertisement in the local newspaper varies according to the size of the ad, measured in column inches, and the number of times the ad is printed per year, known as insertions per year.

**TABLE 1: COST PER COLUMN INCH**

Number of insertions per year

| Number of column inches per ad | 1–3 | 4–6 | 7–9 | 10 or more |
|---|---|---|---|---|
| 6–15 | $7.75 | $7.25 | $6.75 | $6.25 |
| 16–25 | 7.60 | 7.10 | 6.60 | 6.10 |
| 26–35 | 7.45 | 6.95 | 6.45 | 5.95 |
| 36–50 | 7.25 | 6.75 | 6.25 | 5.75 |
| 51–75 | 7.00 | 6.50 | 6.00 | 5.50 |

**TABLE 2**

| Cost per column inch | Answer |
|---|---|
| $5.50–6.05 | a |
| 6.06–6.60 | b |
| 6.61–7.15 | c |
| 7.16–7.75 | d |

65. The owner of The Record Broker, which specializes in records, tapes, cassettes, and stereo equipment, has decided to place five advertisements in the local paper this year. The owner estimates that each ad will be 30 column inches. Using Table 1 and Table 2, determine which answer best indicates the cost of the ads per column inch.

   a) a    b) b    c) c    d) d

66. Kevin Klein's Tavern has been losing customers lately because the new highway bypasses this fine old establishment. The proprietor hopes that repetitive ads will bring back some of the business that has been lost. The owner plans to run an 8-column-inch ad for a year. Using both tables provided, determine which answer indicates the cost of the ads per column inch.

   a) a    b) b    c) c    d) d

In the next 9 questions, select the next item in each sequence.

67. B, D, F, H, ?

   a) J    b) L    c) G    d) K

**68.** AZ, BY, CX, ?

    a) DU    b) DV    c) DW  d) DX

**69.** AC, FH, KM, ?

    a) PQ    b) PR    c) OP    d) OQ

**70.** Z, Y, W, T, P, ?

    a) L    b) M    c) J    d) K

**71.** M, P, O, R, Q, T, ?

    a) R    b) S    c) U    d) W

**72.** read, reader, readers, readiness, ?

    a) ready    b) real    c) reading    d) reality

**73.** support, supportable, supporter, supporting, ?

    a) supposable    b) supportive    c) supported    d) supports

**74.** pat, page, pacer, palace, ?

    a) pace    b) pacify    c) paddle    d) pancake

The chart below shows six items (birds, clothing, fruit, sports, trees, vegetables) grouped into ten various combinations.

| Group | Items |
|---|---|
| 1. | birds, clothing |
| 2. | fruit, vegetables |
| 3. | clothing, sports, trees |
| 4. | sports, birds |
| 5. | clothing, fruit, birds |
| 6. | trees, birds |
| 7. | clothing, sports, birds |
| 8. | birds, fruit |
| 9. | vegetables, birds |
| 10. | vegetables, sports, clothing |

**75.** Select the group number that contains: hat, shoe, tennis, soccer, elm, maple

    a) 1    b) 3    c) 5    d) 7

**76.** Select the group number that contains: robin, blue jay, cardinal, apple, orange, watermelon

    a) 2    b) 4    c) 6    d) 8

**77.** Select the group number that contains: sweater, golf, crow, coat, softball, sparrow

    a) 5    b) 7    c) 2    d) 3

**78.** Select the group number that contains: cantaloupe, woodpecker, grapefruit, whippoorwill, shirt

    a) 8    b) 6    c) 5    d) 2

# LOGIC TEST

Discover if you are skilled in the art of reasoning. Can you find similarities and differences among objects and ideas? Can you systematize and simplify involved problems? Draw conclusions rapidly? Can you infer information?

**Directions:** Read the directions carefully, then work quickly and accurately. Answer as many of the 54 questions as you can within the time limit. Use the answer sheet provided on page 169.

**Time Limit: 25 minutes**

## Analogies

For Questions 1 through 20 select the pair of words that best expresses a relationship similar to the Given Pair.

**1. BED : SLEEP**

    a) car : gasoline
    b) cow : ranch
    c) bird : feather
    d) chair : sit

**2. FATHER : DAUGHTER**

    a) uncle : aunt
    b) son : daughter
    c) grandfather : mother
    d) son-in-law : aunt

**3. ARTIST : PICTURE**

    a) poem : poet
    b) photographer : film
    c) sculptor : statue
    d) gambler : chance

**4. HOUSE : ROOF**

    a) mattress : bed
    b) table : leg
    c) door : barn
    d) foundation : concrete

**5. WARM : HOT**

    a) costly : exorbitant
    b) irregular : regular
    c) simplicity : commonplace
    d) secluded : withdrawn

**6. APERTURE : CLOSURE**

    a) trench : trough
    b) hole : cavity
    c) gap : blockage
    d) sealed : airtight

**7. NUMISMATIST : COIN**

    a) clown : circus
    b) agnostic : prayer
    c) psychologist : psychology
    d) harvest : farmer

**8. FOOD : HUNGER**

    a) clothes : exposure
    b) question : answer
    c) student : school
    d) door : knob

**9. TERRIER : KENNEL**

    a) parakeet : cage
    b) bee : hive
    c) lion : den
    d) bird : nest

**10. LIFE : YOUTH**

    a) birth : death
    b) football game : quarter
    c) sunrise : sunset
    d) pages : book

11. ABUNDANCE : PAUCITY

    a) multiplication : plural
    b) redundance : double
    c) holiday : festival
    d) profusely : sparsely

12. MEMBER : TEAM

    a) baseball : athletics
    b) fiber : fabric
    c) body : knee
    d) seed : tree

13. CUTLERY : HUNTING KNIFE

    a) carving knife : jackknife
    b) dining utensils : spoon
    c) end wrench : monkey wrench
    d) auger bit : cross bit

14. YARDSTICK : MEASUREMENT

    a) depth : width
    b) painter : brush
    c) camera : enlarger
    d) pencil : writing

15. GUN : DEATH

    a) handle : trigger
    b) book : writer
    c) umbrella : rain
    d) sun : heat

16. BODY : RELAX

    a) sleep : hypnosis
    b) runner : fatigued
    c) rope : slacken
    d) limp : muscle

17. SEPARATION : TEAR

    a) musical instrument : violin
    b) progress : advance
    c) expanse : spread
    d) insurance : protection

18. TAR : RAT

    a) black : rodent
    b) spot : tops
    c) black : animal
    d) rabbit : squirrel

19. CHROMATIC : PALLID

    a) animation : spirited
    b) true-blue : faithful
    c) healthy : unsalutary
    d) insignificant : minuscule

20. MOTORIST : ROAD SIGN

    a) vocabulary : letter
    b) quarterback : signals
    c) language : foreign
    d) reader : punctuation

21. On the simultaneous roll of three dice, a total of 17 is obtained. What is the chance that one of the dice is a 5 spot?

    a) one chance in six rolls totaling 17
    b) one chance in three rolls totaling 17
    c) two chances in every three rolls totaling 17
    d) on every roll totaling 17

22. The cost of your hotel room is D dollars for the first day and S dollars for each day thereafter. Your meals cost N dollars per day. What is the total charge if you stay J days?

    a) $D + S + N + J$
    b) $D + S (J - 1) + JN$
    c) $J (D + S + N)$
    d) $JN + JS - JD$

23. On a shelf in a supermarket are G bottles of ketchup. A child running down the aisle accidentally strikes the display and V bottles are broken. What percentage of bottles remains intact?

    a) $100 (G - V)$
    b) $\dfrac{G + V}{100}$
    c) $\dfrac{100 (G - V)}{G}$
    d) $\dfrac{G - V}{100}$

For questions 24 through 41, select the one that is different from the other three.

24. a) spoon
    b) fork
    c) knife
    d) plate

25. a) chair
    b) automobile
    c) airplane
    d) boat

26. a) 973
    b) 739
    c) 379
    d) 374

27. a) waltz
    b) dancer
    c) fox-trot
    d) polka

28. a) crooked
    b) arc
    c) semicircle
    d) curve

29. a) rubber
    b) band
    c) duet
    d) choral

30. a) misjudge
    b) mishandle
    c) misrepresent
    d) miscible

31. a) objectionable
    b) tolerable
    c) bearable
    d) endurable

32. a) scarlet
    b) indigo
    c) vermilion
    d) crimson

33. a) biographer
    b) binoculars
    c) bicycle
    d) biennial

34. a) torrid
    b) scalding
    c) blistering
    d) tepid

35. a) vixen
    b) bitch
    c) drake
    d) filly

36. a) calcium
    b) chlorine
    c) copper
    d) cyanide

37. a) chronometer
    b) metronome
    c) altimeter
    d) calendar

38. a) adeptness
    b) prowess
    c) maladroitness
    d) deftness

39. a) blackjack
    b) weapon
    c) machete
    d) cannon

**40.**  a)  43
    b)  17
    c)  27
    d)  31

**41.**  a)  nodwiw
    b)  leepop
    c)  toeltb
    d)  rromri

**42.**  There are four cities.

Armian lies west of Postich.
Clester lies west of Armian.
Tribo lies west of both Clester and Armian
Which city is farthest east?

    a)  Armian    b)  Clester    c)  Postich    d)  Tribo

**43.**  Given: designer = 8; illustrator = 11; painter = 7;
            then photographer = ?

    a)  8    b)  10    c)  12    d)  14

For questions 44 through 51:

The four Given Frames make a logical series. Select the Answer Frame that should be next in the series.

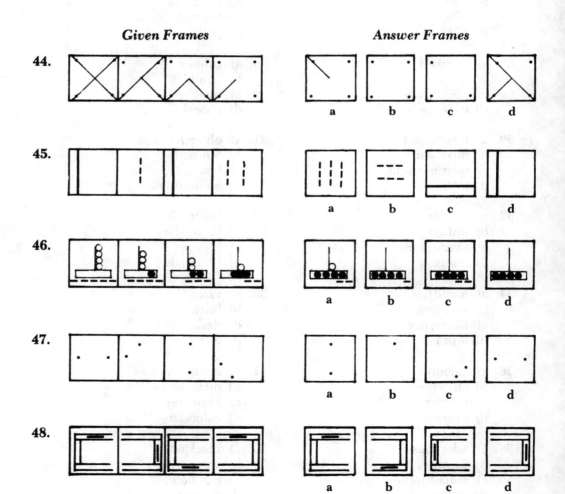

*Given Frames*                    *Answer Frames*

49.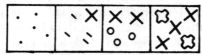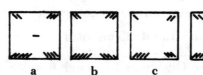

50.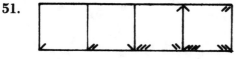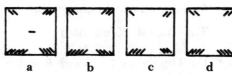

51.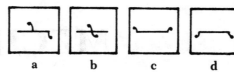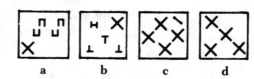

52. Murray, Lisa, and Kira are a marketing-research executive, an oceanographer, and a dispensing optician, but not necessarily in that order. Kira is not the oceanographer. Murray is not the dispensing optician nor the oceanographer. Therefore:

   a) Lisa = marketing; Murray = oceanographer; Kira = optician
   b) Lisa = oceanographer; Murray = marketing; Kira = optician
   c) Lisa = optician; Murray = marketing; Kira = oceanographer
   d) Lisa = oceanographer; Murray = optician; Kira = marketing

53. All red rosebushes have thorns. Some yellow rosebushes have thorns. Pink rosebushes have no thorns. If these statements are true, then it follows that . . .

   a) half of all rosebushes have thorns.
   b) one third of all rosebushes have *no* thorns.
   c) a blind person could determine the color of a rose by feeling the stem for thorns.
   d) none of these.

54. Five computer trainees, Alice, Barbara, Charles, David, and Edward, each had former occupations: assembler, bank teller, salesperson, teacher, and travel agent. Each trainee was born in a different state: Arizona, Illinois, Maine, Utah, and Virginia. Barbara is not from Illinois. The Virginian was a travel agent. Alice was not a banker and was not born in Virginia. The former salesperson was born in Utah. Barbara was a teacher. Edward was born in Illinois. The bank teller is from Arizona and is not David. Which of the following statements is completely true?

   a) Alice is a former assembler from Maine.
   b) Edward is a former assembler from Illinois.
   c) Charles is a former travel agent from Virginia.
   d) Charles is a former salesclerk from Utah.

# MECHANICAL TEST

Discover if tomorrow's technology includes you. Can you follow patterns, understand basic machines, or solve problems involving spatial relationships? Can you develop intricate designs and work with precision?

**Directions:** Read the directions carefully, then work quickly and accurately. Try to answer as many of the 43 questions as you can within the time limit. Use the answer sheet provided on page 170.

**Time Limit: 25 minutes**

For Questions 1 through 6, select the object that is represented by the three-view drawings.

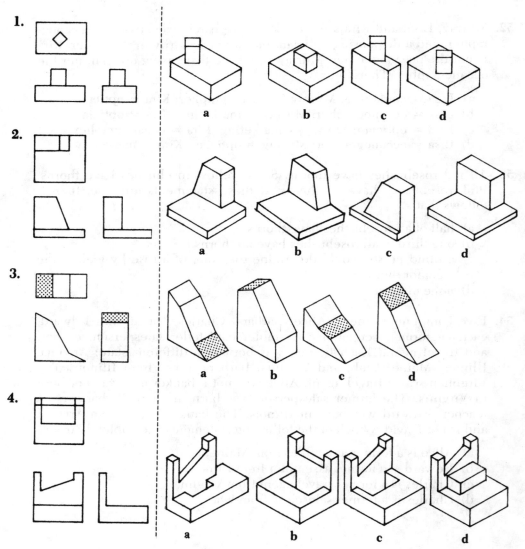

**5.**

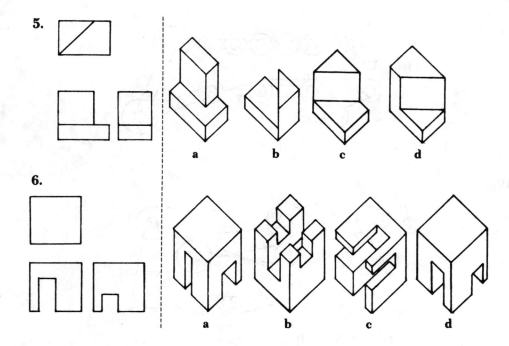

a          b          c          d

**6.**

a          b          c          d

**7.** Each of three connected containers, A, B, and C, has a capacity of twenty-five quarts. Each container has five quarts of water in it. If forty-five more quarts of water are slowly poured into A and allowed to rest, how many quarts would then be in C?

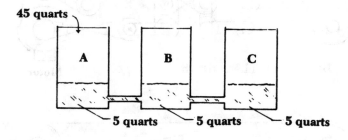

a) twenty quarts          c) ten quarts
b) fifteen quarts         d) five quarts

For questions 8 through 13, determine which numbered wheel is turning clockwise (the same direction as the motor).

**8.**

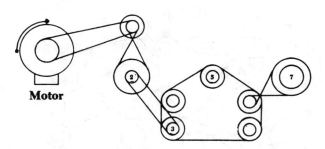

a) 2     b) 3     c) 5     d) 7

**9.**

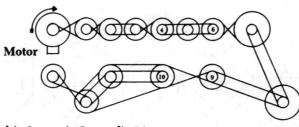

Motor

a) 4     b) 6     c) 9     d) 10

**10.**

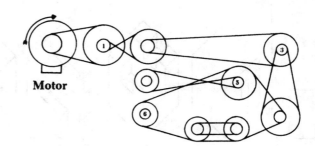

Motor

a) 1     b) 3     c) 5     d) 6

**11.**

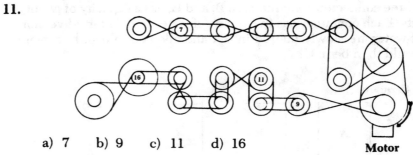

a) 7     b) 9     c) 11     d) 16

Motor

**12.**

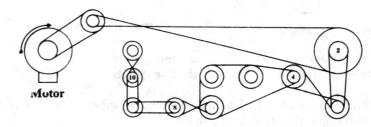

Motor

a) 2     b) 4     c) 8     d) 10

**13.**

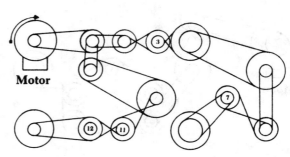

Motor

a) 3     b) 7     c) 11     d) 12

14. How often you lubricate machinery with moving parts depends mainly upon the . . .

  a) weight of the moving parts
  b) speed at which the moving parts rotate
  c) skill of the person doing the lubricating
  d) amount of use of the machinery

15. If you feel an electric shock while using a portable electric hand drill, you should immediately . . .

  a) stand on a piece of paper or scrap lumber
  b) grab on to a metal doorknob
  c) shut off the drill
  d) reverse the plug in the electric outlet

16. As an empty conference room becomes gradually filled by people, the room's . . .

  a) temperature and humidity both decrease
  b) temperature and humidity both increase
  c) temperature decreases and the humidity increases
  d) temperature increases and the humidity decreases

17. An electrical reading of "1,200 watts" is *least* likely to refer to . . .

  a) an automobile's motor
  b) a portable hair dryer
  c) a heat lamp
  d) a toaster

For questions 18 through 26, determine which box *cannot* be constructed from the given pattern.

18.
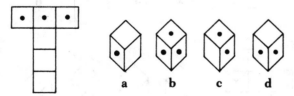
    a       b       c       d

19.
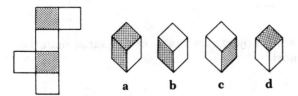
    a       b       c       d

20.
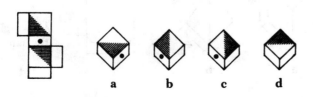
    a       b       c       d

**21.**

**22.**

**23.**

**24.**

**25.**

**26.**

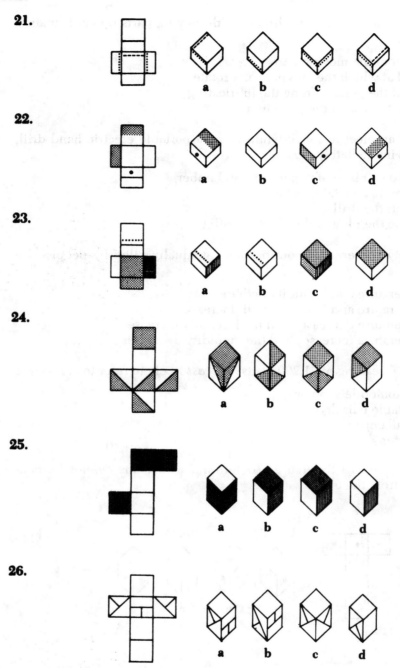

**27. If all three solid objects are made of the same material, which one will weigh the most?**

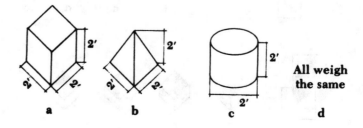

**28.** The shadow cast from a cloud approximates its own size and shape because . . .

    a) the sun's rays are nearly parallel
    b) the moisture in the cloud acts as a mirror and reflects the light upon the earth
    c) all the colors except gray are filtered out
    d) the speed of light is extremely fast

**29.** If the automatic transmission in an automobile is not working properly, a mechanic should *first* . . .

    a) adjust the transmission linkage bands to manufacturer's specifications
    b) administer a liquid pressure test in the transmission lines
    c) check the transmission fluid level
    d) check the engine's vacuum system

**30.** Which of the following is *least* likely to be the cause of a continuous vibration in an operating motor?

    a) loose ball bearings
    b) a faulty ignition circuit
    c) loose belt tension or bolts
    d) an unbalanced armature

**31.** If Gear A makes 10 revolutions, Gear B will make . . .

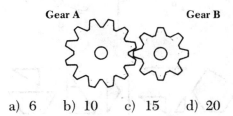

    a) 6    b) 10    c) 15    d) 20

**32.** How much weight is needed to balance this seesaw?

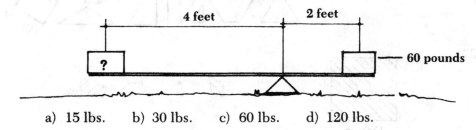

    a) 15 lbs.    b) 30 lbs.    c) 60 lbs.    d) 120 lbs.

**33.** At the mark, the scale reads . . .

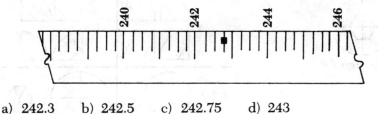

    a) 242.3    b) 242.5    c) 242.75    d) 243

**34.** Which of the following pulley systems will lift the weight most easily?

 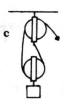 

For questions 35 through 40: Which set of segments best forms the given design?

**35.**

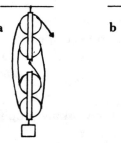

**Design**

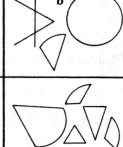

**36.**

**Design**

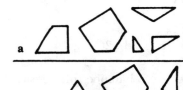

**37.**

**Design**

a   b   c   d

**38.**

**Design**

 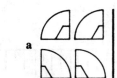 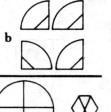

**39.**

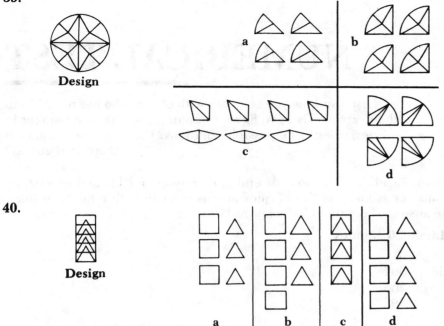

**40.**

**41.** A silver spoon and a wooden pencil are both in the same room and at the same temperature. However, the spoon feels colder when you touch it because . . .

    a) it is heavier.
    b) silver is a good conductor.
    c) silver is quite valuable.
    d) gray objects usually appear cooler.

**42.** A decelerating lane would most probably be used in connection with a . . .

    a) highway exit.
    b) tollbooth.
    c) steep grade on a highway.
    d) sharp curve on a highway.

**43.** A painted wooden ladder is a safety hazard primarily because the paint . . .

    a) becomes slippery after it dries.
    b) may hide weak spots in the ladder's frame.
    c) weakens the cells in the wood.
    d) will peel and cause the wood to decay.

# NUMERICAL TEST

Discover how you compare with others who use numbers in their careers. Can you figure discounts, find the next number in a series, or estimate possible solutions? Can you read numerical charts and graphs?

**Directions:** Read the directions carefully, then work quickly and accurately. Try to answer as many of the 47 questions as you can within the time limit. Use the answer sheet provided on page 170.

**Time Limit: 30 minutes**

1. Add:   307
           268
           197
            93
          425

    a) 1180    b) 1190    c) 1280    d) 1290

2. Add:  $3\frac{2}{9}$
         $5\frac{1}{9}$
         $7\frac{1}{9}$

    a) $15\frac{4}{9}$    b) $15\frac{4}{27}$    c) $^{19}\!/_9$    d) none of these

3. Add:  $\frac{3}{4} + \frac{1}{2} =$

    a) $\frac{4}{6}$    b) $\frac{3}{8}$    c) $1\frac{1}{4}$    d) $1\frac{1}{2}$

4. Add:  $5\frac{2}{3}$
         $6\frac{1}{2}$
       $10\frac{5}{6}$

    a) $21\frac{8}{11}$    b) 22    c) 23    d) $22\frac{1}{3}$

5. Add:   6 ft.   9 in.
       23 ft.  $10\frac{1}{2}$ in.
       16 ft.   6 in.
        1 ft.  $3\frac{1}{2}$ in.

    a) 46 ft. 28 in.      b) 48 ft. 9 in.
    c) 48 ft. 5 in.       d) 46 ft. 11 in.

6. Multiply:    697
             $\times 34$

    a) 23,898    b) 23,698    c) 22,898    d) 22,698

**7.** Which of the following would be greater than (60 × 60)?

    a) (50 × 70)          b) (60 × 60)
    c) (50 × 80)          d) (40 × 90)

**8.** Multiply:    .016
            × .016

    a) .000256    b) .00256    c) .0256    d) .256

**9.** Solve:    4/9 × 3/5 =

    a) ½    b) 20/27    c) 7/45    d) 4/15

**10.** The total number of sixths in 2½ is

    a) 10    b) 11    c) 13    d) 15

**11.** What is the mean (average) of the following numbers?

    5, 12, 3, 8, 2

    a) 3    b) 5    c) 6    d) 30

**12.** The length of a piece of rope is 4 yards, 2 feet, and 3 inches. What is the rope's length expressed in feet?

    a) 6¼    b) 9    c) 14¼    d) none of these

**13.** If you purchase three sweaters that cost $11.95 each, how much change should you receive if you give the clerk forty dollars?

    a) $4.15    b) $5.15    c) $25.05    d) $28.05

**14.** Subtract:     7 hrs. 12 min. 30 sec.
              − 4 hrs. 14 min. 40 sec.

    a) 2 hr. 57 min. 50 sec.       b) 2 hr. 58 min. 50 sec.
    c) 3 hrs. 2 min. 10 sec.       d) 11 hr. 25 min. 70 sec.

**15.** A football team won 6 games and lost 18. What fraction of its games did the team win?

    a) ⅓    b) ¼    c) ⅔    d) ¾

**16.** What *one* number can replace *both* question marks?

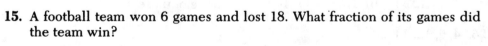

    $\dfrac{5}{?} = \dfrac{?}{45}$

    a) 1    b) 9    c) 15    d) 225

**17.** 5 is what percentage of 4?

    a) 20    b) 80    c) 120    d) 125

18. A particular jogging outfit usually sells for $45.00. However, during a sale it is advertised at 20% off. How much does the outfit cost during the sale?

    a) $9.00    b) $25.00    c) $36.00    d) $54.00

19. A movie begins at seven twenty-three P.M. and ends at nine fourteen P.M. the same evening. How long is the movie?

    a) 1 hour 9 minutes          b) 1 hour 51 minutes
    c) 2 hours 9 minutes         d) 2 hours 51 minutes

20. What is the cost to carpet a room 15 feet long and 12 feet wide, if the carpet cost 18 dollars per square yard?

    a) $3,240    b) $1,080    c) $540    d) $360

21. If *JK* is parallel to *LM*, how many degrees are there in angle y?

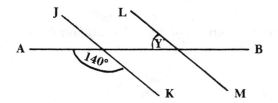

    a) 40    b) 140    c) 220    d) none of these

For questions 22 through 29, select the number that would be next in the series.

22. 1, 4, 7, 10, 13, 16,

    a) 17    b) 18    c) 19    d) none of these

23. 31, 24, 18, 13, 9, 6,

    a) 1    b) 2    c) 3    d) none of these

24. 3, 28, 6, 24, 9, 20, 12, 16, 15,

    a) 12    b) 16    c) 18    d) none of these

25. 7, 13, 24, 45, 86,

    a) 127    b) 167    c) 168    d) none of these

26. 4, 6, 12, 14, 28, 30,

    a) 32    b) 34    c) 60    d) none of these

27. 6.546, 6.659, 6.772, 6.885, 6.998,

    a) 7.111    b) 7.10    c) 7.011    d) none of these

28. 3, 4, 4, 6, 12, 15, 45, 49,

    a) 54    b) 196    c) 205    d) none of these

29. 2, 12, 30, 56, 90, 132,

    a) 150    b) 182    c) 190    d) none of these

For questions 30 through 33, estimate (*do not use paper and pencil*) which of the given computations would result in the largest numerical answer.

**30.** a) 32 × 30          b) 40 × 12
    c) 65 × 9          d) 13 × 52

**31.** a) 4326 × 117          b) 8247 × 14
    c) 6105 × 38          d) 2621 × 119

**32.** a) 10 × 200 × 3½          b) 20 × 400 × 1½
    c) 15 × 400 × 2½          d) 30 × 200 × 4½

**33.** a) 20% of 4,350          b) 36% of 4,000
    c) 70% of 3,100          d) 50% of 2,850

**34.** A television manufacturer offers a distributor successive discounts of 15 percent and 10 percent on one of its new color models. The distributor pays $459 net for the TV set. What was the original price before any discounts?

  a) $612    b) $600    c) $580.65    d) $573.75

**35.** If you can paint three standard-size rooms in two days, how many similar rooms can you and three of your friends paint in three days?

  a) 6    b) 13½    c) 18    d) 54

**36.** A car enters the Connecticut Turnpike at 4:15 P.M. and leaves at an exit 36 miles away at 5:00 P.M. What is the average speed of the car in miles per hour?

  a) 27    b) 36    c) 45    d) 48

The bar graph below shows the number of new contemporary, Colonial, and ranch-style homes recently built in Bachville.

**THE NEW HOMES IN BACHVILLE**

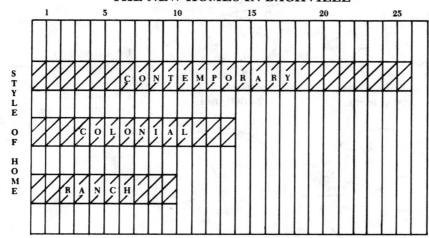

**37.** Find the ratio of new contemporary homes to the total number of new homes in Bachville.

  a) 13 : 12    b) 26 : 24    c) 13 : 25    d) 26 : 12

**38.** What percentage of the new homes is ranch-style?

a) 10    b) 14    c) 20    d) 26

**39.** During the past several years, one of the Midwestern universities has been actively seeking students from other sections of the nation. The campaign has been successful. Now 30% of the student body comes from other areas. New England is the largest supplier, with 60% of the recruited students. The percentage of students from New England is

a) ½    b) 18    c) 30    d) 90

**40.** If the sum of the edges of a cube is 36 inches, the volume of the cube is
a) 12.96 cu. in.                    b) 27 cu. in.
c) 40.5 cu. in.                     d) 81.125 cu. in.

**41.** If two dice are thrown simultaneously, what is the probability that each will turn up 4?

a) 1 : 16    b) 1 : 18    c) 1 : 24    d) 1 : 36

**42.** Three women and three men go to a photographer to have a group picture taken. The photographer places six chairs in a row and insists that no two people of the same sex sit next to each other. How many different pictures could be taken?

a) 18    b) 36    c) 72    d) 144

Questions 43 and 44 pertain to the following graphs.

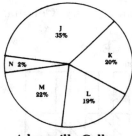

**Adamsville College**
**5,400 students**

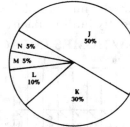

**Scottstown College**
**24,000 students**

KEY:
J = Liberal Arts
K = Business Administration
L = Communications
M = Fine Arts
N = Engineering

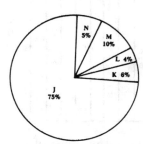

**Valbury College**
**7,000 students**

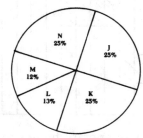

**College of Paulsburg**
**3,600 students**

**43.** Which college has the greatest number of students enrolled in a Liberal Arts program?

    a) Adamsville College      b) Scottstown College
    c) Valbury College         d) College of Paulsburg

**44.** Which college has the *smallest* number of students enrolled in a Fine Arts Program?

    a) Adamsville College      b) Scottstown College
    c) Valbury College         d) College of Paulsburg

**45.** Two cards are drawn, one after the other, from a deck of 52 playing cards. What is the probability that they will be the same suit?

    a) $1:4$     b) $12:51$     c) $11:52$     d) $1:12$

**46.** If snow is falling at the rate of 1½ inches per hour, how many inches of snow will fall in X minutes?

    a) $\dfrac{x}{40}$     b) $\dfrac{x}{30}$     c) $30x$    d) $40x$

**47.** Determine the next number in this series:

    0, 6, 24, 60, 120, 210,

    a) 300     b) 330     c) 336     d) none of these

# SOCIAL TEST

Discover if you have the aptitude for helping others solve personal problems. Can you motivate others? Can you advise, guide, or counsel others?

**Directions:** Read the directions carefully, then work quickly and accurately. Try to answer as many of the 55 questions as you can within the time limit. Use the answer sheet provided on page 170.

**Time Limit: 30 minutes**

1. Early one evening, you see a few young children playing on a construction site with unattended construction equipment. You should . . .

    a) pay no attention; it's not your concern.
    b) tell them to leave; it's not their property and it is a dangerous place to play.
    c) make a citizen's arrest, call the police, press charges, and make sure these children are taught a lesson.
    d) not get involved; probably one of their parents works on this construction site.

2. An individual's socialization process:

    a) continues throughout a lifetime.
    b) is the primary concern of the school.
    c) reverses itself after puberty.
    d) ceases in the teen-age years.

3. The children who are overprotected at home often seem at school to be:

    a) the best workers.
    b) most aggressive.
    c) lacking in independence.
    d) slower in muscular development.

4. You are an eighth-grade teacher and have noticed that during the past several weeks the behavior of one of your students has changed. Until now she had been a model student, always doing the right thing at the right time. Lately she interrupts while others are speaking, hums aloud in class, intentionally drops her books on the floor at least once a day. If you do not pay attention to her, she becomes rude and discourteous. After a few inquiries, you learn that her mother has recently remarried. On the basis of this information, which of the following suppositions is the most likely explanation of her present behavior?

    a) Her behavior has changed because her stepfather insists upon checking her homework every night.
    b) Her behavior is directed toward seeking more attention because she must now share her mother's love.
    c) She is now reacting in school as her "real self." It's like the saying "You show your true colors when the chips are down."
    d) Her mother does not love her anymore.

5. Which of the following environmental conditions is most likely to cause emotional disturbances in children?

   a) disrupted and strained family relationships
   b) a family has a lower income than that of friends, neighbors, or relatives
   c) a family has a higher income than that of friends, neighbors, or relatives
   d) three children sharing one bedroom

6. You are the Executive Director of your state's Mental Health Association. During this month's meeting of department supervisors, you notice that one of your subordinates is asking many good questions and contributing substantially to all the discussions. You should therefore surmise that . . .

   a) this supervisor will eventually cause trouble and object to being controlled by you.
   b) this supervisor is trying to impress you.
   c) this supervisor is having a positive learning experience at the conference.
   d) this supervisor feels that "talk is cheap."

7. You are a psychologist at one of the country's federal penitentiaries, and one of your functions is to try to rehabilitate the inmates. For this to be accomplished, an inmate must . . .

   a) be highly intelligent and free of any neurotic tendencies.
   b) come from a highly moralistic home.
   c) be willing to actively participate in the rehabilitation process.
   d) have interests and aptitudes that do not differ greatly from yours.

8. Which of the following is a characteristic of an immature person? An immature person . . .

   a) has passed through the "taking" stage into the "giving" stage and derives pleasure from giving affection and emotional support.
   b) has an eagerness for immediate gratification of personal needs and fulfilling personal pleasures.
   c) has ambitions and goals that are realistic in comparison with abilities and aptitudes.
   d) can deal with reality, and either accepts circumstances as they are or works purposefully to alter them.

9. The leader of a teen-age club makes a special effort to involve each member in its weekly discussion because teen-agers have a need . . .

   a) to compete with one another.
   b) to contradict one another's statements.
   c) to quarrel with one another.
   d) to belong to the group.

10. If you are described as "skilled in human relations," then you . . .

   a) can persuade others to do things your way.
   b) can recognize interpersonal problems and find a way to solve them.
   c) are usually happy, have many friends, and have few personal problems.
   d) help others find their ancestry and construct a family tree.

11. You are a well-respected, successful, and conscientious executive director of a city agency and are often called upon by other city departments for suggestions concerning proper agency administration. One of your favorite recommendations is that agencies provide an inexperienced worker with definite limits and controls as well as necessary freedoms because controls . . .

   a) will help the inexperienced worker realistically see what life is all about.
   b) give the inexperienced worker specific guidelines which will foster feelings of security and ultimately form a base for future decision making.
   c) will keep the inexperienced worker from advancing up the ladder of success too fast.
   d) will explain agency policy.

12. Which of the following statements is true?

   a) A person's character may be accurately determined from an examination of his or her physical characteristics.
   b) The best applicant for a job is usually the one who most needs the money.
   c) Infant boys are more active than infant girls.
   d) You can have positive and negative feelings toward the same object at the same time.

13. Adolescence is a time of rapid physical growth and change. About how many adolescents are concerned with their physical development?

   a) one out of three
   b) one out of eight
   c) one out of ten
   d) one out of twenty

14. Which of the following is the most necessary element for finding a solution to a problem?

   a) The problem should have only one workable solution.
   b) The person seeking the solution should have a need or desire to do so.
   c) There should be no obstacles between the person seeking the solution and the solution itself.
   d) It must be possible to find the solution in a reasonable length of time.

15. David, one of your acquaintances, asks you to make an important decision for him. Should you . . .

   a) tell him to talk it over with his family?
   b) advise him to go to a psychiatrist?
   c) ask him why he is having such difficulty making the decision himself?
   d) inform him that you have too many problems of your own and you can't handle another problem at this time?

16. During your summer vacation from college you are employed as a summer-camp athletic counselor. You notice that one of the campers, Chuck, appears to be fearful of playing physically active games with the other children. He complains of stomach cramps just before athletic events. As you continue your observations, you soon notice that Chuck is so clumsy when he does play that some of the other campers make fun of him, while others avoid him. What would you do?

    a) Suggest that he read books about the games so he will know the rules and learn how to play better.
    b) Get him involved in the games by giving him an assignment such as keeping score or caring for the equipment.
    c) Demand that he get into the games because he must learn how to play with others and now is as good a time as any.
    d) Just ignore the boy because you'll probably do more harm than good.

17. Of the following, the single most important resource for learning and growth for a college professor will probably come from . . .

    a) the students.
    b) other faculty members.
    c) professional literature.
    d) television news programs.

18. Most criminals . . .

    a) have beady eyes.
    b) look like other people.
    c) have a very high I.Q.
    d) have a good sense of humor.

19. A counseling psychologist is adept at understanding and interpreting what a client says and does, but should not immediately share his or her interpretations with the client. The reason for delaying a response is that the client . . .

    a) will not understand the interpretations.
    b) is not in the right frame of mind to accept or use the interpretations properly.
    c) should be given time to draw some conclusions and make some interpretations without specific directions from the psychologist.
    d) does not want to hear these interpretations, for they only tend to add to the client's problems.

20. When asked to draw another member of their family, young children often distort features in their drawings because . . .

    a) their artistic talents are not perfected.
    b) they exaggerate what they deem important.
    c) their fine motor coordination is still undeveloped.
    d) they are unable to remember all the details.

**21.** As a counseling psychologist, you want to help one of your clients overcome feelings of inferiority. You should . . .

    a) tell your client never to admit defeat but to keep trying to solve all problems no matter how great the odds.

    b) tell your client that all people have some feelings of inferiority.

    c) point out to your client past or present successes, even minor ones, in order to develop some feelings of self-confidence.

    d) refer your client to the latest research studies on inferiority. Reading the studies will help your client understand the dynamics of this problem.

**22.** You are a psychiatric social worker in charge of a small group-therapy session. Sarcastic remarks to one of your clients . . .

    a) should never be used.

    b) should be used when all other methods fail.

    c) should be used with an individual client after the therapy session.

    d) should be used with a client who has shown steady improvement.

**23.** A few parents have expressed anxiety that the quality of their children's education will suffer because there are several minority children in the class. As the teacher, you should . . .

    a) inform the parents that their children will now benefit by helping less capable students.

    b) call for a brief meeting with those parents and discuss the background of the minority children.

    c) answer that education is for all peoples and if they don't like it they can put their children in a private school.

    d) invite the parents to visit your classroom to observe the children at work and at play.

**24.** Which of the following do most single people consider to be the most important factor contributing to their overall happiness?

    a) their present financial situation

    b) their house or apartment and furnishings

    c) their health and physical condition

    d) their friends and social life

**25.** The prime reason that a sizable number of adolescents are prone to use swear words and slang expressions is their . . .

    a) need to defy authority.

    b) need to assert independence.

    c) desire to attain peer approval.

    d) tendency to imitate their parents.

**26.** College students who are highly motivated toward achievement are probably . . .

    a) dominated by their parents.

    b) graduates of a small rural high school.

    c) obtaining intrinsic rewards from their work.

    d) perfectionists.

27. You are a hospital social worker and frequently need to interview patients. The information you receive at an interview should be recorded on the patient's cumulative record form . . .

    a) at the time the client tells it.
    b) the same day as the interview.
    c) about a week later, which will give you sufficient time to think over what was said and weed out the unimportant details.
    d) using your own private coding system to prevent other hospital personnel from reading this information.

28. You are a resident therapist at a state-hospital dormitory for the mildly retarded. In helping your clients learn how to accept and fulfill responsibilities, you may properly permit them to make decisions with respect to all of the following questions *except:*

    a) Should we assign one person to sweep the dormitory for a month, or should we rotate the assignment daily?
    b) Which exits shall we use during fire drills?
    c) What color should we paint the lounge walls?
    d) What flavor ice cream should we serve at the next happy occasion?

29. Generally speaking, if high-school students are treated as responsible people . . .

    a) they will act as responsible people.
    b) they will disappoint you.
    c) their parents will be enraged, for they do not want their children to grow up.
    d) you will be unable to predict the outcome.

30. Research shows that good teachers tend to be:

    a) lenient.
    b) strict and demanding.
    c) flexible and businesslike.
    d) rigid and autocratic.

31. If you believe that hereditary and environmental factors are equally important in the process of learning, then you . . .

    a) regard motivation as a useless technique.
    b) consider the I.Q. to be a fixed number.
    c) would agree to giving a test at the fourth-grade level that would separate the academically oriented students from those who will work with their hands.
    d) would disagree with giving a test at the fourth-grade level that would separate the academically oriented students from those who will work with their hands.

32. The most important qualification of medical social workers is . . .

    a) extensive medical training.
    b) to be bilingual.
    c) a belief in the value of individual human life.
    d) extensive knowledge of all legal and medical community resources.

33. Of the following, the most accurate generalization about human ability is that . . .

    a) it is always changing.
    b) it is constant.
    c) it is affected by the environment.
    d) it is determined at birth.

34. Generally, a youngster's first major source of racial bias is the child's . . .

    a) siblings.
    b) parents.
    c) television programs.
    d) peer group.

35. You are a probation officer who has a counseling group for juvenile offenders, and you want to develop an attitude of cooperation within the group. Which of the following methods is *least* likely to do so?

    a) List all the reasons why cooperation is a necessity in order to get along in this world.
    b) Encourage the youngsters to help plan the counseling sessions.
    c) Provide opportunities for them to help younger children with a special project.
    d) Whenever the opportunity arises, set a proper example by cooperating with them or with your co-workers.

36. If you are considered by others to be a "good person," then applying your own standards and ideals for a proper life is . . .

    a) usually the best way to help someone else.
    b) usually a good way to help someone else.
    c) not a good way to help someone else.
    d) all you really need to help someone else.

37. You are a social worker in the City Department of Welfare, and you learn that one of your clients has been hospitalized. You should first . . .

    a) request that a Welfare Department physician go immediately to see the client in the hospital.
    b) telephone the hospital to find out the probable length of hospitalization.
    c) telephone the relatives and tell them you are sorry.
    d) visit your client at the hospital to assess the extent of the injuries.

38. Pressures for success are usually the strongest upon students from . . .

    a) the lower-income class.
    b) the middle-income class.
    c) the upper-income class.
    d) all of the above.

**39.** Which of the following statements is true?

a) Younger workers are significantly more dissatisfied than older ones with the financial rewards and challenges their jobs provide.
b) Younger workers are significantly more satisfied than older ones with the financial rewards and challenges their jobs provide.
c) Younger and older workers express the same amount of satisfaction concerning the financial rewards and challenges their jobs provide.
d) A person's age and the amount of satisfaction he or she derives from the job have no statistical relationship.

**40.** When you delegate authority to others, you should first give the most consideration to . . .

a) how much power and authority you should entrust to them.
b) what results you expect of them.
c) the selection of the person who will be held responsible for the outcome of this project.
d) the financial compensations that you will have to make as a result of any new job descriptions.

**41.** You are a hospital nursing-service administrator, and one of your newly appointed young nurses shows some symptoms of insecurity, such as excessive talkativeness, unpredictable "freezing up," and being unable to follow directions correctly. Of the following, which would be the most desirable action for you to take?

a) Have a conference with this nurse and state that if there is not an immediate improvement in behavior a replacement will be hired.
b) Have a conference with this nurse and state that you are aware of some problem but that you cannot get involved. He or she must work out the problem alone.
c) Organize the duty schedule in such a way that the nurse in question begins with an activity that is relatively easy.
d) Relieve the nurse of any duties that have to do with caring for patients.

**42.** Which of the following personality traits should be considered most important for someone about to be employed in a "people-helping career"?

a) sociable and cheerful
b) good-natured and hospitable
c) persuasive and strong-willed
d) enthusiastic and eager

**43.** Nearly twenty percent of the young people today state that they want to have a career that is "people-oriented" or "helping others." In order to wisely help others with their personal and emotional problems, which of the following characteristics is needed *least*?

a) knowledge of what makes people behave as they do
b) knowledge of community resources and agencies set up to help people in need
c) an ability to provide a relationship that neither wallows in sympathy nor withholds it as a punishment
d) a good sense of intuition combined with kind intentions

44. Kurt, a college student, is in his dormitory room listening to television. The program is suddenly interrupted for a special news bulletin which tells that the college may be directly in the path of an approaching tornado. Which of the following is Kurt most likely to do? He will probably . . .

   a) rush to the common lounge area to find other students who will be listening to the weather bulletins.
   b) stay in his room alone and continue listening to the weather bulletins.
   c) begin to cry, for he is aware of the devastation a tornado can cause.
   d) telephone the local fire department to find out what to do.

45. Young children often learn to manipulate their parents by crying. This technique is commonly used at bedtime when the children do not want to go to bed, although they are physically quite tired and sleepy. To eliminate the "crying tactics," the parents should . . .

   a) not respond to the child's crying.
   b) occasionally respond to the child's crying.
   c) punish the child for crying.
   d) let the child stay up later at night.

46. If your child insists upon reading only sports books, you should . . .

   a) forbid that type of book in the house because it will limit your child's scope of the real world.
   b) stipulate that for every sports book read, your child must read one book on another topic.
   c) steer and encourage your child to reach the highest level of reading competency using sports books as the tool.
   d) pay no attention. The teacher will correct the situation later.

47. Two groups of high school students are given a lengthy word problem involving some arithmetic. Group A is told the truth, that the solution to the problem may take some time but that the actual mathematical computations involved are relatively simple once they figure out what has to be done. Group B is told that this problem is really for "intellectual giants" and that this "brain teaser" is often given to graduating math students at our nation's best colleges. What results should be expected?

   a) Approximately the same number of students in both groups will get the right answer.
   b) More students in group A will get the right answer.
   c) More students in group B will get the right answer.
   d) Approximately the same number of students in both groups will get a wrong answer.

48. Which of the following statements is true?

   a) Your personality cannot be changed by experiences.
   b) People who have a high I.Q. usually have a low mechanical aptitude.
   c) People who have an extremely low I.Q. usually have one aptitude that is very strong and makes up for their deficiencies.
   d) People who live in a city do not have a higher rate of mental disturbance than those who live in small towns.

**49.** In order to curb the amount of cheating on tests, which of the following would likely be most effective?

    a) Warn the test takers that anyone caught cheating will automatically receive a zero as a grade.
    b) Discuss the various cheating methods, including the ingenious ones other test takers have used that have been unsuccessful.
    c) Prepare two or more forms of the same test and astutely distribute them to the test takers.
    d) Double the number of proctors during the test.

**50.** You are a geriatric psychologist in a hospital for the terminally ill. You tell an aged patient that everything is going to be "just fine," although you and the patient both inwardly know that that is not the truth. This avoidance of the truth, although it may be prompted by pity and kindness, will . . .

    a) be greatly appreciated by your patient.
    b) probably lead to your patient's eventual distrust of you.
    c) probably lead to a reversal in your patient's condition.
    d) be greatly appreciated by other members of the hospital staff.

**51.** Which of the following problems is ordinarily the most difficult to resolve while a major reorganization of a state's social-service agency is in progress?

    a) selecting the new organizational structure
    b) indifference toward the new structure on the part of the agency's clients
    c) overcoming resentment to the new structure on the part of higher-level employees
    d) overcoming resentment to the new structure on the part of lower-level employees

**52.** You are a teacher of children with learning disabilities. One of your students verbally demands too much of your time, causing you to neglect other children in your group. Which of the following would be the best way to resolve this problem?

    a) Refer this case to your immediate supervisor, who has had more experience with this type of problem.
    b) Disregard most of the demands. Soon the student will realize what you are doing and will stop demanding your attention.
    c) Warmly, yet firmly, explain to the student why you will be unable to constantly pay attention to each future demand.
    d) Pay as much attention to this student as demanded. Obviously this student needs more attention than the others.

53. The endeavor in most child abuse cases is to mend and strengthen the relationships within the child's family rather than separating and protecting the child from the family cluster. Therefore, which of the following courses of action would offer the best chance for success in child abuse cases?

    a) Place the child in a foster home and conduct therapeutic counseling sessions for the parents and siblings.
    b) Arrange daytime child-care services at the home, while the parents and siblings have therapeutic counseling services.
    c) Schedule psychiatric treatment for the abusing parent and temporarily place the abused child in a foster home.
    d) Have the court remove the primary abusing parent from the home while you arrange for therapeutic group counseling of the family members remaining at home.

54. You are a college graduate student and the resident counselor of a dormitory. Lately, the students have complained of a rash of petty thefts. This morning when nearly all the students are in class, you observe Russell searching through chests of drawers in several of the dormitory rooms. At first, he protests his innocence. But when pressed, he readily admits the recent thefts. After further discussion with the boy and a few phone calls home, you learn that his parents are recently divorced. Neither of them has sent him any money lately, nor are they planning to be financially responsible for him. What should you do?

    a) Ask the professors, administrators, and students to each contribute a small amount of money so that Russell can stay in college.
    b) Explain to him that sooner or later all thieves get caught. Assure him that although you will let him off easy this time, he will be dismissed from the school if it happens again.
    c) Help Russell find a part-time job. This will enable him to pay for any stolen articles and have enough spending money to at least finish the semester.
    d) Conduct a conference involving the boy, his parents, the college dean, and the police in order to determine what punishment Russell should receive.

55. You are a junior-high-school principal. Lately there has been a significant increase in the number of classroom windows broken at night. Certainly you didn't want this situation to occur, but as long as it did you feel that you should take advantage of the recent circumstances and help your students learn to respect public and private property. Which of the following would be the best learning technique?

    a) During an assembly period explain assertively, but without anger, that destruction of public and private property is a crime and warrants specific punishments.
    b) During an assembly period have the local police captain give a presentation concerning "crime and punishment."
    c) Request your school's parents' organization to set up night patrols around the school. If the parents are inconvenienced, they will make sure their children will not continue to break windows.
    d) Request that your social-studies teachers formulate a teaching program that incorporates the concept of responsibility for the care of public and private property.

# PART III

# SCORING

Before you begin to score your test results, we'd like to share an observation with you. Throughout our years of testing we have noticed many people who will solve test problems carefully and painstakingly, only to spoil their efforts by scoring their answers inaccurately. Whether through haste or anxiety, they do themselves a real disservice by being careless about scoring. We urge you to avoid this trap. Compute your scores with the same care you used on taking the test, following the directions step by step. You will notice that you are required to deduct a "correction factor" figure from your right answers. This is a simple procedure which allows for the fact that you may have done some guessing. Unless you have guessed wildly, you will not be penalized, so don't worry about this step. It is standard procedure in all test scoring.

Scoring instructions for all the six sections of the test are exactly the same. Score each test separately.

1. Compare each of your answers on each section with the answer keys on pages 75–76. Mark those you answered right with an R and those answered wrong with a W. Do not score questions you did not attempt, or did not have time to complete.
2. Total your *right* answers.
3. Total your *wrong* answers.
4. Apply the number of *wrong* answers from step 3 to the "Correction for Guessing" table below to determine a Score Correction Factor.
5. Subtract your Score Correction Factor from your total of *right* answers. You now have your final score for that section of the test.

| If Your Number Wrong Is: | 0–1 | 2–6 | 7–10 | 11–14 | 15–18 | 19–22 | 23–26 | 27–30 | 31–34 |
|---|---|---|---|---|---|---|---|---|---|
| Your Score Correction Factor is: | 0 | 1 | 2 | 3 | 4 | 5 | 6 | 7 | 8 |

Sample Scoring:

Business Test: 42 R
9 W
(7 not answered)
Score Correction Factor = 2
Final Score = 42 (R)
−2 (Score Correction Factor)
40

Transfer 40 to the space opposite Business, and score the rest of the tests in exactly the same way.

6. Transfer your test scores to this page.

BUSINESS _____ CLERICAL _____ LOGIC _____
MECHANICAL _____ NUMERICAL _____ SOCIAL _____

Below are two aptitude-test profile charts: one for high school juniors and seniors and another for adults. Select the chart that applies to you, and use a large X to plot your test scores within the appropriate boxes. You will need this chart when you determine your Career Cluster in part IV.

## HIGH SCHOOL JUNIOR OR SENIOR

| | Very low | Low | Below Average | Low Average | Average | High Average | Well Above Average | Superior | Very Superior |
|---|---|---|---|---|---|---|---|---|---|
| BUSINESS | 0–9 | 10–13 | 14–18 | 19–23 | 24–29 | 30–34 | 35–38 | 39–41 | 42–58 |
| CLERICAL | 0–29 | 30–34 | 35–42 | 43–48 | 49–55 | 56–60 | 61–64 | 65–68 | 69–78 |
| LOGIC | 0–8 | 9–13 | 14–18 | 19–24 | 25–30 | 31–35 | 36–39 | 40–43 | 44–54 |
| MECHANICAL | 0–10 | 11–13 | 14–17 | 18–22 | 23–28 | 29–32 | 33–35 | 36–38 | 39–43 |
| NUMERICAL | 0–7 | 8–11 | 12–15 | 16–19 | 20–24 | 25–29 | 30–32 | 33–36 | 37–47 |
| SOCIAL | 0–13 | 14–17 | 18–21 | 22–26 | 27–31 | 32–35 | 36–39 | 40–42 | 43–55 |

## ADULT

| | Very low | Low | Below Average | Low Average | Average | High Average | Well Above Average | Superior | Very Superior |
|---|---|---|---|---|---|---|---|---|---|
| BUSINESS | 0–12 | 13–16 | 17–20 | 21–25 | 26–30 | 31–35 | 36–39 | 40–43 | 44–58 |
| CLERICAL | 0–30 | 31–36 | 37–45 | 46–51 | 52–57 | 58–62 | 63–66 | 67–71 | 72–78 |
| LOGIC | 0–11 | 12–15 | 16–20 | 21–25 | 26–31 | 32–36 | 37–40 | 41–44 | 45–54 |
| MECHANICAL | 0–10 | 11–13 | 14–17 | 18–22 | 23–28 | 29–32 | 33–36 | 37–39 | 40–43 |
| NUMERICAL | 0–7 | 8–11 | 12–15 | 16–20 | 21–25 | 26–30 | 31–34 | 35–39 | 40–47 |
| SOCIAL | 0–16 | 17–20 | 21–25 | 26–30 | 31–35 | 36–39 | 40–42 | 43–45 | 46–55 |

## BUSINESS ANSWER KEY

| 1. b___ | 13. c___ | 25. d___ | 37. a___ | 49. a___ |
|---------|----------|----------|----------|----------|
| 2. b___ | 14. b___ | 26. b___ | 38. b___ | 50. d___ |
| 3. d___ | 15. c___ | 27. c___ | 39. b___ | 51. d___ |
| 4. d___ | 16. c___ | 28. a___ | 40. c___ | 52. b___ |
| 5. c___ | 17. d___ | 29. c___ | 41. c___ | 53. a___ |
| 6. a___ | 18. c___ | 30. d___ | 42. b___ | 54. c___ |
| 7. b___ | 19. a___ | 31. a___ | 43. b___ | 55. d___ |
| 8. a___ | 20. c___ | 32. d___ | 44. a___ | 56. d___ |
| 9. a___ | 21. b___ | 33. b___ | 45. c___ | 57. a___ |
| 10. c___ | 22. a___ | 34. c___ | 46. c___ | 58. a___ |
| 11. b___ | 23. b___ | 35. d___ | 47. d___ | |
| 12. c___ | 24. b___ | 36. d___ | 48. d___ | |

## CLERICAL ANSWER KEY

| 1. c___ | 17. b___ | 33. b___ | 49. a___ | 65. c___ |
|---------|----------|----------|----------|----------|
| 2. a___ | 18. d___ | 34. c___ | 50. c___ | 66. b___ |
| 3. d___ | 19. b___ | 35. c___ | 51. d___ | 67. a___ |
| 4. c___ | 20. c___ | 36. d___ | 52. b___ | 68. c___ |
| 5. b___ | 21. c___ | 37. a___ | 53. b___ | 69. b___ |
| 6. b___ | 22. d___ | 38. a___ | 54. b___ | 70. d___ |
| 7. a___ | 23. c___ | 39. c___ | 55. c___ | 71. b___ |
| 8. c___ | 24. a___ | 40. a___ | 56. d___ | 72. c___ |
| 9. d___ | 25. c___ | 41. c___ | 57. d___ | 73. b___ |
| 10. d___ | 26. c___ | 42. b___ | 58. a___ | 74. d___ |
| 11. b___ | 27. a___ | 43. c___ | 59. b___ | 75. b___ |
| 12. b___ | 28. c___ | 44. a___ | 60. c___ | 76. d___ |
| 13. a___ | 29. d___ | 45. b___ | 61. d___ | 77. b___ |
| 14. b___ | 30. b___ | 46. b___ | 62. b___ | 78. c___ |
| 15. c___ | 31. d___ | 47. b___ | 63. b___ | |
| 16. d___ | 32. a___ | 48. d___ | 64. a___ | |

## LOGIC ANSWER KEY

| 1. d___ | 12. b___ | 23. c___ | 34. d___ | 45. d___ |
|---------|----------|----------|----------|----------|
| 2. c___ | 13. b___ | 24. d___ | 35. c___ | 46. b___ |
| 3. c___ | 14. d___ | 25. a___ | 36. d___ | 47. d___ |
| 4. b___ | 15. d___ | 26. d___ | 37. c___ | 48. c___ |
| 5. a___ | 16. c___ | 27. b___ | 38. c___ | 49. b___ |
| 6. c___ | 17. a___ | 28. a___ | 39. b___ | 50. c___ |
| 7. c___ | 18. b___ | 29. a___ | 40. c___ | 51. a___ |
| 8. a___ | 19. c___ | 30. d___ | 41. b___ | 52. b___ |
| 9. a___ | 20. d___ | 31. a___ | 42. c___ | 53. d___ |
| 10. b___ | 21. d___ | 32. b___ | 43. c___ | 54. b___ |
| 11. d___ | 22. b___ | 33. a___ | 44. b___ | |

## MECHANICAL ANSWER KEY

| | | | | |
|---|---|---|---|---|
| 1. d___ | 10. a___ | 19. a___ | 28. a___ | 37. c___ |
| 2. b___ | 11. a___ | 20. c___ | 29. c___ | 38. a___ |
| 3. d___ | 12. b___ | 21. c___ | 30. b___ | 39. b___ |
| 4. c___ | 13. d___ | 22. d___ | 31. c___ | 40. d___ |
| 5. c___ | 14. d___ | 23. b___ | 32. b___ | 41. b___ |
| 6. d___ | 15. c___ | 24. c___ | 33. c___ | 42. a___ |
| 7. a___ | 16. b___ | 25. b___ | 34. d___ | 43. b___ |
| 8. d___ | 17. a___ | 26. c___ | 35. a___ | |
| 9. c___ | 18. b___ | 27. a___ | 36. a___ | |

## NUMERICAL ANSWER KEY

| | | | | |
|---|---|---|---|---|
| 1. d___ | 11. c___ | 21. a___ | 31. a___ | 41. d___ |
| 2. a___ | 12. c___ | 22. c___ | 32. d___ | 42. c___ |
| 3. c___ | 13. a___ | 23. d___ | 33. c___ | 43. b___ |
| 4. c___ | 14. a___ | 24. a___ | 34. b___ | 44. d___ |
| 5. c___ | 15. b___ | 25. b___ | 35. c___ | 45. b___ |
| 6. b___ | 16. c___ | 26. c___ | 36. d___ | 46. a___ |
| 7. c___ | 17. d___ | 27. a___ | 37. c___ | 47. c___ |
| 8. a___ | 18. c___ | 28. b___ | 38. c___ | |
| 9. d___ | 19. b___ | 29. b___ | 39. b___ | |
| 10. d___ | 20. d___ | 30. a___ | 40. b___ | |

## SOCIAL ANSWER KEY

| | | | | |
|---|---|---|---|---|
| 1. b___ | 12. d___ | 23. d___ | 34. b___ | 45. a___ |
| 2. a___ | 13. a___ | 24. d___ | 35. a___ | 46. c___ |
| 3. c___ | 14. b___ | 25. c___ | 36. c___ | 47. b___ |
| 4. b___ | 15. c___ | 26. c___ | 37. b___ | 48. d___ |
| 5. a___ | 16. b___ | 27. a___ | 38. b___ | 49. c___ |
| 6. c___ | 17. a___ | 28. b___ | 39. a___ | 50. b___ |
| 7. c___ | 18. b___ | 29. a___ | 40. b___ | 51. c___ |
| 8. b___ | 19. c___ | 30. c___ | 41. c___ | 52. c___ |
| 9. d___ | 20. b___ | 31. d___ | 42. d___ | 53. b___ |
| 10. b___ | 21. c___ | 32. c___ | 43. d___ | 54. c___ |
| 11. b___ | 22. a___ | 33. a___ | 44. a___ | 55. d___ |

## WHAT YOUR SCORES TELL YOU

You will probably have scored better on some tests than on others. As you study your results, keep in mind that your higher scores reflect your comparative strengths and that this information will suggest career areas you should investigate. Your lower scores do not prohibit you from finding some success in those areas but are indications that you may have a tougher time and will not reach as high a level of success.

First let's take a look at your ability to handle BUSINESS situations. If you have done well on this test, you most likely will be able to: administer programs, advertise merchandise, conduct meetings, confront others, coordinate activities, delegate responsibilities, distribute products, handle complaints, hire workers, manage organizations, mediate between departments, monitor others' progress, motivate people, negotiate contracts, organize a company, persuade others, plan company needs, promote products, sell consumer goods, supervise workers, prepare a public-relations campaign, evaluate employee performance, and oversee production.

Your potential for working rapidly and accurately with minute details was evidenced on the CLERICAL test. It shows your aptitude to: alphabetize lists, arrange information, catalog data, collate materials, compile statistics, discriminate minute details, dispense information, examine notices, file particulars, handle details, index topics, inspect objects, proofread publications, recall minutiae, record data, remember minor details, repeat set procedures, schedule events, sort information, update files, work at a relatively fast pace, and keep projects within a preset timetable.

Using different forms of reasoning to solve abstract problems is the key to the LOGIC section. Doing well here shows you most likely have the ability to: adjudicate disagreements, analyze data, categorize information, classify materials, condense lengthy reports, create new ideas, deduce conclusions, design data systems, devise a research plan, edit publications, extract main ideas, evaluate proposals, identify problem areas, invent solutions, link similarities, organize a plan, predict outcomes, question others, recommend actions, systematize an involved process, think strategically, identify the pros and cons of a proposal, and judge the value of property.

Your score on the MECHANICAL test indicates your ability to: adjust electrical equipment, assemble apparatus, construct buildings, design data systems, design patterns, display artistic ideas, exhibit artifacts, follow a pattern, illustrate diagrams, invent new machinery, measure areas, memorize designs, operate heavy-duty equipment, overhaul motors, repair appliances, service appliances, sketch diagrams, visualize new applications, work with precision, operate television studio equipment, and design company logos.

Your NUMERICAL test score shows your aptitude for solving and estimating solutions to mathematical problems. So if you've done well on this test, you most likely will be able to: approximate amounts, assess property, audit financial records, balance budgets, budget expenses, calculate depreciations, compile statistics, compute solutions, determine fees, estimate solutions, evaluate net worth, figure discounts, gauge probabilities, measure boundaries, program computers, project future needs, quantify materials, set prices, survey land areas, tabulate surveys, verify measurements, prepare tax forms, and plan tax strategies.

And lastly you showed your aptitude for understanding, analyzing, and resolving others' personal or social problems on the SOCIAL test. So if you've done well here, you should be quite able to: advise people, assess personal progress, be considerate of others' feelings, coach teams, counsel people, encourage others, express feelings, guide conversations, instruct pupils, interview people, listen to others, mediate between sides, motivate others, organize groups, persuade others, provide consultations, recommend a course of action, reflect feelings, rehabilitate others, respond to situations, supervise others, build a sense of trust, convince others to believe something you hold to be true, and resolve personal conflicts.

# CHOOSING YOUR CAREER: The Career Clusters

Just as we believe that successful career selection should be based on an appraisal of your strengths and weaknesses, we also think that any systematized grouping of careers should have the same emphasis on aptitudes. So we have compiled groups of careers that "cluster" around the use of specific combinations of aptitudes. A Career Cluster, then, is a group of careers that are related because they tend to need the same combination of aptitudes.

You will notice that some of the Clusters contain as many as 90 careers. At first glance it may be difficult to imagine how a few of the careers are related to the others. For example who would ever think of a carpet installer, optician, construction estimator, geodesist, and agricultural-engineering technician as having the same aptitudes? They deal with different problems, work in different surroundings, need varying amounts of schooling, use different tools, and have different on-the-job experiences. However, as you begin to analyze which aptitudes they most likely need to function properly on the job, you will see how they are interrelated. Each of these five careers tends to need the same combination of aptitudes—Mechanical and Numerical ones.

Some career titles appear in more than one cluster, because not all careers fit neatly into just one cluster. Many of them overlap. And it is impossible to include every conceivable career but there is a large number of possibilities for you to consider.

Some professionals, such as musicians, professional athletes, and movie stunt persons, rely heavily upon talents impossible to evaluate with this test. We have omitted them from the Career Clusters.

You will notice that for your convenience we have subdivided the Clusters by educational requirements. In each Cluster you will find a variety of jobs requiring a high school diploma (frequently followed by an apprenticeship), a certificate from a two-year college or certified, specialized training school, a college degree, or a graduate school degree. We want to emphasize that these divisions are not rigid. They are generalizations and may vary from one employer to another, or from one area of the country to another, or they may fluctuate according to supply and de-

mand. However, although there may be exceptions to these educational requirements, basic standards do exist and you should use them as guidelines. You will therefore be able to plan any further education or training with an eye to your financial position, your family obligations, or your interest in further schooling.

## HOW TO FIND YOUR CAREER CLUSTER

The Career Cluster system uses the first letter of the name of each section of the test. Each different combination of these letters represents a specific Career Cluster. Career Clusters are always given in alphabetical order. For example careers that require primarily Clerical aptitudes are in the C Cluster. Similarly those that rely on both Logic and Mechanical aptitudes would be represented by the LM Cluster. The BCS Cluster contains those careers that involve Business aptitudes, plus Clerical, plus Social.

Refer to your Aptitude Test Profile on page 74. Choose your strongest scores. Usually only two or three will stand out, although you may have more. Use the seven examples on the following pages to help you determine your Career Cluster. The examples go from one to four strong aptitudes and show how you can arrange them into Career Clusters.

If you score very well on several of the tests, you may find you can choose from more than one Career Cluster. If you do have that choice, then of course you will have more options when deciding which career to pursue. You can be guided by several factors in making your final decision—your financial position, your educational background and the possibility of further schooling, where you live, your family responsibility, your personal preference, and so on. You might do well to consult a career counselor as well.

To select your Career Cluster, remember:

1. A Cluster may consist of one, two, or three aptitudes.
2. Always include only your strongest scores.
3. Keep the Clusters in alphabetical order.
4. You may have more than one Cluster (see examples 4 through 7).

**EXAMPLE 1.**
**ONE STRONG APTITUDE:**
**SINGLE-LETTERED CLUSTER**

| | Very low | Low | Below Average | Low Average | Average | High Average | Well Above Average | Superior | Very Superior |
|---|---|---|---|---|---|---|---|---|---|
| BUSINESS | | | | | | | | X | |
| CLERICAL | | | | X | | | | | |
| LOGIC | | | X | | | | | | |
| MECHANICAL | | | X | | | | | | |
| NUMERICAL | | | X | | | | | | |
| SOCIAL | | | | X | | | | | |

Business is clearly the strongest score on this profile, and there are no other scores worthy of note. Thus the singular B Cluster is the choice.

**EXAMPLE 2.**
**TWO STRONG APTITUDES:**
**DOUBLE-LETTERED CLUSTER**

| | Very low | Low | Below Average | Low Average | Average | High Average | Well Above Average | Superior | Very Superior |
|---|---|---|---|---|---|---|---|---|---|
| BUSINESS | | X | | | | | | | |
| CLERICAL | | | | | X | | | | |
| LOGIC | | | | | X | | | | |
| MECHANICAL | X | | | | | | | | |
| NUMERICAL | | X | | | | | | | |
| SOCIAL | | X | | | | | | | |

Here both the Clerical *and* the Logic scores are comparatively higher than the others. This indicates the use of the combination CL Cluster.

(Note: LC cannot be used: there is no such cluster; the components must be kept in alphabetical order—rule 3.)

EXAMPLE 3.
THREE STRONG APTITUDES:
TRIPLE-LETTERED CLUSTER

|  | Very low | Low | Below Average | Low Average | Average | High Average | Well Above Average | Superior | Very Superior |
|---|---|---|---|---|---|---|---|---|---|
| BUSINESS |  |  |  |  |  |  |  | X |  |
| CLERICAL |  |  |  |  |  |  |  |  | X |
| LOGIC |  |  |  | X |  |  |  |  |  |
| MECHANICAL |  |  | X |  |  |  |  |  |  |
| NUMERICAL |  |  |  | X |  |  |  |  |  |
| SOCIAL |  |  |  |  |  |  | X |  |  |

The Clerical score is the highest and must be used —rule 1. Both the Business *and* the Social scores stand well above the rest and should be incorporated into the cluster . . . the BCS Cluster. (Note: the three components are in alphabetical order—rule 3.)

EXAMPLE 4.
THREE STRONG APTITUDES:
TWO DOUBLE-LETTERED CLUSTERS

|  | Very low | Low | Below Average | Low Average | Average | High Average | Well Above Average | Superior | Very Superior |
|---|---|---|---|---|---|---|---|---|---|
| BUSINESS |  |  | X |  |  |  |  |  |  |
| CLERICAL |  |  |  | X |  |  |  |  |  |
| LOGIC |  |  |  |  |  | X |  |  |  |
| MECHANICAL |  |  |  |  |  |  |  | X |  |
| NUMERICAL |  |  |  |  |  | X |  |  |  |
| SOCIAL |  |  | X |  |  |  |  |  |  |

In this case there are several clusters to consider. The combination of the three highest scores indicates the use of the LMN Cluster (in alphabetical order). We do *not* suggest the use of the singular M Cluster, since both Logic and Numerical are high enough above the rest to be included in the cluster.

Another worthy selection is the Logic *and* Mechanical, LM, combination. It contains the highest score, M, and one of the other comparatively strong scores.

Similarly the MN Cluster is worth mention for it also contains the highest, M, and one of the other strengths, N.

Caution: the LN Cluster cannot be used, because the highest score, Mechanical, must be included in each cluster.

**EXAMPLE 5.**
**FOUR STRONGER APTITUDES:**
**THREE TRIPLE-LETTERED CLUSTERS**

|  | Very low | Low | Below Average | Low Average | Average | High Average | Well Above Average | Superior | Very Superior |
|---|---|---|---|---|---|---|---|---|---|
| BUSINESS |  |  |  |  | X |  |  |  |  |
| CLERICAL |  |  |  |  |  | X |  |  |  |
| LOGIC |  |  |  |  | X |  |  |  |  |
| MECHANICAL |  | X |  |  |  |  |  |  |  |
| NUMERICAL |  | X |  |  |  |  |  |  |  |
| SOCIAL |  |  |  |  | X |  |  |  |  |

This profile chart reveals Clerical to be the leading aptitude, with three others following closely behind. Since clusters may contain no more than three components (rule 2), and Clerical, the highest, must be included (rule 1), this limits the results to the following three clusters: Business + Clerical + Logic, BCL; Business + Clerical + Social, BCS; Clerical + Logic + Social, CLS.

**EXAMPLE 6.**
**FOUR STRONGER APTITUDES:**
**TWO TRIPLE-LETTERED CLUSTERS**

|  | Very low | Low | Below Average | Low Average | Average | High Average | Well Above Average | Superior | Very Superior |
|---|---|---|---|---|---|---|---|---|---|
| BUSINESS |  |  |  |  |  | X |  |  |  |
| CLERICAL |  |  |  |  |  |  |  | X |  |
| LOGIC |  |  |  |  |  |  |  |  | X |
| MECHANICAL |  |  |  |  |  |  |  | X |  |
| NUMERICAL |  |  |  |  |  |  |  |  | X |
| SOCIAL |  |  |  |  |  | X |  |  |  |

This example is similar to the previous one but shows four power-packed aptitudes. Logic *and* Numerical are the strongest and must both be included in the cluster (rule 1). Either Clerical *or* Mechanical should be added, since the cluster limit is three components (rule 2). The resultant clusters are: Clerical + Logic + Numerical, CLN; and Logic + Mechanical + Numerical, LMN.

**EXAMPLE 7.**
**FOUR STRONGER APTITUDES:**
**FOUR TRIPLE-LETTERED CLUSTERS**

|  | Very low | Low | Below Average | Low Average | Average | High Average | Well Above Average | Superior | Very Superior |
|---|---|---|---|---|---|---|---|---|---|
| BUSINESS |  |  |  | X |  |  |  |  |  |
| CLERICAL |  |  |  |  |  |  | X |  |  |
| LOGIC |  |  |  |  |  |  | X |  |  |
| MECHANICAL |  |  |  |  |  |  | X |  |  |
| NUMERICAL |  |  |  |  |  |  | X |  |  |
| SOCIAL |  |  |  |  | X |  |  |  |  |

This last, and rather uncommon, example shows four equally measured strengths. However, only three can be used at one time (rule 2), and they must be kept in alphabetical order (rule 3).

This results in the following Clusters: CLM, CLN, CMN, and LMN.

Before you go on to look at the careers in your cluster, a few final words of advice:

As you scan the careers in your cluster, remember that you may need more education to succeed in several of these careers. Keep in mind too your financial requirements, flexibility, geographic preferences; your inclination to gamble or play it safe, ideal working conditions for you, your depth of determination, the present state of the economy. All these will influence your career decision, now that you know what areas of employment will be best for you.

The Career Directory following the section on Career Clusters will help you compare job descriptions; these are general, composite definitions and describe all the careers mentioned in the book. There may be slight variations from one es-tablishment to another, but the glossary should give you a pretty good idea of what each career entails.

**PROFIT FROM YOUR RESULTS**

- Your scores and Career Cluster are valuable tools, and should be used in conjunction with the advice of career guidance counselors, management consultants, placement agencies, and job counselors. This could be the single most important piece of objective information you can give them about yourself.
- Include the results on your résumé.
- Discuss your aptitudes with possible employers with assurance, and back up the discussion with your test results.
- You can use your results to help plan your curriculum in high school, college, adult-education evening school, professional school, courses in the armed forces, or graduate school.

# The 41 Career Clusters

## THE B CLUSTER

### High School/Apprenticeship:

Advertising Sales Representative
Agri-Business Salesperson
Appliance Salesperson
Automobile Dealer
Automobile Salesperson
Book Salesperson
Carpet Representative
Circulation Manager
Club Manager

Commercial Broker
Cosmetic Salesperson
Customer-Service Representative
Dental-Equipment Sales
  Representative
Electrical-Appliance Salesperson
Food Broker
Livestock-Workers Supervisor
Membership Solicitor

Mobile-Canteen Operator
Office-Machine Sales
  Representative
Pawnbroker
Produce-Department Manager
Skating-Rink Manager
Sporting-Goods Salesperson
Wholesaler

### Two-Year College/Certificate Program:

Bakery Manager
Broadcasting Announcer
Claims Adjuster
Communications Consultant
Dairy Farmer
Executive Chef
Garden-Center Manager

Grain Broker
Health-Club Manager
Industrial-Cafeteria Manager
Jeweler
Livestock Rancher
Mutuel Department Manager
Office Manager

Order-Department Supervisor
Police Chief
Recreation Facility Manager
Real-Estate Agent
Sports Marketer
Stockbroker

### Four-Year College:

Advertising Account Executive
Advertising Copywriter
Advertising Manager
Advertising Worker
Agri-Business Agent
Agricultural Communications
  Specialist
Agricultural Marketing Specialist
Agricultural Teacher
Arboretum Curator
Bank Cashier
City Manager
College Athletic Director
College Recruiter
Computer Sales Representative
Corporate Benefits Manager

County Agricultural Agent
County Manager
Customer Technical-Services
  Manager
Department-Store Manager
Economic-Development
  Coordinator
Escrow Officer
Farm Manager
Film Producer
Front-Office Hotel Manager
Fruit-and-Vegetable Manager
Historic-Site Administrator
Hotel Manager
Information Marketing Manager

Insurance Agent
Insurance Sales Representative
Life-Insurance Sales Agent
Literary Agent
Lobbyist
Natural-Gas Utilization Manager
Park Superintendent
Personnel Administrator
Pharmaceutical Detailer
Public-Relations Representative
Sales Manager
Securities-Brokerage Manager
Social-Services Director
Television Producer
Welfare Director

**Graduate School:**

| | | |
|---|---|---|
| College President | High-School Principal | School Superintendent |

## THE BC CLUSTER

### High School/Apprenticeship:

| | | |
|---|---|---|
| Airline Ramp Agent | Classified-Ad Clerk | Mail-Room Supervisor |
| Airline Ticket Agent | Coding-Clerk Supervisor | Pawnbroker |
| Ammunition Safety Inspector | Correspondence Clerk | Procurement Clerk |
| Automobile-Rental Representative | Dispatcher | Stockroom Supervisor |
| Automobile-Parts Sales Manager | Hotel Bell Captain | Travel Agent |
| Bus-Station Manager | Import-Export Agent | Warehouse Manager |

### Two-Year College/Certificate Program:

| | | |
|---|---|---|
| Airline Schedule Analyst | Foundry Supervisor | Logging Contractor |
| Bank Secretary | Freight Traffic Consultant | Micrographics Services Supervisor |
| Data-Control Supervisor | Hospital Central-Supply Supervisor | Office Manager |
| Dietetic Assistant | Hospital Food-Service | Personal Manager |
| Executive Secretary | Administrator | Postmaster |
| Fire Inspector | International Freight Forwarder | Railroad Station Agent |
| Forest Nursery Supervisor | Legal Assistant | Secretary |

### Four-Year College:

| | | |
|---|---|---|
| Bank Cashier | Custom House Broker | Fund Raiser |
| Brokerage Manager | Dietitian Administrator | Health Record Administrator |
| Collections Manager | Fish-Hatchery Manager | Quality-Control Coordinator |

### Graduate School:

| | |
|---|---|
| Art Librarian | Business Librarian |

## THE BCL CLUSTER

### Two-Year College/Certificate Program:

| | | |
|---|---|---|
| Accounts-Receivable Supervisor | Executive Secretary | Shopping Investigator |
| Airline Schedule Analyst | Forms Analyst and Designer | |

## Four-Year College:

Accountant
Accounting Teacher
Book Editor
Brokerage Manager
Business Manager
Certified Public Accountant

Fund-Raising Director
Head Nurse
Health Officer
Hydroponics-Nursery Manager
Industrial Editor

Information Manager
Medical Record Administrator
News Reporter
Nursing-Home Dietitian
Technical Training Coordinator

## Graduate School:

Head Public Librarian
Librarian

Market-Research Analyst

Patent Attorney

## THE BCM CLUSTER

### High School/Apprenticeship:

Ammunitions Safety Inspector

Building Inspector

Handicraft/Hobby-Shop Manager

### Two-Year College/Certificate Program:

Aircraft Electronic-Instrument
    Inspector
Automobile Service Manager
Fire Inspector

Forms Analyst and Designer
Foundry Supervisor
Gemologist
Industrial-Cafeteria Manager

Micrographics Services Supervisor
Proof-Machine-Operator Supervisor

### Four-Year College:

Agricultural Teacher
County Agricultural Agent
Educational Audiovisual Specialist

Fashion-Design Teacher
Production-Control Supervisor
Quality-Control Coordinator

Safety Inspector
Theater Stage Manager

## THE BCN CLUSTER

### High School/Apprenticeship

Accounting Clerk
Export Clerk
Garden-Center Buyer

Procurement Clerk
Services Clerk

Shipping-and-Receiving Clerk
Ticket Broker

## Two-Year College/Certificate Program:

| | | |
|---|---|---|
| Accounts-Receivable Supervisor | Production-Clerk Supervisor | Tax Preparer |
| Grain Manager | Rate Supervisor | Trust-Evaluation Clerk |
| Order-Department Supervisor | Real-Estate Appraiser | |

## Four-Year College:

| | | |
|---|---|---|
| Accountant | Certified Public Accountant | Quality-Control Coordinator |
| Actuary | Economist | Tax Accountant |
| Auditor | Export Manager | Tax Auditor |
| Bank Cashier | Purchasing Agent | |

## Graduate School:

Community Pharmacist

# THE BCS CLUSTER

## High School/Apprenticeship:

| | | |
|---|---|---|
| Airline-Lounge Receptionist | Correspondence Clerk | Travel-Information-Center Supervisor |

## Two-Year College/Certificate Program:

| | | |
|---|---|---|
| Child-Care Supervisor | Medical Secretary | Reception Clerk |
| Executive Secretary | Passenger-Service Representative | Social Director |
| Legal Assistant | Personal Manager | Summer-Camp Director |
| Legal Secretary | | |

## Four-Year College:

| | | |
|---|---|---|
| Accounting Teacher | Educational-Course Sales | Home Extension Agent |
| Advertising Copywriter | Employment Interviewer | Hospital Personnel Director |
| College Financial-Aid Officer | Head Nurse | Secondary-School Teacher |

## Graduate School:

Community Pharmacist

## THE BL CLUSTER

### Two-Year College/Certificate Program:

Accounts-Receivable Supervisor       Embalmer                              Garden-Center Plant Doctor

---

### Four-Year College:

Accounting Systems Expert            Consumer-Affairs Director             Information Manager
Advertising Worker                   County Agricultural Agent             Insurance Sales Underwriter
Agri-Business Agent                  Credit Analyst                        Job Analyst
Agricultural Economist               Credit-Union Manager                  Job Development Specialist
Agricultural Extension Agent         Ecology Ranger                        Labor-Union Business Agent
Airport Manager                      Educational Programming Director      Law-Enforcement Director
Animal Scientist                     Finance-Company Manager               Literary Agent
Arbitrator                           Floriculturist                        Loan Officer
Bank Lending Officer                 Foreign Correspondent                 Logistics Engineer
Book Editor                          Forest Ranger                         Management Analyst
Branch-Bank Operations Manager       Fruit-and-Vegetable Field Servicer    Newspaper Editorial Writer
Business Analyst                     Harbor Master                         Park Ranger
Chief Medical Technologist           Health Administrator                  Political Scientist
City Editor                          Hydroponics-Nursery Manager           Right-of-Way Agent
Computer Sales Representative        Industrial Editor                     Silviculturist
Conservationist                      Information Consultant                Wage-and-Salary Administrator

---

### Graduate School:

Academic Dean                        Dean of Students                      Market-Research Analyst
Avian Veterinarian                   Hospital Administrator                Newspaper Editor
Bank Comptroller                     Immigration Lawyer                    Patent Attorney
Bank Credit Analyst                  International Lawyer

## THE BLM CLUSTER

### High School/Apprenticeship:

Building Contractor                  Highway Contractor

---

### Two-Year College/Certificate Program:

Embalmer                             Industrial-Engineering Technician

---

### Four-Year College:

Advertising Worker                   Environmentalist                     Industrial Engineer
Art Director                         Environmental Planner                Landscape Architect
City Planner                         Fire-Protection Engineer             Media Director
City-Planning Engineer               Forester                             Surgical-Appliance Salesperson
Dental-Laboratory Manager

**Graduate School:**

| | | |
|---|---|---|
| Architect | Clinical Engineer | Patent Attorney |

## THE BLN CLUSTER

**High School/Apprenticeship:**

Highway Contractor

**Two-Year College/Certificate Program:**

Industrial-Engineering Technician

**Four-Year College:**

| | | |
|---|---|---|
| Accountant | Credit Analyst | Internal Auditor |
| Accounting Systems Expert | Dairy Technologist | Loan Officer |
| Accounting Teacher | Economist | Marine Economist |
| Agricultural Economist | Finance-Company Manager | Operations Research Analyst |
| Bank Lending Officer | Financial Analyst | Purchasing Manager |
| Bond Analyst | Financial Planner | Silviculturist |
| Certified Public Accountant | Grant Coordinator | Tax Accountant |
| City-Planning Engineer | Industrial Economist | Wage-and-Salary Administrator |
| Contract Specialist | Industrial Engineer | |

**Graduate School:**

| | | |
|---|---|---|
| Bank Comptroller | Economic Analyst | Probate Lawyer |
| Bank Credit Analyst | Hospital Pharmacist Administrator | Tax Attorney |
| Conciliator | | |

## THE BLS CLUSTER

**Four-Year College:**

| | | |
|---|---|---|
| Advertising Manager | Employment-Agency Manager | Penologist |
| Branch-Bank Operations Manager | Employment Counselor | Personnel Recruiter |
| Business Consultant | Employment Supervisor | Religious-Activities Director |
| Business Manager | Football Coach | Retirement Officer |
| Consumer-Affairs Director | Head Nurse | Security Consultant |
| Cooperative-Extension-Adviser Specialist | Occupational Therapist | Welfare Director |

**Graduate School:**

Dean of Students
Educational Consultant
Employee Relations Specialist
Engineering Psychologist
Human Resource Adviser

Immigration Lawyer
Industrial Psychologist
Industrial Sociologist
Labor-Relations Consultant

Lawyer
Political-Science Professor
Vocational Rehabilitation
 Consultant

## The BM Cluster

**High School/Apprenticeship:**

Aircraft-Parts Sales Representative
Apartment-Building Superintendent
Arcade Attendant
Communications-Equipment
 Salesperson
Construction Superintendent
Electric-Motors Salesperson
Electronic-Parts Sales
 Representative

Farm-Equipment Dealer
Farmer
Fishing-Boat Captain
Forge Shop Supervisor
Furniture Designer
Handicraft/Hobby-Shop Manager
Hardware Salesperson

House Builder
Industrial-Equipment Sales
 Representative
Jeweler
Masseur/Masseuse
Office-Machine Sales
 Representative

**Two-Year College/Certificate Program:**

Automobile Service Manager
Barber/Stylist
Chef
Commercial Artist
Commercial Photographer
Condominium Manager
Cosmetologist

Fashion Designer
Floral Designer
Garden-Center Landscape Designer
Geothermal-Power-Plant Supervisor
Hairpiece Stylist
Heating-Plant Superintendent
Hospital Engineer

Memorial Designer
Mine Superintendent
Newspaper Art Director
Oil-Field Pipeline Supervisor
Promotion Designer
Retail-Store Art Director
Yacht Designer

**Four-Year College:**

Agricultural Teacher
Art Conservator
Broadcasting Director
Clothes Designer
Display Director

Educational Audiovisual Specialist
Fashion Coordinator
Fashion Designer
Fashion-Design Teacher
Fashion Display Specialist

Film-Laboratory Supervisor
Fire Chief
Interior Designer
Oil-Well Services Supervisor
Television Director

## The BMN Cluster

**High-School/Apprenticeship:**

Building Contractor
Cabinetmaker

Carpenter
Floor-Covering Salesperson

Hardware Salesperson
House Builder

**Two-Year College/Certificate Program:**

| | | |
|---|---|---|
| Architectural Graphic Designer | Dispensing Optician | Hospital Engineer |
| Construction Estimator | Geothermal-Power-Plant Supervisor | Real-Estate Appraiser |

**Four-Year College:**

| | | |
|---|---|---|
| Chief Petroleum Engineer | Landscape Architect | Public-Utilities Sales |
| City-Planning Engineer | Pollution-Control Engineer | Representative |
| Film-Laboratory Supervisor | Project Engineer | Textile Stylist |

**Graduate School:**

| | | |
|---|---|---|
| Architect | Industrial Health Physicist | Manufacturing Engineer |

## The BMS Cluster

**High School/Apprenticeship:**

Hearing-Aids Salesperson

**Two-Year College/Certificate Program:**

| | | |
|---|---|---|
| Electrologist | Paraoptometric | Technical-Course Sales |
| Hairpiece Stylist | Psychiatric-Hospital Cook | Representative |
| Health-Club Manager | Psychiatric-Hospital Groundskeeper | Wardrobe Supervisor |

**Four-Year College:**

| | | |
|---|---|---|
| Advertising Manager | Corrective Therapist | Nursing-Home Food-Service |
| Agricultural Teacher | County Agricultural Agent | Supervisor |
| Artist's Agent | Fashion-Design Teacher | Television Director |
| Art Therapist | Industrial-Arts Teacher | |

**Graduate School:**

| | |
|---|---|
| Public-Health Dentist | Youth Correctional-Education Supervisor |

## The BN Cluster

**High School/Apprenticeship:**

| | | |
|---|---|---|
| Advertising Sales Representative | Caterer | Garden-Center Buyer |
| Auctioneer | Cost Estimator | |

## Two-Year College/Certificate Program:

| | | |
|---|---|---|
| Appraiser | Food-and-Beverage Manager | Mutuel Department Manager |
| Estimator | Golf-Club Manager | Real-Estate Appraiser |
| Executive Chef | Industrial-Cafeteria Manager | Stockbroker |

## Four-Year College:

| | | |
|---|---|---|
| Actuary | Escrow Officer | Personnel Administrator |
| Agricultural Loan Examiner | Financial-Services Sales Agent | Purchasing Agent |
| Agricultural Marketing Specialist | Group-Insurance Sales Agent | Schedule Planning Manager |
| Budget Officer | Hospital Personnel Director | Weighting-and-Measurements- |
| Buyer | Hospital Purchasing Director | Instruments Salesperson |
| Credit-Collections Supervisor | International Banker | |

## Graduate School:

Public-Finance Specialist

## The BNS Cluster

### Two-Year College/Certificate Program:

| | |
|---|---|
| Taxpayer Service Representative | Technical-Course Sales Representative |

### Four-Year College:

| | | |
|---|---|---|
| Accounting Teacher | Consumer Financial Adviser | Financial-Aid Counselor |
| Agricultural Loan Examiner | Consumer Services Consultant | Insurance Sales Underwriter |
| Bank Manager | Corporate Benefits Manager | Nutritionist |
| Branch-Bank Operations Officer | Credit-Collections Supervisor | Personnel Administrator |
| Business Agent | Credit Counselor | Retirement Officer |
| Business Manager | Demographer | |

### Graduate School:

| | | |
|---|---|---|
| Conciliator | Tax Attorney | Probate Lawyer |
| Druggist | | |

## The BS Cluster

### High School/Apprenticeship:

| | | |
|---|---|---|
| Automobile Driving Instructor | Burial-Needs Salesperson | Hearing-Aids Salesperson |

## Two-Year College/Certificate Program:

Child-Care Supervisor
Funeral Director
Group Leader

Modeling Instructor
Passenger Service Representative
Personal Manager

Preparole-Counseling Aide
Wedding Consultant

## Four-Year College:

Advertising Account Executive
Advertising Copywriter
Advertising Manager
Artist's Agent
Business Communicator
Business Education Instructor
Casework Supervisor
City Manager
College Athletic Director

College Recruiter
Consumer-Services Consultant
Corporate Benefits Manager
Day-Care-Center Director
Dramatic Coach
Educational-Course Sales
    Representative
Employee-Welfare Manager
Employer Relations Representative

Farm-Management Adviser
Home Economist
Home Extension Agent
Nursing-Home Social-Work
    Supervisor
Public-Health Educator
Retirement Officer
Secondary-School Teacher
Theater-Arts Teacher

## Graduate School

Educational Supervisor
Employee Relations Specialist

High-School Principal

Special-Education Director

## The C Cluster

## High School/Apprenticeship:

Agricultural Commodity Grader
Aircraft Inspector
Airline-Lounge Receptionist
Automatic-Typewriter Operator
Billing Typist
Cashier
Check-Processing Clerk
Clerk-Typist
Collections Clerk
Customs Inspector
Customs-Patrol Officer
Directory-Assistance Operator

Educational Attendance Clerk
File Clerk
Financial-Statement Clerk
Freight Clerk
Glass Inspector
Hospital Insurance Clerk
Information Clerk
Insurance Clerk
Journal Clerk
Letter Carrier
Mail Clerk

Media Clerk
Medical-Records Clerk
Office Clerk
Order Clerk
Parcel-Post Clerk
Parts-Order and Stock Clerk
PBX Operator
Postal Clerk
Receptionist
Wharfinger
Word-Processing Specialist

## Two-Year College/Certificate Program:

Airline Dispatcher
Airline Schedule Analyst
Blood-Bank Technologist
Broadcast-Secretary Specialist
Conference Typist
Court Clerk
Court Reporter
Customs Import Specialist
Data Typist
Digitizer Operator

Fingerprint Classifier
Health-Care-Facilities Inspector
Keypunch Operator
Laboratory-Animal Technician
Legal Assistant
Legal Secretary
Legal Stenographer
Legislative Reporter
Library Technical Assistant
Medical Office Receptionist

Medical Secretary
Notereader
Passport-Application Examiner
Proofreader
Reservation Clerk
School Secretary
Secretary
Stenotype Operator
Title Searcher
Veterinary-Hospital Attendant

**Four-Year College:**

| | | |
|---|---|---|
| Bank Teller | Food-and-Drug Inspector | Insurance Claims Examiner |
| Conference Interpreter | | |

**Graduate School:**

Catalog Librarian

## The CL Cluster

**Two-Year College/Certificate Program:**

| | | |
|---|---|---|
| Computer Programmer | Forest Technician | Legal Assistant |
| Fishery Technician | Game Warden | Wildlife-Control Agent |

**Four-Year College:**

| | | |
|---|---|---|
| Abstractor | Cytotechnologist | Intelligence Research Specialist |
| Agricultural Microbiologist | Detective | Meteorologist |
| Applications Programmer | Documents Examiner | Microbiologist |
| Archivist | Emergency Medical Technician | Nematologist |
| Bacteriologist | Forest Ecologist | News Assistant |
| Biological Systemist | Geo-Microbiologist | Newspaper Columnist |
| College Registrar | Historian | Pesticide-Control Inspector |
| Cryptanalyst | Industrial Occupational Analyst | Veterinary Bacteriologist |
| Cytotechnician | | |

**Graduate School:**

| | | |
|---|---|---|
| Aerospace Librarian | FBI Agent | Medical Parasitologist |
| Behavioral Pharmacologist | Film Librarian | Music Librarian |
| Biological-Science Librarian | Health-Science Librarian | News Analyst |
| Chemical Librarian | Librarian | Pathologist |
| Communications Librarian | | |

## The CLM Cluster

**Two-Year College/Certificate Program:**

| | | |
|---|---|---|
| Aerial-Photograph Interpreter | Electrocardiograph Technician | Maintenance Data Analyst |
| Aircraft Electronic-Instruments | Electronic Technician | Preservationist |
|   Inspector | Laboratory Assistant | Records Management Analyst |
| Drafter | Laboratory Test Mechanic | Tire Technician |

**Four-Year College:**

Air-Traffic Controller
Fashion Writer

Geo-Microbiologist
Information-Processing Engineer

Mineralogist
Technical Writer

**Graduate School:**

Patent Attorney

# THE <u>CLN</u> CLUSTER

**Two-Year College/Certificate Program:**

Clinical Laboratory Assistant
Computer Programmer

Laboratory Assistant
Production Planning Supervisor

Statistical Clerk

**Four-Year College:**

Dietetic Researcher
Economist
Forest Ecologist

Geo-Microbiologist
Industrial Microbiologist
Internal-Revenue Agent

Medical Technologist
Nuclear Medical Technologist

**Graduate School:**

Epidemiologist
Forensic Pathologist
Forensic Toxicologist

Hospital Pharmacist
Industrial Pharmacologist
Medical Parasitologist

Oral Pathologist
Pharmacist
Pharmacologist

# THE <u>CLS</u> CLUSTER

**High School/Apprenticeship:**

Airport Security Officer

Border-Patrol Agent

**Two-Year College/Certificate Program:**

Dietetic Technician
Legal Assistant

Medical Assistant
Medical Secretary

Mental-Health Technician
Referral Aide

**Four-Year College:**

Career-Information Specialist
Detective
Dietetics Instructor
Dietitian

Internal Affairs Investigator
News Reporter
Office Nurse
Polygraph Examiner

Prisoner Classification Interviewer
Religious-Activities Director
School Media Specialist
Social-Group Worker

**Graduate School:**

Epidemiologist
Geriatric Social Worker

Guidance Counselor
Medical Social Worker

Psychiatric Social Worker
School Social Worker

## THE CM CLUSTER

**High School/Apprenticeship:**

Aircraft Inspector
Animator
Building Inspector
Braille Coder

Calibrator
Construction Inspector
Duplicating-Machine Operator
Electrotyper

Highway Inspector
Meter Inspector
Offset-Duplicating-Machine
   Operator

**Two-Year College/ Certificate Program:**

Aircraft Electronic-Instruments
   Inspector
Aviation Technician
Book Designer
Computer Operator
Electrocardiograph Technician
Electroencephalographic
   Technician

Electromyographic Technician
Electronic-Communications
   Technician
Electronic Technician
Electronics Mechanic
Map Editor

Medical Photographer
News Photographer
Occupational Safety-and-Health
   Inspector
Ophthalmic-Lens Inspector
Water-Treatment-Plant Operator

**Four-Year College:**

Safety Inspector

## THE CMN CLUSTER

**High School/Apprenticeship:**

Calibrator
Construction-Materials Supervisor

Mechanical Inspector
Planimeter Operator

Volume Computer

**Two-Year College/Certificate Program:**

Highway Inspector
Laboratory Assistant
Land Surveyor
Lens Prescription Clerk
Meteorological Technician

Order Detailer
Petroleum Inspector
Photographic-Equipment
   Technician
Provider

Storage-Battery Inspector
Water-Treatment-Plant Operator
Weapons Instrument Mechanic

**Four-Year College:**

| | | |
|---|---|---|
| Electrical Inspector | Engineering Surveyor | Mathematical Technician |

## THE CMS CLUSTER

**High School/Apprenticeship:**

| | |
|---|---|
| Playroom Attendant | Tourist-Information Assistant |

**Two-Year College/Certificate Program:**

| | | |
|---|---|---|
| Audiological Technician | Occupational Safety-and-Health | Physical-Therapy Aide |
| Dental Assistant | Inspector | Secretary of Town Health Services |
| Flying Instructor | Optometric Assistant | |

**Four-Year College:**

| | | |
|---|---|---|
| Airline Pilots' Instructor | Dental Hygienist | Physical Therapist |
| Air-Traffic Controller | Fashion-Design Teacher | Sanitation Officer |
| Art Teacher | Geriatric Physical Therapist | Teacher of Visually Handicapped |

**Graduate School:**

| | |
|---|---|
| Osteopathic Physician | Youth Correctional-Education |
| | Supervisor |

## THE CN CLUSTER

**High School/Apprenticeship:**

| | | |
|---|---|---|
| Accounting Clerk | Insurance Clerk | Mortgage Accounting Clerk |
| Bookkeeper | Manifest Clerk | Policy-Loan Calculator |
| Calculating-Machine Operator | Mechanical Inspector | Record Clerk |
| Charge-Account Clerk | Media Clerk | Services Clerk |
| Financial-Statement Clerk | Medical Voucher Clerk | Shipping-and-Receiving Clerk |
| Fruit-and-Vegetable Grader | Molded-Parts Inspector | Traffic Rate Clerk |
| Foreign-Exchange Clerk | | |

**Two-Year College/Certificate Program:**

| | | |
|---|---|---|
| Brokerage Clerk | Order Detailer | Roulette Dealer |
| Custom House Broker | Payroll Clerk | Survey Worker |
| Foreign-Exchange Teller | Production-Planning Supervisor | Tax Preparer |
| Hotel Night Auditor | Proofreader | Traffic Manager |

**Four-Year College:**

Auditor                          Bank Teller                        Tax Auditor

## THE <u>CNS</u> CLUSTER

**High School/Apprenticeship:**

Bank Receptionist               Educational Attendance Clerk

**Two-Year College/Certificate Program:**

Audit Accounting Aide           Personnel Scheduler               Tax-Fraud Investigative Aide
Credit-Collections Secretary    Tax-Attorney Secretary            Taxpayer Service Representative

**Four-Year College:**

Bookkeeping Instructor          Geriatric Nurse                   Nutritionist
Financial-Aid Counselor         Loan Interviewer                  Veterinary Laboratory Technician

**Graduate School:**

Economics Professor             Patients' Librarian               Tax Attorney
Geriatric Nurse Practitioner    Probate Lawyer

## THE <u>CS</u> CLUSTER

**High School/Apprenticeship:**

Airline-Lounge Receptionist     Hospital Admitting Clerk          Receptionist
Airport Security Officer        Nurse Aide                        Teacher Aide
Border-Patrol Agent             Playroom Attendant                Tourist-Information Assistant

**Two-Year College/Certificate Program:**

Airplane Flight Attendant       Medical Secretary                 Referral Aide
Laboratory-Animal Technician    Mental-Health Technician          School Secretary
Medical Assistant               Police Inspector                  Social Director
Medical-Office Receptionist

**Four-Year College:**

College Financial-Aid Officer   Religious-Activities Director

**Graduate School:**

Patients' Librarian


## THE L CLUSTER

**Two-Year College/Certificate Program:**

Applications Programmer        Plant Breeder        Pulp and Paper Tester
Computer Programmer

**Four-Year College:**

Agricultural Entomologist       Dairy Scientist                  Microbiologist
Agricultural Microbiologist     Data-Base Manager                Nematologist
Agronomist                      Earth Scientist                  Ornithologist
Anthropologist                  Ecologist                        Paleontologist
Apiculturist                    Fishery Scientist                Parasitologist
Applications Programmer         Helminthologist                  Physical Anthropologist
Aquatic Biologist               Herpetologist                    Physiologist
Arboretum Researcher            Horticulturist                   Plant Physiologist
Archaeologist                   Ichthyologist                    Political Scientist
Bacteriologist                  Intelligence-Research Specialist Protozoologist
Biologist                       Invertebrate Paleontologist      Range Manager
Botanist                        Legislative Assistant            Seed Analyst
Climatologist                   Logistics Engineer               Soil Scientist
Computational Linguist          Mammalian Physiologist           Stratigrapher
Criminalist                     Marine Biologist                 Vector Control Assistant
Criminologist                   Marine Ecologist                 Veterinary Bacteriologist
Cyberneticist                   Marine Meteorologist             Zoologist

**Graduate School:**

Behavioral Pharmacologist       Endocrine Pharmacologist         Plant Pathologist
Clinical Pharmacologist         Pathologist                      Veterinarian


## THE LM CLUSTER

**High School/Apprenticeship:**

Automobile Mechanic             Electrician

**Two-Year College/Certificate Program:**

Acupuncturist                   Corporate Pilot                  Production Engineer
Aerial-Photograph Interpreter   Graphics Designer                Radiologic Technologist
Air-Conditioning Technician     Industrial Designer              Surgical Technologist
Computer-Aided Design Technician Laboratory-Test Mechanic        Theatrical Special-Effects
Computer-Systems Service        Marine Engineer                     Technician
   Technician                   Medical Illustrator              Tool-and-Die Maker

## Four-Year College:

Agricultural Engineer
Airline Pilot
Airline Pilots' Instructor
Anatomist
Architectural Graphic Designer
Cephalometric Analyst
Ceramic Design Engineer
Cinematographer
Controls Designer
Costume Specialist
Design Engineer

Diagnostic Medical Sonographer
Diagnostic X-Ray Technologist
Electronic Packaging Engineer
Fashion Display Specialist
Film Editor
Fire-Protection Engineer
Information-Processing Engineer
Instructional Technologist
Irrigation Engineer
Marine Geologist

Mechanical-Design Engineer
Mineral-Processing Engineer
Open-Pit-Mining Engineer
Optical-Effects-Camera Operator
Parking Analyst
Petrologist
Photojournalist
Reliability Engineer
Technical Illustrator
Technical Writer

## Graduate School:

Cardiovascular Perfusionist

Neurosurgeon

Safety Engineer

## THE LMN CLUSTER

## Two-Year College/Certificate Program:

Aerial-Photograph Interpreter
Biomedical Engineering Technician
Cartographic Technician
Civil Engineering Technician
Drafter
Electronics Communications
    Technician

Engineering Technician
Environmental Engineering
    Technician
Environmental Health Technician
Film-Laboratory Technician
Industrial Engineering Technician

Laser Technician
Metallurgical Engineering
    Technician
Oceanographic Technician
Tool-and-Die Maker
Tool Designer

## Four-Year College:

Aeronautical Engineer
Aerospace Engineer
Aerospace Scientist
Aircraft Stress Analyst
Biomedical Engineer
Cartographer
Chemical Engineer
Civil Engineer
Coal-Mining Engineer
Computer-Applications Engineer
Design Engineer
Drilling Engineer
Electrical Engineer
Electrical Test Engineer
Electronics Engineer
Engineer
Engineering Geologist

Engineering Technical Writer
Environmental Engineer
Environmental Health Specialist
Environmental Planner
Geological Engineer
Geologist
Geomorphologist
Highway Engineer
Industrial Engineer
Information Scientist
Irrigation Engineer
Marine Engineer
Marine Geologist
Marine Surveyor
Materials Engineer
Materials Scientist

Mechanical-Design Engineer
Mechanical Engineer
Metallographer
Metrologist
Mineral-Processing Engineer
Mining Engineer
Ocean Engineer
Oceanographer
Optical Engineer
Petroleum Engineer
Petroleum Geologist
Petroleum Researcher
Photogrammetrist
Plastics Engineer
Pollution-Control Engineer
Weight Engineer

**Graduate School:**

Aerospace Research Engineer
Anesthesiologist
Biophysicist
Electro-Optics Physicist
Environmental Scientist
Exploration Geophysicist

Geophysicist
Health Physicist
Industrial Health Physicist
Medical Physicist
Metallurgical Engineer
Naval Architect

Nuclear Engineer
Nurse Anesthetist
Optical Physicist
Physicist
Plasma Physicist
Seismologist

## THE LMS CLUSTER

**High School/Apprenticeship:**

Cartoonist

**Two-Year College/Certificate Program:**

Acupuncturist
Flying Instructor

Naprapathist
Radiologic Technologist

Respiratory Therapist
Ultrasound Technologist

**Four-Year College:**

Airline Pilots' Instructor
Audiologist
Exercise Physiologist

Geriatric Physical Therapist
Industrial Hygienist

Physical Therapist
Prosthetist

**Graduate School:**

Chiropractor
Dentist
Endodontist
Gynecologist
Neurosurgeon
Ophthalmologist

Oral Surgeon
Orthopedic Surgeon
Osteopathic Physician
Otolaryngologist
Periodontist

Plastic Surgeon
Proctologist
Radiation Therapist
Surgeon
Urologist

## THE LN CLUSTER

**Two-Year College/Certificate Program:**

Chemical Laboratory Technician
Medical Chemistry Technologist

Pulp and Paper Tester
Quality-Control Technician

Water-Pollution Technician

## Four-Year College:

Acoustics Physicist
Analytical Chemist
Analytical Statistician
Apiculturist
Applied Mathematician
Biochemist
Biostatistician
Budget Analyst
Chemical Oceanographer
Chemist
Computer Systems Analyst
Customer Support Specialist
Cytologist
Dairy Technologist
Data-Base Manager

Data-Processing Systems Analyst
Data-Reduction Technician
Demographer
Dietetic Researcher
Earth Scientist
Economic Geographer
Entomologist
Fiber Technologist
Food Scientist
Gas Dynamics Researcher
Geographer
Geothermal Geologist
Histologist
Information-System Programmer
Insurance Analyst

Intelligence Research Specialist
Internal Auditor
Limnologist
Mycologist
Oceanographer
Performance Analyst
Physical Chemist
Poultry Scientist
Purchasing Agent
Quality-Control Engineer
Rate and Cost Analyst
Reservoir Engineer
Systems Analyst
Wood Technologist
Zoologist

## Graduate School:

Astronomer
Extractive Metallurgist
Geneticist
Health Physicist
Industrial Health Physicist
Mathematical Statistician

Metallurgical Analyst
Neuropharmacologist
Nuclear-Fuels Research Engineer
Nuclear Physicist
Oral Pathologist
Pharmacist

Pharmacologist
Physical Metallurgist
Physicist
Poultry Veterinarian
Radiobiologist
Research Mathematician

## THE LNS CLUSTER

### Four-Year College:

Demographer
Geriatric Nurse

Mathematics Teacher

Psychiatric Nurse

### Graduate School:

Allergist
Aviation Physician
Cardiologist
Cardiovascular Physician
Druggist
Educational Psychologist
Engineering Psychologist

Experimental Psychologist
Geriatric Nurse Practitioner
Internist
Naturopathic Physician
Neuropharmacologist
Pediatrician
Physician

Probate Lawyer
Professor of Educational Statistics
Psychiatrist
Social Psychologist
Toxicologist
Urban Sociologist

## THE LS CLUSTER

### Two-Year College/Certificate Program:

Animal Technician
Emergency Medical Technician

Emergency Specialist
Home Health Technician

Mental-Health Technician
Police-Academy Instructor

## Four-Year College:

Athletic Trainer
Audiologist
Biology Teacher
Clergy Member
College Planning and Placement
Correctional Treatment Specialist
Dietetics Instructor
Educational Therapist
Elementary-School Teacher

Football Coach
Music Therapist
Newspaper Editorial Writer
Nurse Clinician
Nurse-Midwife
Occupational Therapist
Office Nurse
Parole Officer

Penologist
Police Officer
Polygraph Examiner
Psychiatric Nurse
Recreational Therapist
School Nurse
Social-Group Worker
Teacher of the Deaf

## Graduate School:

Allergist
Cardiologist
Cardiovascular Physician
Child Psychologist
Clinical Child Psychologist
Clinical Psychologist
Counseling Psychologist
Dermatologist
Engineering Psychologist
Geriatric Psychologist
Geriatric Social Worker

Guidance Counselor
Gynecologist
Hypnotherapist
Internist
Judge
Lawyer
Medical Social Worker
Naturopathic Physician
Neurologist
Pediatrician

Physician
Podiatrist
Psychiatric Social Worker
Psychiatrist
School Social Worker
Social Psychologist
Sociologist
Speech Pathologist
Veterinarian
Voice Pathologist

## THE M CLUSTER

## High School/Apprenticeship:

Agricultural Pilot
Animator
Appliance Installer
Artificial-Eye Maker
Asbestos Removal Worker
Assembler
Automobile Mechanic
Bricklayer
Burglar-Alarm Repairer

Cabinetmaker
Carpenter
Composing-Machine Operator
Construction Electrician
Electrical-Control Assembler
Elevator Constructor
Farm Mechanic
Fire-Sprinkler Installer

Glass Decorator
Goldsmith
Health-Equipment Servicer
Hydraulic Repairer
Lens Grinder
Manugrapher
Meter Installer
Motion-Picture Projectionist

## Two-Year College/Certificate Program:

Agricultural Engineering
   Technician
Air-Conditioning Mechanic
Audio Technician
Audiovisual Technician
Book-Jacket Designer
Computer-Systems Service
   Technician
Dental Ceramist
Die Maker

Electronics Photo Technician
Field Engineer
Industrial X-Ray Operator
Laser-Beam-Color-Scanner Operator
Lithographer
Marine Machinist
Mobile-Crane Operator
Museum Ceramic Restorer
Museum Exhibit Designer
Music Mixer

News Photographer
Optician
Orthodontic Technician
Orthoptist
Package Designer
Photolithographer
Prosthetics Technician
Recording Engineer
Stationary Engineer
Test Fixture Designer

**Four-Year College:**

| | | |
|---|---|---|
| Art Teacher | Fishery Engineer | Set Designer |
| Costume Designer | Orthotist | Technical Illustrator |
| Diagnostic X-Ray Technologist | Printed Circuit Designer | |

**Graduate School:**

| | | |
|---|---|---|
| Oral Surgeon | Orthodontist | Orthopedic Surgeon |

## THE MN CLUSTER

**High School/Apprenticeship:**

| | | |
|---|---|---|
| Carpenter | Electroplater | Tabulating-Machine Operator |
| Carpet Installer | Model Maker | |

**Two-Year College/Certificate Program:**

| | | |
|---|---|---|
| Agricultural Engineering Technician | Glass Technologist | Oceanographic Technician |
| Construction Estimator | Heating and Air-Conditioning Drafter | Optician |
| Drafter | Hydrographic-Survey Technician | Tool-and-Die Maker |
| Drafting Technician | Meteorological-Equipment Repairer | Topographic Surveyor |
| Electromechanisms Design Drafter | Microfilm Technologist | Video Operator |

**Four-Year College:**

| | | |
|---|---|---|
| Geodesist | Mathematical Technician | Petroleum Engineer |
| Hydraulic Engineer | Microwave Engineer | Petroleum Geologist |
| Illuminating Engineer | Noise Technologist | Photogrammetrist |
| Manufacturing Engineer | Ocean Engineer | Photographic Engineer |
| Marine Engineer | Optical Engineer | Weight Engineer |

## THE MNS CLUSTER

**Two-Year College/Certificate Program:**

| | | |
|---|---|---|
| Dialysis Technician | Inhalation Therapist | Paraoptometric |
| Emergency Medical Technician | Orthoptist | Ultrasound Technologist |

**Four-Year College:**

| | | |
|---|---|---|
| Dental Hygienist | Industrial-Arts Teacher | Photography Teacher |
| Drafting Instructor | | |

**Graduate School:**

Anesthesiologist
Astronomy Professor
Dentist

Optometrist
Otolaryngologist
Periodontist

Petroleum-Engineering Professor
Public-Health Dentist

# THE MS CLUSTER

**High-School/Apprenticeship:**

Cartoonist

Respiratory-Therapy Aide

**Two-Year College/Certificate Program:**

Dental Assistant
Dialysis Technician
Electrologist
Inhalation Therapist

Manual-Arts Therapist
Orientation and Mobility Instructor
Naprapathist

Orthoptist
Paraoptometric
Respiratory Therapist

**Four-Year College:**

Art Teacher
Art Therapist
Corrective Therapist

Dental Hygienist
Industrial-Arts Teacher

Orthotist
Physiatrist

**Graduate School:**

Optometrist
Oral Surgeon

Orthodontist

Orthopedic Surgeon

# THE N CLUSTER

**High School/Apprenticeship:**

Accounting Clerk

Charge-Account Clerk

Policy-Loan Calculator

**Two-Year College/Certificate Program:**

Estate Appraiser
Estimator
Foreign-Exchange Teller

Hosiery Dye-Lab Technician
Real-Estate Appraiser

Statistical Clerk
Traffic-Rate Clerk

**Four-Year College:**

Acoustics Physicist
Actuary
Analytical Statistician
Applied Mathematician

Biostatistician
Computer-Applications Engineer
Mathematical Technician

Physical Chemist
Spectographer
Statistician

**Graduate School:**

Astronomer
High-Energy Physicist
Mathematical Statistician

Molecular Pharmacologist
Nuclear Physicist

Solid-State Physicist
Space Physicist

# THE NS CLUSTER

**Two-Year College/Certificate Program:**

Tax-Fraud Investigative Aide

Taxpayer Service Representative

**Four-Year College:**

Accounting Teacher
Bookkeeping Instructor
Consumer Financial Adviser

Credit Counselor
Demographer
Mathematics Teacher

Nutritionist
Retirement Officer

**Graduate School:**

Astronomy Professor
Druggist
Economics Professor

Educational Psychologist
Experimental Psychologist
Professor of Educational Statistics

Quantitative Psychologist
Tax Attorney

# THE S CLUSTER

**High School/Apprenticeship:**

Child-Care Attendant

Child-Care Supervisor

Nurse Aide

**Two-Year College/Certificate Program:**

Manual-Arts Therapist
Orientation and Mobility Instructor
Modeling Instructor

Nursing-Home Recreational
   Therapist

Preparole-Counseling Aide
Recreation Leader

**Four-Year College:**

Child-Development Associate
Clergy Member
Correctional-Treatment Specialist
Corrections Officer
Dance Therapist
Elementary-School Teacher
Foreign-Student Adviser

Kindergarten Teacher
Music Therapist
Nursing-Home Social-Worker
   Supervisor
Occupational Therapist
Parole Officer

Physical-Education Instructor
Recreation Specialist
Residence Counselor
Secondary-School Teacher
Social-Group Worker
Theater-Arts Teacher

**Graduate School:**

Medical Social Worker

Clinical Psychologist

Psychiatric Social Worker

# LEARNING ABOUT YOUR CAREER:

## A Directory of More Than 1,100 Careers Identified and Explained

This new revised edition expands upon the original glossary which now contains composite definitions of more than 1,100 careers.

The Cluster designations placed at the end of each definition are another new feature that will lead you into new areas and expand your career choices. Here is how it can help you: Consider, for example, that you have tested and scored yourself, and the results indicate an aptitude for the BCN Cluster. You then refer to Part IV, to the job titles listed for that Career Cluster, and perhaps Purchasing Agent catches your eye. Next you turn to Part V and this directory to discover the typical duties and responsibilities for this occupation. At the end of the job description you will find an additional Career Cluster designated BN. We encourage you to then refer to the BN Cluster and to note the careers listed there. While they may not be as closely aligned to your abilities as your primary Career Cluster, they are compatible and clearly worthy of your investigation. Choosing or changing a career is one of your most important decisions in life, and you don't want to overlook any appropriate category.

Selecting the right occupation is the final step in our program to help you discover what you're best at. With that knowledge you can feel confident that you finally have the competitive edge when you move into the marketplace to build your career.

# The Career Directory

**Abstractor.** Processes the intellectual content of documents for convenient purposes of examination, proof, or ready reference. CL

**Academic Dean.** Develops academic policies and programs for college or university. Directs and coordinates activities of chairpersons of individual colleges or academic departments. BL

**Accountant.** Examines, analyzes, and interprets accounting records for the purpose of giving advice or preparing statements. Applies principles of accounting to analyze past and present financial operations and estimates future revenues and expenditures to prepare budget. BCL—BCN—BLN

**Accounting Clerk.** Performs any combination of routine calculating, posting, and verifying duties to obtain primary financial data for use in maintaining accounting records. BCN—CN—N

**Accounting Systems Expert.** Devises and installs special accounting systems and related procedures in establishment which cannot use standardized system. Conducts survey of operations to ascertain needs of establishment. Sets up classification of accounts and organizes accounting procedures and machine methods support. BL—BLN

**Accounting Teacher.** Studies, organizes, and teaches accounting principles, and methods. Frequently teaches logic, mathematics, finance, marketing, management, behavioral sciences, and economics. College teachers of accounting are often governmental advisers or consultants to business firms. BCL—BCS —BLN—BNS—NS

**Accounts-Receivable Supervisor.** Supervises and coordinates activities of workers engaged in tracing sources of error and correcting billing records for customers, and in processing records for advance or final billings. BCL—BL

**Acoustics Physicist.** Investigates the nature of sound and how it affects us. Conducts studies of effects of noise, musical instruments, audio equipment, and certain newly devised medical equipment. May also work in areas including noise pollution and underwater sound. LN—N

**Actuary.** Applies knowledge of mathematics, probability, statistics, and principles of finance and business to problems in life, health, and casualty insurance, annuities, and pensions. BCN—BN—N

**Acupuncturist.** Uses traditional Chinese therapeutic technique whereby the patient's body is punctured with fine needles to relieve discomfort associated with painful disorders. LM—LMS

**Advertising Account Executive.** Develops advertising programs for client firms and individuals. Studies the client's sales, public image, and advertising problems, and then creates a program that suits the client's needs. In some small agencies, may be responsible for developing the actual artwork and advertising copy. B—BS

**Advertising Copywriter.** Writes advertising copy for use by publications or broadcast media to promote sale of goods and services. B—BCS—BS

**Advertising Manager.** Directs sale of display and classified advertising services for a publication. Consults with department heads and other officials to plan special campaigns and to promote sale of advertising services to various industry or trade groups. B—BLS— BMS—BS

**Advertising Sales Representative.** Sells classified and display advertising space for publication. Using rate charts, computes cost of advertisement, based on size, date, position, and number of insertions. B—BN

**Advertising Worker.** Creative individual such as a writer, artist, or designer who develops and produces advertisements to persuade people to buy a company's product or use its services. B—BL—BLM

**Aerial-Photograph Interpreter.** Draws maps and analyzes and interprets aerial photographs to detect significant military, industrial, resource, or topographical data. CLM—LM—LMN

**Aeronautical Engineer.** Designs, develops, and tests aircraft, space vehicles, surface effect vehicles, and missiles, applying engineering principles and techniques. Tests models and prototypes to study and evaluate operational characteristics and effects of stress imposed during flight conditions. LMN

**Aerospace Engineer.** Designs, develops, tests, and helps produce commercial and military aircraft, missiles, and spacecraft. Often specializes in structural design, navigational guidance and control, instrumentation and communication, or production methods. May specialize in one type of aerospace product such as passenger planes, helicopters, satellites, or rockets. LMN

**Aerospace Librarian.** Provides research personnel with available scientific knowledge in physics and related disciplines to solve problems dealing with flight in space. CL

**Aerospace Research Engineer.** Conducts research in many areas, such as developing vehicles with greater speeds, ranges, and reliability; engines with more power; and more advanced sources of rocket propulsion, such as nuclear and electric energy. Metals and plastics also are continually being developed for wider capabilities, as are electronic communications systems. LMN

**Aerospace Scientist.** Does research on how materials withstand certain conditions, such as intense heat or velocity, or creates new materials that are needed. Contributes to developing designs for aircraft, missiles, and spacecraft. LMN

**Agri-Business Agent.** Advises and instructs farmers and individuals engaged in agribusiness in applications of agricultural research findings. Collects, analyzes, and evaluates data to advise farmers on farm management and soil conservation. B—BL

**Agri-Business Salesperson.** Can be involved as a retail salesperson, who sells directly to farmers; a dealer resalesperson, who helps both the farmer and dealer to do a better job; or a salesperson who sells to dealers only. Most agribusiness salespersons are a combination of all three. B

**Agricultural Commodity Grader.** Inspects samples of agricultural products to determine their quality and grade, and then issues grading certificates. C

**Agricultural Communications Specialist.** Develops advertisements and public relations bulletins to inform farm residents and agricultural institutions of recent prices, sales, and grades of agricultural produce in movement from the farm to the market. B

**Agricultural Economist.** Deals with problems related to production, financing, pricing, and marketing of farm products. Formulates recommendations for agricultural financing and other monetary policies. BL—BLN

**Agricultural Engineer.** Applies engineering technology and knowledge of biological sciences to agricultural problems concerned with power and machinery, electrification, structures, soil and water conservation, and processing of agricultural products. LM

**Agricultural-Engineering Technician.** Prepares original layout and completes detailed drawings of agricultural machinery and equipment. M—MN

**Agricultural Entomologist.** Identifies the populations and distributions of insects that injure agricultural products during growth, shipping, storage, processing, and distribution. Research is directed toward finding ways to control and manage beneficial ones. L

**Agricultural Loan Examiner.** Examines the loan portfolio of the federal land banks, federal intermediate credit banks, and banks for cooperatives. The agricultural loan examiner must know agricultural conditions, price trends, production factors, farming practices, and changes in the agricultural industry. BN—BNS

**Agricultural-Marketing Specialist.** Surveys wholesalers, retailers, and consumers; analyzes data on products and sales; and prepares sales forecasts used by businesses to make decisions relating to product design and advertising. B—BN

**Agricultural Microbiologist.** Studies bacteria and other microorganisms to better understand their relation to human, plant, and animal health. CL—L

**Agricultural Pilot.** Pilots airplane or helicopter, at low altitudes, over agricultural fields to dust or spray fields with seeds, fertilizers, or pesticides. M

**Agricultural Teacher.** Instructs secondary school and adult-education classes in farm management, agricultural production, agricultural supplies and services, operation and repair of farm equipment and structures, inspection and processing of farm products, and ornamental horticulture. B—BCM—BM—BMS

**Agronomist.** Conducts experiments or investigations in field-crop problems and develops new methods of growing crops to secure more efficient production, higher yield, and improved quality. Often develops methods for control of noxious weeds, crop diseases, and insect pests. L

**Air-Conditioning Mechanic.** Installs, services, and repairs environmental-control systems in residences, department stores, office buildings, and commercial establishments, utilizing knowledge of refrigeration theory, pipefitting, and structural layout. M

**Air-Conditioning Technician.** Plans requirements for fabricating, installing, testing, and servicing climate-control and heat-transfer assemblies and systems to assist engineering personnel, utilizing knowledge of heat-transfer technology and engineering methods. LM

**Aircraft Electronic-Instruments Inspector.** Inspects, tests, and adjusts electronic instruments according to specifications, using hand tools and precision-testing equipment. BCM—CLM—CM

**Aircraft Inspector.** Keeps records of usage and time intervals between inspection and maintenance of designated airplane parts. Compiles data from flight schedules to compute time that airplane parts are in use. C—CM

**Aircraft-Parts Sales Representative.** Sells aircraft equipment and parts to individuals and to business and industrial establishments. BM

**Aircraft Stress Analyst.** Conducts stress analysis on designs of experimental, prototype, or production aircraft, space vehicles, surface effect vehicles, missiles, and related components to evaluate ability to withstand stresses imposed during flight or ground operation. LMN

**Airline Dispatcher.** Authorizes, regulates, and controls commercial airline flights according to government and company regulations to expedite and ensure safety of flight. C

**Airline-Lounge Receptionist.** Admits members and guests to airline lounge, serves beverages and snacks, and provides other personal services as requested. Answers questions regarding scheduled flights and terminal facilities. Verifies passengers' reservations. BCS—C—CS

**Airline Pilot.** Pilots airplane to transport passengers, mail, or freight, or for other commercial purposes. Reviews ship's papers to ascertain factors, such as load weight, fuel supply, weather conditions, and flight route and schedule. Contacts control tower by radio to obtain takeoff clearance and instructions. Logs information, such as time in flight, altitude flown, and fuel consumed. LM

**Airline Pilots' Instructor.** Trains new and experienced company airline pilots in policy and in use of equipment. May conduct review courses in navigation and meteorology. CMS—LM—LMS

**Airline Ramp Agent.** Directs and coordinates, through subordinate supervisory personnel, air-transport-terminal cargo and ramp activities to provide fast and efficient services for clients and passengers. BC

**Airline Schedule Analyst.** Keeps track of the whereabouts of aircraft and crews; receives and relays reports of delays due to weather and mechanical problems; notifies all concerned regarding delays or changes; gives orders for substitution of aircraft when required. BC—BCL—C

**Airline Ticket Agent.** Sells tickets to airline passengers at airport and city ticket offices. Uses computers to determine schedules, rates, and seats available. BC

**Airplane Flight Attendant.** Performs a variety of personal services conducive to safety and comfort of airline passengers during flight. Greets passengers, verifies tickets, records destinations, and explains use of safety equipment aboard airplane. CS

**Airport Manager.** Plans, directs, and coordinates, through subordinate personnel, activities concerned with construction and maintenance of airport facilities and operation of airport in accordance with governmental agency or commission policies and regulations. BL

**Airport Security Officer.** Patrols an assigned beat, on foot or using motorcycle or patrol car, to control traffic; prevents crime or disturbance of peace; and arrests violators. CLS—CS

**Air-Traffic Controller.** Controls air traffic on and within vicinity of airport according to established procedures and policies to prevent collisions and to minimize delays arising from traffic congestion. CLM—CMS

**Allergist.** Diagnoses and treats diseases and conditions with allergic or immunologic causes. Uses diagnostic aids, such as X-ray, patch tests, and blood tests, to prescribe treatments and medication. LNS—LS

**Ammunition Safety Inspector.** Supervises and inspects activities of workers engaged in storing, issuing, and accounting for ammunition or explosives. BC—BCM

**Analytical Chemist.** Determines the structure, composition, and nature of substances. Develops new techniques, new procedures, and application of new products. LN

**Analytical Statistician.** Plans data collection, and analyzes and interprets numerical data from experiments, studies, surveys, and other sources, and applies statistical methodology to provide information for scientific research and statistical analysis. LN—N

**Anatomist.** Studies form and structure of animal bodies. Determines ability of animal bodies to regenerate destroyed or damaged parts, and investigates possibility of transplanting organs and skin segments from one living body to another. LM

**Anesthesiologist.** Administers anesthetics to render patients insensible to pain during surgical, obstetrical, and other medical procedures. Examines patient to determine degree of surgical risk and type of anesthesia to administer. LMN—MNS

**Animal Scientist.** Conducts research in selection, breeding, feeding, management, and marketing of beef and dual-purpose cattle, horses, mules, sheep, goats, dogs, and other pet animals. BL

**Animal Technician.** Works under the supervision of professional personnel such as veterinarians, physiologists, or microbiologists, performing routine laboratory and clinical procedures in a veterinary clinic. May take samples of various body fluids or tissues and make chemical analyses. LS

**Animator.** Draws animated cartoons for use in motion pictures or television. Renders series of sequential drawings which when projected at specific speed, become animated. CM—M

**Anthropologist.** Makes comparative studies in relation to distribution, origin, evolution, and races of humans, cultures they have created, and their distribution and physical characteristics. L

**Apartment-Building Superintendent.** Directs activities of workers engaged in operating and maintaining facilities and equipment in apartment buildings. BM

**Apiculturist.** Studies bee culture and breeding. Conducts experiments regarding causes and controls of bee diseases and factors affecting yields of nectar and pollen on various plants visited by bees. L—LN

**Appliance Installer.** Installs fixtures and appliances and lays floor covering in mobile and modular homes and travel-trailer coaches, using hand tools and power tools. M

**Appliance Salesperson.** Sells, explains, and demonstrates appliances such as radios, television sets, stoves, refrigerators, vacuum cleaners, and washing machines to customer. B

**Applications Programmer.** Writes detailed instructions for processing data, using one of the languages specially developed for computers. Checks program and "debugs" any errors. Usually specializes in business or scientific operations. CL—L

**Applied Mathematician.** Conducts logical analysis of scientific, engineering, and other technical problems; and formulates mathematical models of problems for solution by digital computer. LN—N

**Appraiser.** Appraises merchandise, fixtures, machinery, and equipment of business firms to ascertain values for such purposes as approval of loans, issuance of insurance policies, disposition of estates, and liquidation of assets of bankrupt firms. BN

**Aquatic Biologist.** Studies plants and animals living in water and environmental conditions affecting them. Investigates temperature, salinity, oxygen content and other physical conditions of water to determine their relationship to aquatic life. L

**Arbitrator.** Settles disputes between labor and management to bind both to specific terms and conditions of a labor contract. Conducts hearings to evaluate disputed contract provisions. BL

**Arboretum Curator.** Directs and coordinates activities of workers engaged in operating exhibiting institutions, such as botanical gardens, arboretums, and herbariums. B

**Arboretum Researcher.** Seeks to improve horticultural crops through plant breeding, or by developing more economical and effective techniques for growing, handling, and marketing horticultural crops. L

**Arcade Attendant.** Assists patrons of amusement facility; performs minor repairs on game machines; explains operation of game machines to patrons. BM

**Archaeologist.** Reconstructs record of extinct cultures, especially preliterature cultures. Studies, classifies, and interprets artifacts recovered by excavation. L

**Architect.** Provides professional services in research, development, design, construction, alteration, or repair of real property, such as private residences, office buildings, theaters, public buildings, and factories. BLM—BMN

**Architectural Graphic Designer.** Works with architects, using type and color to design the graphic symbols that identify buildings. Depending on the purpose of a building or complex, the architectural graphic designer may also design presentation brochures, stationery, marquees, or shopping bags. A knowledge of typography, color reproduction skill, and an understanding of contemporary architecture and building materials are required. BMN—LM

**Archivist.** Collects, evaluates, systemizes, preserves, and makes available for reference public records and documents of historical significance. Appraises and edits permanent records and historically valuable documents. CL

**Art Conservator.** Coordinates activities of subordinates engaged in examination, repair, and conservation of art objects. BM

**Art Director.** Formulates concepts and supervises workers engaged in executing layout designs for artwork and copy to be presented by visual communications media, such as magazines, books, newspapers, television, posters, and packaging. BLM

**Artificial-Eye Maker.** Fabricates artificial glass or plastic eyes according to physician's prescription or customer specifications. M

**Artist's Agent.** Manages affairs of entertainers by participating in negotiations with others concerning contracts and business matters affecting clients' interests, and advises clients on career development and advancement. BMS—BS

**Art Librarian.** Manages library or section containing specialized materials for industrial, commercial, or governmental organizations, or for such institutions as schools and hospitals. BC

**Art Teacher.** Instructs pupils in art, such as painting, sketching, designing, and sculpturing. Observes pupils' work to make criticisms and corrections. May plan and supervise student contests and arrange art exhibits. CMS—M—MS

**Art Therapist.** Plans and conducts art-therapy programs in public and private institutions to rehabilitate mentally ill and physically disabled patients. BMS—MS

**Asbestos Removal Worker.** Removes asbestos from ceilings, walls, beams, and boilers, following hazardous waste handling guidelines. M

**Assembler.** Performs one or more repetitive bench or line assembly operations to mass-produce products such as automobile or tractor radiators, refrigerators, or gas stoves. Places parts in specified relationships to each other. M

**Astronomer.** Observes and interprets celestial phenomena and relates research to basic scientific knowledge or to practical problems, such as navigation. Uses optical, radio, or other telescopes equipped with spectrometers or radiometers, which may be above atmosphere on satellites or space probes. LN—N

**Astronomy Professor.** Teaches astronomy at a college or university and is frequently involved in research MNS—NS

**Athletic Trainer.** Evaluates physical condition and advises and treats professional and amateur athletes to maintain maximum physical fitness for participation in athletic competition. LS

**Auctioneer.** Appraises and sells articles at auction to highest bidder. Estimates value of individual pieces. May write auction catalog. BN

**Audiological Technician.** Determines range, nature, and degree of hearing function related to patient's auditory efficiency using electroacoustic instruments and impedance equipment. CMS

**Audiologist.** Specializes in diagnostic evaluation of hearing; prevention, habilitative, and rehabilitative services for auditory problems; and research related to hearing and attendant disorders. LMS—LS

**Audio Technician.** Controls audio equipment to regulate volume level and quality of sound during radio or television broadcasts, according to script and instructions of radio or television broadcasting technical director. M

**Audiovisual Technician.** Operates audiovisual or sound-reproducing equipment to provide or complement educational or public service programs offered by institutions such as museums, zoos, or libraries. Coordinates equipment operation with material presented; maintains equipment in good working condition. M

**Audit Accounting Aide.**   Assists in the examination of a taxpayer's records by preparing exhibits, schedules, and computations of taxpayer's records. CNS

**Auditor.**   Examines and analyzes accounting records of establishment and prepares reports concerning its financial status and operating procedures. Analyzes data to check for duplication of effort, extravagance, fraud, or lack of compliance with management's established policies. BCN—CN

**Automatic-Typewriter Operator.**   Operates special typewriter that perforates tape or paper for subsequent automatic reproduction of data, such as letters, reports, and other material, from master copy. C

**Automobile Dealer.**   Must have a thorough knowledge of the automotive business in addition to being a trained business person, an able salesperson, and a good manager of people and operations. B

**Automobile Driving Instructor.**   Instructs individuals and groups in theory and application of automobile-driving skills. BS

**Automobile Mechanic.**   Repairs and overhauls automobiles, buses, trucks, and other automotive vehicles. Other important assets are the ability to make quick and accurate diagnoses, as well as good reasoning ability and thorough knowledge of automobiles. LM—M

**Automobile-Rental Representative.**   Rents automobiles to customers at airports, hotels, marinas, and other locations. BC

**Automobile Salesperson.**   Sells new or used automobiles on premises of automobile agency. Explains features and demonstrates operation of car. Suggests optional equipment for customer to purchase. Computes and quotes sales price, including tax, trade-in allowance, license fee, and discount, and requirements for financing payment of car on credit. B

**Automobile Service Manager.**   Directs and coordinates activities concerned with acquisition of automotive equipment and operation and maintenance of automotive fleet and repair and storage facilities for public utility, transportation, commercial, or industrial company. BCM—BM

**Automotive-Parts Sales Manager.**   Supervises automotive-parts sales department, keeps records of inventory sold or received from the factory, and handles customers' needs and problems. BC

**Avian Veterinarian.**   Advises individual poultry raisers on poultry problems pertaining to health, feed, and reproduction. BL

**Aviation Physician.**   Practices preventive medicine in the fields of aviation and space flight. LNS

**Aviation Technician.**   Inspects, tests, adjusts, and repairs aircraft communication, navigation, and flight-control systems. CM

**Bacteriologist.**   Studies growth, structure, development, and general characteristics of bacteria and other microorganisms. CL—L

**Bakery Manager.**   Directs and coordinates activities involved with production, sale, and distribution of bakery products. Plans product distribution to customers and negotiates with suppliers to arrange purchase and delivery of bakery supplies. B

**Bank Cashier.**   Directs and coordinates activities relative to creating and administering private, corporate, probate, and court-ordered guardianship trusts in accordance with terms creating trust, decedent's will, probate court, or court order. B—BC—BCN

**Bank Comptroller.**   Directs financial affairs of an organization. Prepares financial analyses of operations for guidance of management. Establishes major economic objectives and policies for company. Prepares reports which outline company's financial position in areas of income, expenses, and earnings, based on past, present, and future operations. BL—BLN

**Bank Credit Analyst.**   Analyzes detailed financial reports submitted by the applicant, interviews a representative of the company about its management, and reviews credit-agency reports to determine the firm's record in repaying debts. BL—BLN

**Bank Lending Officer.**   Evaluates the credit and collateral of individuals and businesses applying for a loan. May handle installment, commercial, real estate, or agricultural loans. BL—BLN

**Bank Manager.**   Manages, directs, and coordinates activities of workers engaged in accounting and recording of financial transactions, setting up trust or escrow accounts, probating estates, and administering trust or mortgage accounts. Develops relationships with customers and business, community, and civic organizations to promote goodwill and generate new business. BN

**Bank Secretary.**   Performs secretarial duties, utilizing knowledge of banking terminology. Prepares loan papers and documents, opens new savings or checking accounts, and aids those having difficulty balancing monthly statements. BC

**Bank Teller.**   Receives and pays out money and keeps records of money and negotiable instruments involved in various banking and other financial transactions, performing any combination of following tasks: receives checks and cash for deposit, verifies amounts, and examines checks for endorsements. C—CN

**Barber/Stylist.**   Cuts and styles hair to suit each customer and may color or straighten hair and fit hairpieces. May offer hair and scalp treatments, shaves, facial massages, and shampoos. BM

**Behavioral Pharmacologist.**   Studies effects of drugs on the behavior of intact organisms, generally rats, mice, monkeys, or other species of laboratory animals. CL—L

**Billing Typist.**   Compiles data and types invoices to be sent to customers, itemizing items sold, amounts due, credit terms, and date of shipment. C

**Biochemist.**   Studies chemical process of living organisms. Conducts research to determine action of foods, drugs, serums, hormones, and other substances on tissues and vital processes of living organisms. LN

**Biological-Science Librarian.** Combines scientific and humanistic interests in the health profession by giving accurate and up-to-date information for the health sciences. CL

**Biological Systematist.** Collates data from other specialties of biology and then deduces specific relationships of material obtained. Often involved in creating new methods of control for infectious diseases, poisons, and biological pests. CL

**Biologist.** Studies origin, growth, relationship, development, anatomy, evolution, functions, and other basic principles of plant and animal life. May specialize in research centering on particular plant, animal, or aspect of biology. L

**Biology Teacher.** Teaches the science of life and life processes, including the study of structure, functioning, growth, origin, evolution, and distribution of living organisms, utilizing various teaching methods, such as lecture, demonstration, and audiovisual aids to supplement presentations. LS

**Biomedical Engineer.** Conducts research into biological aspects of humans or other animals to develop new theories and facts, or to test, prove, or modify known theories of life systems, and to design life-support apparatus, utilizing principles of engineering and bio-behavioral sciences. LMN

**Biomedical Engineering Technician.** Repairs, calibrates, and maintains medical equipment and instrumentation used in health-care-delivery field. LMN

**Biophysicist.** Studies physical principles of living cells and organisms, their electrical and mechanical energy, and related phenomena. LMN

**Biostatistician.** Uses statistical theory, techniques, and methods to determine useful measurements or meaningful relationships of information relating to health or disease. LN—N

**Blood-Bank Technologist.** Medical technologist who collects, classifies, stores, and processes blood. May also select and deliver suitable blood for transfusion. C

**Bond Analyst.** Conducts statistical analysis of information affecting investment programs of public, industrial, and financial institutions, such as banks, insurance companies, and brokerage and investment houses. BLN

**Book Designer.** Specializes in the use of typography to transform a typewritten manuscript into a typeset book, balancing type and illustration on a page in order to produce the most effective publication possible. CM

**Book Editor.** Secures and selects manuscripts and coordinates their publication in book form. Reviews submitted manuscripts, determines demand on the basis of consumer trends and personal knowledge, and makes recommendations regarding procurement and revision. Confers with publisher and author to arrange purchase and details, such as publication date, royalties, and number of copies to be printed. BCL—BL

**Book-Jacket Designer.** Needs a strong sense of design and a knowledge of the latest developments in typography and lettering to create the cover of a book. M

**Bookkeeper.** Keeps complete set of records of financial transactions of establishment. May maintain records in journals or ledgers or on accounting forms. Duties vary with the size of the business. CN

**Bookkeeping Instructor.** Instructs students in bookkeeping procedures, utilizing various teaching methods. Assigns lessons, corrects homework papers, prepares tests, and assists students having difficulty. CNS—NS

**Book Salesperson.** Sells books in book or department store. Suggests selection of books, on the basis of knowledge of current literature and familiarity with publishers' catalogs and book reviews. B

**Border-Patrol Agent.** Patrols on foot or by motor vehicle, powerboat, or aircraft along border or seacoast of United States to detect persons attempting to enter country illegally. CLS—CS

**Botanist.** Studies development and life processes, physiology, heredity, environment, distribution, anatomy, morphology, and economic value of plants for application in such fields as agronomy, forestry, horticulture, and pharmacology. L

**Braille Coder.** Transcribes reading matter into braille for use by the blind, using hand stylus. Reads copy and manipulates hand stylus to emboss special paper with various combinations of dots that characterize the braille alphabet, using braille code form. CM

**Branch-Bank Operations Officer.** Plans, coordinates, controls the work flow, updates systems, strives for administrative efficiency, and is responsible for all functions of a branch office. BL—BLS—BNS

**Bricklayer.** Builds walls, partitions, fireplaces, and other structures with brick, cinder block, and other masonry materials. M

**Broadcasting Announcer.** Introduces musical selections, guests, and programs, and delivers most of the live commercial messages. In small stations the broadcasting announcer may also operate the control board, sell time, and write commercial and news copy. B

**Broadcasting Director.** Plans and supervises individual programs or series of programs, coordinates the shows, selects artists and studio personnel, schedules and conducts rehearsals, and directs on-the-air shows. BM

**Broadcast-Secretary Specialist.** Is highly specialized to utilize the special vocabulary, procedures, and interdepartment communication that are required to work in the broadcasting profession. C

**Brokerage Clerk.** Records purchases and sales of securities, such as stocks and bonds, in investment firm. Telephones customers to inform them of market fluctuations and of stock purchases and sales affecting customers' accounts. Totals daily transactions and summarizes effects on broker's holdings. CN

**Brokerage Manager.** Directs and coordinates brokerage activities concerned with buying or selling commodities, contracts, or securities and mutual funds for clients. Screens, selects, and hires sales representatives and other employees. Directs in-service training to increase effectiveness of client services and increase trade volume. BC—BCL

**Budget Analyst.** Analyzes current and past budgets, prepares and justifies budget requests, and allocates funds according to spending priorities. Analyzes accounting records to determine financial resources required to implement program and submits recommendations for budget allocations. LN

**Budget Officer.** Directs and coordinates activities of personnel responsible for formulation and presentation of budgets for controlling funds to implement program objectives of governmental organization. BN

**Building Contractor.** Contracts to perform specified construction work in accordance with architect's plans, blueprints, codes, and other specifications. Estimates costs of materials, labor, and use of equipment required to fulfill provisions of contract and prepares bids. Confers with clients to negotiate terms of contract. Supervises workers directly or through subordinate supervisors. BLM—BMN

**Building Inspector.** Inspects new and existing buildings and structures to enforce conformance to building, grading, and zoning laws and approved plans, specifications, and standards. Keeps inspection records and prepares reports for use by administrative or judicial authorities. BCM—CM

**Buglar-Alarm Repairer.** Inspects, repairs, and replaces electrical burglar-alarm protective-signaling systems. Examines signaling installations to ensure sound connections. Tests circuits, following wiring specifications, and adjusts controls that transmit signals to police or fire departments. M

**Burial-Needs Salesperson.** Sells burial needs, such as cemetery plots and crypts, grave coverings, markers, and mausoleums. Contacts prospects at their homes in response to telephone inquiries, referrals from funeral homes, and leads from obituary notices. BS

**Business Agent.** Manages financial affairs of entertainers and negotiates with agents and representatives for contracts and appearances. BNS

**Business Analyst.** Is responsible for developing and applying sound analytical techniques to business problems, providing input to investment decisions and acting as financial consultant to product managers. Assists the marketing organizations in terms of the most economical means of getting products to customers, determines whether certain products should be continued or abandoned, analyzes recent trends, and forecasts future results. BL

**Business Communicator.** Often informs, explains, motivates, or surveys employees, using bulletin board displays, question-and-answer programs, paycheck inserts. Frequently works in personnel, public relations, or public-information departments. BS

**Business Consultant.** Consults with clients to define business needs or problems, conducts studies and surveys to obtain data, and analyzes data to advise on or recommend solutions, utilizing knowledge of theory principles, or technology of specific discipline. BLS

**Business Education Instructor.** Instructs students in commercial subjects such as typing, filing, secretarial procedures, business mathematics, office-equipment use, and personality development. BS

**Business Librarian.** Manages library or section containing specialized materials for corporate headquarters and organizations that affect our economic environment. BC

**Business Manager.** Directs and coordinates activities of industrial organization to obtain optimum efficiency and economy of operations and to maximize profits. Directs and coordinates preparation of sales promotion of products manufactured or services performed to develop new markets, increase share of market, and obtain competitive position in industry. BLS—BNS

**Bus-Station Manager.** Directs and coordinates activities of motorbus company to provide passengers with fast, efficient, and safe transportation. BC

**Buyer.** Purchases, inspects, and grades or appraises merchandise or commodities for resale. Selects and orders merchandise from showings by manufacturing representatives, growers, or other sellers, or purchases on open market for cash, basing selection on nature of clientele. BN

**Cabinetmaker.** Sets up and operates variety of woodworking machines and uses various hand tools to fabricate and repair wooden cabinets and high-grade furniture. BMN—M

**Calculating-Machine Operator.** Computes and records statistical, accounting, and other numerical data, utilizing knowledge of mathematics and using machine that automatically performs most mathematical processes. CN

**Calibrator.** Inspects, tests, and calibrates control instruments and devices, such as thermostats, pressure regulators, temperature controls, and furnace, burner, and water controls to ensure specified operating performance, using specialized tools and test devices. CMN—CM

**Cardiologist.** Treats diseases of the heart and its functions. Prescribes medications and recommends dietary and work-activity program, as indicated. May engage in research to study anatomy of, and diseases peculiar to, the heart. LNS—LS

**Cardiovascular Perfusionist.** Operates cardiovascular perfusion equipment during any medical situation necessary to support the patient's cardiovascular function. Responsible for conducting extracorporeal circulation and ensuring the safe management of cardiorespiratory functions by monitoring the necessary physiologic variables. Provides consultation to the physician in the selection of the appropriate equipment and techniques to be used. May administer blood products and anesthetic agents during cardiopulmonary bypass, or drugs through the extracorporeal circulation on prescription. LM

**Cardiovascular Physician.** Diagnoses and treats diseases of the heart and blood vessels. LNS—LS

**Career-Information Specialist.** Collects and organizes occupational data to provide source materials for school career-information center and assists students and teachers in locating and obtaining materials. Keeps records of students enrolled in work-experience program and other vocational programs. CLS

**Carpenter.** Constructs, erects, installs, and repairs structures and fixtures of wood, plywood, and wallboard, using carpenter's hand tools and power tools, and conforming to local building codes. BMN—M—MN

**Carpet Installer.** Inspects floor to determine its condition and plans the layout after allowing for expected traffic patterns so that best appearance and long wear will be obtained. MN

**Carpet Representative.** Performs a variety of tasks including: establishing contacts, implementing promotions in the field, visiting key retailers to offer merchandising advice and to do direct selling, and working with certain national accounts. B

**Cartographer.** Compiles and interprets data and designs and constructs maps and charts. Researches surveying and mapping techniques and procedures. LMN

**Cartographic Technician.** Analyzes source data and prepares mosaic prints, contour maps, profile sheets, and related cartographic materials requiring technical mastery of photogrammetric techniques and principles. LMN

**Cartoonist.** Possesses a unique, humorous or dramatic point of view and the ability to illustrate it in a direct and economical pen-and-ink technique. In most cases the ability to write is essential. May do spot drawings or gag or satirical cartoons on a free-lance basis, have a staff job for a publication, or be syndicated as a comic-strip artist or political cartoonist. LMS—MS

**Caseworker Supervisor.** Coordinates activities of and supervises social-service-agency staff and volunteers, and students of school of social work. Counsels clients individually or in groups on planned or experimental basis and in emergencies. BS

**Cashier.** Receives cash from customers or employees in payment for goods or services and records amounts received. Makes change, cashes checks, and issues receipts or tickets to customers. Reads and records totals shown on cash-register tape and verifies against cash on hand. C

**Catalog Librarian.** Compiles information on library materials, such as books and periodicals, and prepares catalog cards to identify materials and to integrate information into library catalog. Records new information, such as death date of author and revised edition date, to amend catalogued cards. C

**Caterer.** Coordinates food-service activities of hotel, restaurant, or similar establishment or at social functions. Estimates food and beverage costs and requisitions or purchases supplies. Directs hiring and assignment of personnel. Investigates and resolves food quality and service complaints. BN

**Cephalometric Analyst.** Traces head X-rays and illustrates cosmetic result of proposed orthodontic treatment. Records cephalometric measurements to prepare data for computer analysis, using electronic data-recording equipment. Compiles data from tracings and computer plot sheets to illustrate results of proposed surgery or other orthodontic treatment. LM

**Ceramic Design Engineer.** Conducts research, designs machinery, develops processing techniques, and directs technical work concerned with manufacture of ceramic products. LM

**Certified Public Accountant.** Prepares and analyzes financial reports for clients. A certified public accountant may work for accounting firm or have own business. BCL—BCN—BLN

**Charge-Account Clerk.** Processes records of department store transactions that cannot be applied to customer's account by routine procedures in order that charges, cash payments, and refunds may be recorded, collected, or credited. Corrects or adds information to customer accounts as necessary. CN—N

**Check-Processing Clerk.** Examines and processes incoming checks and credit-card payment coupons in bank. Computes and checks totals for each account, compares total with account balance, and notifies supervisor of insufficient funds. C

**Chef.** Supervises, coordinates, and participates in activities of cooks and other kitchen personnel engaged in preparing and cooking foods in hotel restaurant, cafeteria, or other establishment. BM

**Chemical Engineer.** Designs equipment and develops processes for manufacturing chemicals and related products, utilizing principles and technology of chemistry, physics, mathematics, engineering, and related physical and natural sciences. LMN

**Chemical-Laboratory Technician.** Conducts chemical and physical laboratory tests and makes qualitative and quantitative analyses of materials, liquids, and gases for such purposes as research and development of new products and materials. LN

**Chemical Librarian.** Works in the field of physical sciences by providing the research and engineering staffs with information on new developments as well as reviews of past discoveries. CL

**Chemical Oceanographer.** Investigates the chemical compositions of ocean water and sediments as well as chemical reactions in the sea. LN

**Chemist.** Conducts research and analysis on substances for the purpose of product development. Devises new equipment and formulae for solution of technical problems. LN

**Chief Petroleum Engineer.** Plans and directs engineering activities of a petroleum company to develop oil fields and produce oil and gas. BMN

**Chief Medical Technologist.** Supervises and coordinates activities of workers engaged in performing chemical, microscopic, and bacteriologic tests to obtain data for use in diagnosis and treatment of diseases. BL

**Child-Care Attendant.** Cares for group of children housed in city, county, private, or other similar institution, under supervision of superintendent of home. May counsel or provide similar diagnostic or therapeutic services to mentally disturbed, delinquent, or handicapped children. S

**Child-Care Supervisor.** Supervises and organizes activities of prekindergarten children in nursery schools or in playrooms operated for patrons of theaters, department stores, hotels, and similar organizations. BCS—BS—S

**Child-Development Associate.** Takes care of a group of children, helping them to learn and develop, and keeps in contact with their parents, helping them to become involved in the center's program. S

**Child Psychologist.** Diagnoses or evaluates mental and emotional disorders of children and administers programs of treatment. Conducts diagnostic studies to identify child's needs, limitations, and potentials, observing child in play or other situations. May administer and score psychological tests. LS

**Chiropractor.** Adjusts spinal column and other articulations of body to prevent disease and correct abnormalities of human body believed to be caused by interference with nervous system. May utilize supplementary measures, such as exercise, rest, water, light, heat, and nutritional therapy. LMS

**Cinematographer.** Plans, directs, and coordinates motion-picture filming. Confers with motion-picture director regarding interpretation of scene and desired effects. Observes set or location and reviews drawings and other information relating to natural or artificial conditions to determine filming and lighting requirements. Views film after processing and makes adjustments as necessary to achieve desired effects. LM

**Circulation Manager.** Directs sale and distribution of newspapers, books, and periodicals. Directs staffing, training, and performance evaluations to develop and control sales and distribution programs. Establishes geographical areas of responsibility for subordinates to coordinate sales and distribution activities. B

**City Editor.** Directs and supervises personnel engaged in selecting, gathering, and editing local news and news photographs for edition of newspaper. BL

**City Manager.** Directs and coordinates administration of city or county government in accordance with policies determined by city council or other authorized elected officials. B—BS

**City Planner.** Develops comprehensive plans and programs for utilization of land and physical facilities of cities, counties, and metropolitan areas. BLM

**City-Planning Engineer.** Develops comprehensive plans and programs for utilization of land and physical facilities of cities, counties, and metropolitan areas. Compiles and analyzes data on economic, social, and physical factors affecting land use, and prepares or requisitions graphic and narrative reports on data. Confers with local authorities, civic leaders, social scientists, and land planning and development specialists to devise and recommend arrangements of land and physical facilities for residential, commercial, industrial, and community uses. BLM—BLN—BMN

**Civil Engineer.** Plans, designs, and directs construction and maintenance of structures and facilities, such as roads, railroads, airports, bridges, harbors, water and sewage systems, and waste-disposal units. May perform technical research and utilize computers as aids in developing solutions to engineering problems. LMN

**Civil-Engineering Technician.** Assists civil engineers in planning, designing, and constructing highways, bridges, dams, harbors, airports, pipelines, and other structures. May specialize in one area, such as highway or structural technology. Estimates costs, prepares specifications for materials, or participates in surveying, drafting, or designing. Once construction begins, may assist the contractor in scheduling construction activities and inspecting the work in order to ensure that it conforms to blueprints and specifications. LMN

**Claims Adjuster.** Investigates claims against insurance or other companies for personal, casualty, or property loss or damages and attempts to effect out-of-court settlement with claimant. Prepares report of findings and negotiates settlement with claimant. B

**Classified-Ad Clerk.** Receives orders for classified advertising for newspaper or magazine by telephone or in person. Talks to customer to determine wording and dates of publication of classified advertisement. Determines word, line, or day rates, using rate schedule, and calculates total charge for customer. BC

**Clergy Member.** Conducts religious worship and performs other spiritual functions associated with beliefs and practices of religious faith or denomination and provides spiritual and moral guidance and assistance to members. Conducts wedding and funeral services. Visits sick and shut-ins, and helps poor. Counsels those in spiritual need and comforts bereaved. LS—S

**Clerk-Typist.** Compiles data and operates typewriter in performance of routine clerical duties to maintain business records and reports. C

**Climatologist.** Studies climatic trends and analyzes past records of wind, rainfall, sunshine, and temperature to determine the general pattern of weather that makes up an area's climate. L

**Clinical Child Psychologist.** Uses psychological tests and interview and observational techniques to diagnose, evaluate, and treat behavioral disorders in children. May work with an individual child or with groups of children, and with their parents. May conduct research projects delving into the causes of such disorders. LS

**Clinical Engineer.** Uses technology to improve health-care-delivery systems in hospitals, clinics, government installations, universities, and industry. Besides sound engineering skills, a clinical engineer should have good management and communication skills. BLM

**Clinical Laboratory Assistant.** Assists medical technologists and technicians in routine tests and related work that can be learned in a relatively short time. May store and label plasma; clean and sterilize laboratory equipment, glassware, and instruments; prepare solutions, following standard laboratory formulas and procedures; keep records of tests; and identify specimens. CLN

**Clinical Pharmacologist.** Defines therapeutic regimes; determines valid methods of observation of drug effect; draws scientific conclusions from testing; employs drugs as diagnostic agents; creates new purposes for old drugs; disseminates the results of patient-oriented research; and helps medical therapists recognize the shortcomings and dangers of drugs and how to monitor their effects so as to minimize risks and maximize benefits. May act as a therapeutic consultant to guide developing doctors in what they can expect from drugs and how disease can alter the disposition and effects of drugs. L

**Clinical Psychologist.** Diagnoses or evaluates mental and emotional disorders of individuals, and administers programs of treatment. Interviews patients and studies medical and social case histories. Observes patients and selects, administers, and interprets tests to diagnose disorders and formulate plans of treatment. Treats psychological disorders to effect improved adjustment. LS—S

**Clothes Designer.** Designs garments, shoes, handbags, and other apparel and accessories. Makes rough and detailed drawings and writes specifications describing such factors as color scheme, construction, and type of material to be used. Analyzes trends, confers with sales and management executives, compares apparel materials, and integrates findings with personal interests, tastes, and knowledge of design to create new apparel designs. BM

**Club Manager.** Estimates and orders food products and coordinates activities of workers engaged in selling alcoholic and nonalcoholic beverages for consumption on premises. B

**Coal-Mining Engineer.** Examines coal seams for depth and purity, determines the type of mine to be built, and supervises the construction and maintenance of mines. LMN

**Coding-Clerk Supervisor.** Supervises and coordinates activities of workers engaged in converting routine items of information from source documents into codes to prepare records for data processing. Modifies, revises, or designs forms and initiates procedures

to develop more efficient methods of data input. BC

**Collections Clerk.** Receives and processes collection items (negotiable instruments), such as checks, drafts, and coupons, presented to bank by customers or correspondent banks. Traces unpaid items to determine reasons for nonpayment and notifies customer of disposition. C

**Collections Manager.** Directs and coordinates credit-card operations for bank, commercial concern, or credit-card company. Develops and establishes procedures for verifying data on application form, such as applicant bank references, established credit rating, and personal data, to ascertain if applicant meets prescribed criteria for credit. BC

**College Athletic Director.** Administers intercollegiate athletic program, hires staff, draws up a budget, and authorizes department expenditures. Directs preparation and dissemination of publicity to promote athletic events. B—BS

**College Financial-Aid Officer.** Directs scholarship, grant-in-aid, and loan programs to provide financial assistance to students in college or university. Selects candidates and determines types and amounts of aid. Organizes and oversees student-financial-counseling activities. BCS—CS

**College Planning and Placement Counselor.** Helps bridge the gap between education and work by assisting students in all phases of career decision making and planning. Arranges for job recruiters to visit the campus to discuss their firm's personnel needs and to interview applicants. LS

**College President.** Formulates plans and programs for and directs administration of college, school, or university, within authority delegated by governing board. Negotiates with administrative officials and representatives of business, community, and civic groups to promote educational research and public-service objectives and policies of institution as formulated by board of control. B

**College Recruiter.** Travels to high schools to present admission data and outline college programs. Interviews prospective students. B—BS

**College Registrar.** Directs and coordinates college registration activities. Prepares student transcripts and commencement list. Directs preparation of statistical reports on educational activities for government and educational agencies and interprets registration policies to faculty and students. Coordinates class schedules with room assignments for optimum use of buildings and equipment. CL

**Commercial Artist.** Draws or paints illustrations for use by various media to explain or adorn printed or spoken word. Studies layouts and sketches of proposed illustrations and determines style, technique, and medium best suited to produce desired effects and conform with reproduction requirements. BM

**Commercial Broker.** Specializes in selling or leasing income-producing business properties, such as apartment and office buildings, retail stores, and warehouses. B

**Commercial Photographer.** May specialize in a particular type of photography, such as illustrative, fashion, architectural, or portrait. BM

**Communications Consultant.** Contacts residential, commercial, and industrial telephone-company subscribers to ascertain communications problems and needs and promote use of telephone services, utilizing knowledge of marketing conditions, contacts, sales methods, and communications services and equipment. B

**Communications-Equipment Salesperson.** Sells telephone services to business accounts. Contacts and visits commercial customers to review telephone service. Analyzes communication needs of business establishments, recommends services and equipment, quotes rates, and writes up orders. May specialize in selling services to a particular industry. BM

**Communications Librarian.** Provides information to the specialists who create the ideas and produce the formats of communications. CL

**Community Pharmacist.** Compounds and dispenses medications, following prescriptions issued by physicians, dentists, or other authorized medical practitioners. A community pharmacist may also buy and sell nonpharmaceutical merchandise. BCN—BCS

**Composing-Machine Operator.** Operates machine to cast complete lines of type from type metal and deposit them in galley in composed form for printing. M

**Computational Linguist.** Analyzes words and language structure to determine how the computer can manipulate text for indexing, classification, abstracting, search, and retrieval. L

**Computer-Aided Design Technician.** Operates computer-aided design (CAD) system and peripheral equipment to resize or modify integrated circuit designs and to generate computer tape of artwork for use in producing mask plates used in manufacturing integrated circuits. LM

**Computer-Applications Engineer.** Formulates mathematical models of systems, and sets up and controls analog or hybrid computer system to solve scientific and engineering problems. Prepares technical reports describing step-by-step solution of problems. Develops new techniques for solving problems. LMN—N

**Computer Operator.** Monitors and controls electronic computer to process business, scientific, engineering, or other data, according to operating instructions. CM

**Computer Programmer.** Designs and tests computer programs, and may assist sales personnel in determining data-processing needs of customers. CL—CLN—L

**Computer Sales Representative.** Sells computers and electronic data-processing systems to business or industrial establishments. Analyzes customer's needs and recommends computer system that best meets customer's requirements. B—BL

**Computer Systems Analyst.** Conducts logical analyses of scientific, engineering, and other problems and formulates mathematical models of problems for solution by digital computer. LN

**Computer-Systems Service Technician.** Services machines or systems to keep them operating efficiently. LM—M

**Conciliator.** Mediates and conciliates disputes in negotiation of labor agreements. Promotes use of fact-finding and advisory services to prevent labor disputes and to maintain sound labor relations. BLN—BNS

**Condominium Manager.** Manages condominium complex in accordance with homeowner's property management contract. Confers with representatives of homeowners' association or board of directors to review financial status of association and to determine management priorities. Directs collection of monthly assessments from residents and payment of incurred operating expenses. Directs maintenance staff in routine repairs. BM

**Conference Interpreter.** Often works in a glass-enclosed booth while listening through earphones to what is said. Simultaneously translates idea by idea, or by phrases, as the speaker continues to talk. Requires speed and fluency. C

**Conference Typist.** Records, transcribes, and disseminates minutes of meetings to the participants. C

**Conservationist.** Protects, develops, and manages forests, rangelands, wildlife, and soil and water resources to ensure that future ecological needs will be met. BL

**Construction Electrician.** Assembles, installs, and wires electrical systems that operate heating, lighting, power, air-conditioning, and refrigeration components. M

**Construction Estimator.** Must have detailed knowledge of the costs involved in all of the dozens of building crafts. BMN—MN

**Construction Inspector.** Ensures compliance with building codes and ordinances, zoning regulations, and contract specifications, in public and private construction. CM

**Construction-Materials Supervisor.** Is responsible for ordering building supplies, such as steel, lumber, cement and gravel, asbestos, glass. CMN

**Construction Superintendent.** Directs activities of workers concerned with construction of buildings, dams, highways, pipelines, or other construction projects. BM

**Consumer-Affairs Director.** Administers consumer-affairs program. Develops and conducts a program to inform public of departmental objectives. Conducts investigations and cooperates with federal, state, and local agencies, the business community, and private organizations to resolve violations of consumer-protection laws. Recommends changes in legislation affecting consumer protection. BL—BLS

**Consumer Financial Adviser.** Assists consumers in wise management of their monetary resources in financial clinics and institutions, community programs, and cooperative extension services. BNS—NS

**Consumer Services Consultant.** Organizes and conducts consumer education service or research program for equipment, food, textile, or utility company. May engage in research in government, private industry, and colleges and universities, to explore family relations or child development; develop new products for home, discover facts on nutrition, and test serviceability of new materials. BNS—BS

**Contract Specialist.** Negotiates with suppliers to draw up procurement contracts. Formulates and coordinates procurement policies and procedures. Analyzes price proposals, financial reports, and other data to determine reasonableness of prices. BLN

**Controls Designer.** Designs and drafts systems of electrical, hydraulic, and pneumatic controls for machines and equipment, such as arc welders, robots, conveyors, applying knowledge of electricity, electronics, and hydraulics. LM

**Cooperative-Extension-Adviser Specialist.** Instructs extension workers and develops specialized service activities in area of agriculture or home economics. Plans, develops, organizes, and evaluates training programs in subjects such as home management, horticulture, and consumer information. BLS

**Corporate Benefits Manager.** Manages employee benefits program for establishment. Plans and directs implementation and administration of benefits programs designed to insure employees against loss of income because of illness, injury, layoff, or retirement. Directs preparation and distribution of informational literature and oral presentations to notify and advise employees of eligibility for benefits programs. B—BNS—BS

**Corporate Pilot.** Flies aircraft owned by business and industrial firms, transporting company executives on cross-country flights to branch plants and business conferences. LM

**Corrections Officer.** Is responsible for the safekeeping of persons who have been arrested and are awaiting trial, or who have been tried, convicted of a crime, and sentenced to serve time in a correctional institution. S

**Correctional-Treatment Specialist.** Provides casework services for inmates of penal or correctional institution. Interviews inmate and confers with attorneys, judges, and probation officers to compile social history reflecting such factors as nature and extent of inmate's criminality and current and prospective social problems. Analyzes collected data and develops and initiates treatment plan. LS—S

**Corrective Therapist.** Provides medically prescribed program of physical exercises and activities designed to prevent muscular deterioration resulting from long convalescence or inactivity due to chronic illness. BMS—MS

**Correspondence Clerk.** Composes letters in reply to correspondence concerning such matters as requests for merchandise, credit information, delinquent accounts, and unsatisfactory service, or to request information. BC—BCS

**Cosmetics Salesperson.** Sells cosmetics and toiletries, such as skin creams, hair preparations, face powder, lipstick, and perfume, to customers in department store or specialty shop. B

**Cosmetologist.** Provides beauty services for customers. May lighten or darken the color of the hair to better suit the patron's skin color. Suggests cosmetics for conditions, such as dry or oily skin. Cosmetologists may give manicures, facial and scalp treatments; shape and color eyebrows or eyelashes; remove unwanted hair, apply solutions that straighten hair or retain curls or waves in hair; and provide makeup analysis for customers. BM

**Cost Estimator.** Prepares cost estimates for manufacturing of products, construction projects, or services requested to aid management in bidding on, or determining price of product or service. BN

**Costume Designer.** Conducts research and designs authentic period, country, or social-class costumes to be worn by motion picture, television, concert, stage, and other media performers. M

**Costume Specialist.** Employed as a consultant to historical restorations, museum collections, historical societies, and organizations that re-create historical events. Researches and specializes in the identification process involving styles and fabrics and the authentic reconstruction of era attire. LM

**Counseling Psychologist.** Provides individual and group counseling services to assist individuals in achieving more effective personal, social, educational, and vocational development and adjustment. May engage in research to develop and improve diagnostic and counseling techniques. May administer and score psychological tests. LS

**County Agricultural Agent.** Organizes and conducts cooperative extension program to advise and instruct farmers and individuals engaged in agribusiness in applications of agricultural research findings. B—BCM—BL—BMS

**County Manager.** Directs and coordinates administration of government. Appoints department heads and staffs as provided by state laws or local ordinances. Supervises activities of departments performing functions such as collection and disbursement of taxes, law enforcement, maintenance of public health, construction of public works, and purchases of supplies and equipment. May recommend zoning regulations controlling location and development of residential and commercial areas. B

**Court Clerk.** Performs clerical duties in court of law. Prepares docket or calendar of cases to be called, using typewriter. Examines legal documents submitted to court, prepares case folders, and posts, files, or routes documents. Secures information for judges, and contacts witnesses, attorneys, and litigants to obtain information for court, and instructs parties when to appear in court. Records minutes of court proceedings, using a stenotype or shorthand, and transcribes testimony, using typewriter. Collects and records court fees. C

**Court Reporter.** Records examination, testimony, judicial opinions, judge's charge to jury, judgment or sentence of court, or other proceedings in court of law by machine, or reports proceedings into steno-mask. Reads portions of transcript during trial on judge's request and asks speakers to clarify inaudible statements. C

**Credit Analyst.** Analyzes paying habits of customers who are delinquent in payment of bills and recommends action. Evaluates customer records and recommends that account be closed, credit limit reduced or extended, or collection attempted, on the basis of earnings and savings data, payment history, and purchase acitivity of customer. BL—BLN

**Credit-Collections Secretary.** Performs secretarial duties utilizing knowledge of credit-collections terminology. Prepares papers pertinent to overdue charge accounts, loans, or other credit-issuing companies. Gives advice to callers and relieves officials of the need to give minor forms of advice. CNS

**Credit-Collections Supervisor.** Supervises and coordinates activities of workers engaged in collection of overdue charge-account payments from credit-card or loan customers of banks, loan companies, department stores, oil companies, or other credit-card-issuing companies. Reviews delinquent account records to determine which customers must be contacted for collection of overdue accounts. BN—BNS

**Credit Counselor.** Provides financial counseling to individuals in debt. Confers with client to ascertain available monthly income in order to meet credit obligations. Calculates amount of debt and funds available to plan method of payoff and estimate time for debt liquidation. Contacts creditors to arrange for payment adjustments. Keeps records of account activity. BNS—NS

**Credit-Union Manager.** Directs and coordinates activities of credit union engaged in providing savings-and-loan services to members. Reviews applications for loans and recommends to loan committee approval or denial, considering such factors as amount of loan requested, credit rating of member, salary, and length of employment. Performs related managerial duties, such as recommending to board securities for investment of excess funds, arranging for bank credit, negotiating loans, and purchase and sale of securities, as authorized. BL

**Criminologist.** Specializes in research on relationship between criminal law and social order in causes of crime and behavior of criminals. L

**Criminalist.** Applies scientific principles to analysis, identification, and classification of mechanical devices, chemical and physical substances, materials, liquids, or other physical evidence related to criminology, law enforcement, or investigative work. L

**Cryptanalyst.** Analyzes secret coding systems and decodes messages for military, political, or law-enforcement agencies or organizations. CL

**Custom House Broker.** Records purchases and sales of securities. Informs customers of market fluctuations and effects upon their accounts. BC

**Customer-Service Representative.** Interviews applicants for water, gas, electric, or telephone service. Adjusts complaints concerning billing or service rendered, referring the complaints of service failures. B

**Customer-Support Specialist.** Converts client's manual accounting systems to computerized systems. Trains client's employees to program systems and diagnoses computer hardware malfunctions. LN

**Customer Technical-Services Manager.** Directs and coordinates activities of department in manufacturing establishment concerned with providing customers technical services in conjunction with marketing activities. B

**Customs Import Specialist.** Examines, classifies, and appraises imported merchandise according to federal revenue laws, in order to enforce regulations of U.S. Customs Service. C

**Customs Inspector.** Inspects cargo, baggage, articles worn or carried by persons, and vessels, vehicles, or aircraft entering or leaving the United States to enforce customs and related laws. C

**Customs Patrol Officer.** Conducts surveillance, inspection, and patrols by foot, vehicle, boat, or aircraft at assigned points of entry into the United States to prohibit smuggled merchandise and contraband, and to detect violations of customs and related laws. C

**Cyberneticist.** Studies communication and manipulation of information and its use in controlling the behavior of biological, physical, and chemical systems. L

**Cytologist.** Studies plant and animal cells. Selects and sections minute particles of animal or plant tissue for microscopic study. Conducts research in physiology of unicellular organisms, such as protozoa, to ascertain physical and chemical factors involved in growth. Studies influence of physical and chemical factors upon malignant and normal cells. LN

**Cytotechnician.** Performs routine tests in medical laboratory for use in treatment and diagnosis of disease. Prepares tissue samples for pathologist. Takes blood samples. Executes such laboratory tests as urinalysis and blood counts. CL

**Cytotechnologist.** Stains, mounts, and studies cells of human body to determine pathological condition. Examines specimen and diagnoses nature and extent of disease or cellular damage. Executes variety of laboratory tests and analyses to confirm findings. CL

**Dairy Farmer.** Breeds and raises dairy cattle. Operates farm machinery to plant, cultivate, and harvest feed crops. Sterilizes milking machines and equipment. Cools milk to prevent spoilage. Arranges for sale of animals and products. Maintains cost and operation records. B

**Dairy Scientist.** Researches breeding, feeding, and management of dairy cattle. Carries out experiments to determine effects of different kinds of feed and environmental conditions on quantity, quality, and nutritive value of milk produced. Studies physiology of reproduction and lactation, and carries out breeding programs to improve dairy breeds. L

**Dairy Technologist.** Applies principles of bacteriology, chemistry, physics, engineering, and economics to develop new and improved methods in productions, preservation, and utilization of milk, cheese, and other dairy products. BLN—LN

**Dance Therapist.** Applies the principles and techniques of the art to the rehabilitation of physically and mentally ill patients. S

**Data-Base Manager.** Analyzes, manipulates, and coordinates "hard" data for efficient use by researchers and management. L—LN

**Data-Control Supervisor.** Supervises and coordinates activities of workers engaged in keeping control records and scheduling data to be processed on keypunch or electronic data-processing machines. Examines data for discrepancies, corrects errors, and reconciles data to ensure accuracy at various stages of data processing. BC

**Data-Processing Systems Analyst.** Plans efficient methods of processing data and handles the results found in either business or scientific and engineering applications. Discusses data-processing problems with managers or specialists to determine the exact nature of the problem and to break it down into its component parts. Analysts use various techniques, such as cost accounting, sampling, and mathematical model building, to analyze a problem and devise a new system. LN

**Data-Reduction Technician.** Applies standardized mathematical formulas, principles, and methodology to technological problems in engineering and physical sciences in relation to specific industrial and research objectives, processes, equipment, and products. Translates data into numerical values, equations, flow charts, graphs, or other media. Analyzes processed data to detect errors. LN

**Data Typist.** Operates special-purpose electric typewriter to convert alphabetic, numeric, and symbolic data into coded form on punch cards or tapes. C

**Day-Care-Center Director.** Directs activities of preschool day-care center to prepare children for primary school. Prepares and submits facility budget to board of trustees; authorizes purchase of instructional materials and teaching aids; interviews and recommends hiring of teaching and service staff; confers with teaching staff regarding child's behavioral or learning problems. BS

**Dean of Students.** Directs and coordinates student programs of college or university. Formulates and develops student-personnel policies. Advises staff members on problems relating to policy, program, and administration. Counsels or advises individuals and groups on matters pertaining to personal problems, educational and vocational objectives, social and recreational activities, and financial assistance. BL—BLS

**Demographer.** Plans and conducts demographic research, surveys, and experiments to study human populations and affecting trends. BNS—LN—LNS—NS

**Dental Assistant.** Assists dentist engaged in diagnostic, operative, surgical, periodontal, preventive, orthodontic, removable and fixed prosthodontic, endodontic, and pedodontic procedures during examination and treatment of patients. CMS—MS

**Dental Ceramist.** Applies layers of porcelain paste or acrylic resins over metal framework to form dental prostheses, such as crowns, bridges, and tooth facings, according to dentist's prescriptions, using spatula, brushes, and baking oven. M

**Dental-Equipment Sales Representative.** Sells dental equipment and supplies, except drugs and medicines, to dentists, hospitals, dental schools, and retail establishments. Provides customers with advice in such areas as office layout, legal and insurance regulations, cost analysis, and collection methods to develop goodwill and promote sales. B

**Dental Hygienist.** Performs preventive and therapeutic services, such as removing deposits and dental stains, and application of medicine for prevention of tooth decay. CMS—MNS—MS

**Dental-Laboratory Manager.** Coordinates activities of workers in dental laboratory engaged in making and repairing full or partial dentures, crowns, inlays, and bridgework. Analyzes cost and production records to ensure that operation is efficient and profitable. BLM

**Dentist.** Diagnoses and treats diseases, injuries, and malformations of teeth and gums, and related oral structures. Cleans, fills, extracts, and replaces teeth, using rotary and hand instruments, dental appliances, medications, and surgical implements. LMS—MNS

**Department-Store Manager.** Directs and coordinates, through subordinate managerial personnel, activities of department store selling lines of merchandise in specialized departments. Formulates pricing policies for sale of merchandise or implements policies set forth by merchandising board. Negotiates or approves contracts with suppliers of merchandise, or with other establishments providing security, maintenance, or cleaning service. B

**Dermatologist.** Diagnoses and treats diseases of human skin. Examines skin to determine nature of disease, taking blood samples and smears from affected areas and performing other laboratory procedures. LS

**Design Engineer.** Designs machinery, products, systems, and processes for efficient and economical performance. Designs industrial machinery and equipment used to manufacture goods; designs, plans, and supervises the construction of buildings, highways, and rapid-transit systems; designs and develops consumer products such as automobiles, television sets, and refrigerators, and systems for control and automation of manufacturing, business, and management processes. LM—LMN

**Detective.**   Conducts private investigations to locate missing persons, obtain confidential information, and solve crimes. Reports criminal information to police and testifies in court. May arrange lie-detector tests for witnesses or clients' employees. May be employed by commercial or industrial establishments. CL—CLS

**Diagnostic Medical Sonographer.**   Gathers appropriate knowledge of the patient's history and available clinical data. Uses this information to position the patient in a manner that will facilitate optimum diagnostic results. Surveys the area being studied to obtain preliminary sonographic information with respect to the acoustical properties of the patient as well as anatomical and pathological relationships. Performs a diagnostic scan and makes a permanent record of the significant functional and anatomical and pathological data obtained. LM

**Diagnostic-X-Ray Technologist.**   Operates X-ray equipment to make radiographs (on X-ray film) of various parts of the body. These are used by the physician in determining the extent of the patient's illness or injury. LM—M

**Dialysis Technician.**   Sets up and operates artificial-kidney machine to provide dialysis treatment for patients with kidney disorders or failure. May assist with surgical insertion of shunts into vein and artery of patient's arm or leg. May explain dialysis procedure and operation of kidney machine to patient before first treatment to allay apprehension or fear of dialysis. MNS—MS

**Die Maker.**   Constructs metal forms (dies) to shape metal in stamping and forging operations. Engages in making metal molds for die-casting and for molding plastics. M

**Dietetic Assistant.**   Writes food menus following dietetic specifications, oversees the work of food-service employees in health-care facilities, and performs many other duties. BC

**Dietetic Researcher.**   Conducts nutritional research to expand knowledge in one or more phases of dietetics. CLN—LN

**Dietetics Instructor.**   Plans, organizes, and conducts educational programs in dietetics, nutrition, and institutional management for dietetic interns, nursing students, and other medical personnel. CLS—LS

**Dietetic Technician.**   Provides services in assigned areas of food-service management, teaches principles of food and nutrition, and provides dietary counseling, under direction of dietitian. CLS

**Dietitian.**   Plans nutritious and appetizing meals to help people maintain or recover good health. Confers with physicians about patients' nutritional care and instructs patients and their families on importance of diet. CLS

**Dietitian Administrator.**   Directs activities of institutional department providing quantity food-service and nutritional care. Establishes policies and procedures, and provides administrative direction for menu formulation, food preparation and service, purchasing, sanitation standards, safety practices, and personnel utilization. Selects professional dietetic staff, and directs departmental professional activities. BC

**Digitizer Operator.**   Operates encoding machine to trace coordinates on documents such as maps or drawings and encodes document points into computer. C

**Directory-Assistance Operator.**   Provides telephone information from cord or cordless central-office switchboard. May keep record of calls received, and alphabetical or geographical reels and directories up-to-date. C

**Dispatcher.**   Coordinates the movement of trucks and freight into and out of terminals; makes up loads for specific destinations; assigns drivers and develops delivery schedules; handles customers' requests for pickup of freight; and provides information on deliveries. BC

**Dispensing Optician.**   Reads prescription of optometrist or ophthalmologist to obtain lens specifications. Measures and fits customer with eyeglass frames and lenses. BMN

**Display Director.**   Supervises and coordinates the activities of each department in large stores. Also confers with executives, such as advertising and sales managers, to select merchandise for promotion and to plan displays. BM

**Documents Examiner.**   Examines data contained in public documents to gather facts, verify correctness, or establish authenticity. Interviews persons, visits establishments, or confers with technical or professional specialists, to obtain information or clarify facts. CL

**Drafter.**   Develops detailed design drawings and related specifications of mechanical equipment, according to engineering sketches and design-proposal specifications. Often calculates the strength, quality, quantity, and cost of materials. Drafters usually specialize in a particular field of work, such as mechanical, electrical, electronic, aeronautical, structural, or architectural drafting. CLM—LMN—MN

**Drafting Instructor.**   Teaches courses, usually at two-year college, to prepare students for a career in drafting or related areas utilizing knowledge and techniques of the field. MNS

**Drafting Technician.**   Assists engineers and scientists in research for and development of experimental equipment and models by making drawings and sketches and, frequently, by doing routine design work. MN

**Dramatic Coach.**   Coaches performers in acting techniques. Adapts training methods to improve and develop performers' competence. Advises clients regarding wardrobe, grooming, and audition methods, to prepare them for professional contacts. BS

**Drilling Engineer.**   Analyzes technical and cost factors to plan methods to recover maximum oil and gas in oil-field operations, utilizing knowledge of petroleum engineering and related technologies. LMN

**Druggist.** Compounds and dispenses medications, following prescriptions issued by physician, dentist, or other authorized medical practitioner. Dispenses nonprescription medication to public. Advises self-diagnosing and self-medicating patients, or provides information on potential drug interactions, potential adverse drug reactions, and elements of patient's history that might bear on prescribing decision when in advisory capacity to physician. BNS—LNS—NS

**Duplicating-Machine Operator.** Operates equipment such as stencil and copying machines that can reproduce letters, bills, invoices, and other documents. CM

**Earth Scientist.** Is concerned with the history, composition, and characteristics of the earth's surface, interior, and atmosphere. Conducts research on physical and climatic aspects of area, observing landforms, climates, soils, vegetation, and animals. L—LN

**Ecologist.** Studies the relationship between organisms and their environments, particularly the effects on them of such environmental influences as rainfall, temperature, and altitude. L

**Ecology Ranger.** Manages, improves, and protects range resources to maximize their use without incurring ecological destruction. BL

**Economic Analyst.** Reviews, analyzes, and organizes data into report format and arranges for preparation of graphic illustrations of research findings. Formulates recommendations, policies, or plans to aid in market interpretation or solution of economic problems. BLN

**Economic-Development Coordinator.** Directs economic-development planning activities for city, state, or region. Negotiates with industry representatives to encourage location in area. Confers with governmental officials to effect changes in local policies or ordinances discouraging effective development. B

**Economic Geographer.** Deals with the geographic distribution of economic activities including manufacturing, mining, agriculture, trade, and communications. LN

**Economics Professor.** Teaches economics within a prescribed curriculum. Prepares and delivers lectures, compiles and grades examinations. May advise students on academic and vocational plans. CNS—NS

**Economist.** Plans, designs, and conducts research to aid in interpretation of economic relationships and in solution of problems arising in production and distribution of goods and services. Compiles data relating to research area, such as employment, productivity, and wages and hours. BCN—BLN—CLN

**Educational Attendance Clerk.** Compiles attendance records for school district, issues attendance permits, and answers inquiries from parents and school officials, using state education code as guide. Prepares special reports, such as ethnic- or racial-distribution

surveys, requested by state or district education officials. C—CNS

**Educational Audiovisual Specialist.** Directs and coordinates preparation, development, and use of educational materials in public school system. Coordinates activities of workers engaged in cataloging, distributing, and maintaining educational materials and equipment in curriculum library and laboratory. BCM —BM

**Educational Consultant.** Plans and coordinates educational policies for specific subject area or grade level. Develops programs for in-service education of teaching personnel. Confers with federal, state, and local school officials to develop curricula and establish guidelines for educational programs. BLS

**Educational-Course Sales Representative.** Solicits applications for enrollment in technical, commercial, and industrial schools. Advises prospective students on selection of courses on the basis of their education and vocational objectives. BCS—BS

**Educational Programming Director.** Plans, develops, and administers programs to promote educational uses of television programs and auxiliary services of public broadcasting station. Reviews past and current educational and instructional programs, then analyzes data to determine prospective users, audiences, and potential funding sources. BL

**Educational Psychologist.** Investigates processes of learning and teaching and develops psychological principles and techniques applicable to educational problems to foster intellectual, social, and emotional development of individuals. Administers standardized tests to diagnose disabilities and difficulties among students and to develop special methods of remedial instruction. May specialize in educational measurement, school adjustment, learning, or special education. LNS—NS

**Educational Supervisor.** Develops program curriculum and directs teaching personnel of school system. Evaluates teaching techniques and recommends changes for improving them. Conducts workshops and conferences for teachers to study new classroom procedures, new instructional materials, and other aids to teaching. BS

**Educational Therapist.** Teaches elementary and secondary school subjects to educationally handicapped students with neurological or emotional disabilities in schools, institutions, or other specialized facilities. LS

**Electric-Motors Salesperson.** Sells new and used fractional- and integral-horsepower electric motors and estimates cost of repairs in manufacturing, retail, or repair establishment. BM

**Electrical-Appliance Salesperson.** Primary function is to sell merchandise. Often answers questions, demonstrates uses, and shows various models and colors. B

**Electrical-Control Assembler.** Assembles protection, communication, and control devices, such as switches, relays, rheostats, transmitters, and switch-boards, as laid out in drawings and wiring diagrams. M

**Electrical Engineer.**  Conducts research and development activities concerned with design, manufacture, and testing of electrical components, equipment, and systems; application of equipment to new uses; and manufacture, construction, and installation of electrical equipment, facilities, and systems. LMN

**Electrical Inspector.**  Tests electrical devices to determine voltage required to break down insulation at simulated altitudes, using power supply, galvanometer, and oscilloscope. Determines resistance values at specified temperatures, using electric oven, bridges, galvanometer, and power supply. Keeps inspection records and writes procedure reports. CMN

**Electrical Test Engineer.**  Conducts tests on electrical equipment that is applied to controls, instruments, and systems of new commercial, domestic, and industrial uses. LMN

**Electrician.**  Plans layout and installs electrical fixtures, apparatus, and control equipment. Repairs and maintains electrical systems and equipment such as motors, transformers, and switches. LM

**Electrocardiograph Technician.**  Operates and maintains electrocardiograph machines, records electromotive variation in heart-muscle action, and provides data to physicians for diagnosis and treatment of heart ailments. CLM—CM

**Electroencephalographic Technician.**  Operates and maintains electroencephalographic machines, recording brain waves on a graph to be used by physicians in the diagnosis of brain disorders. CM

**Electrologist.**  Removes unwanted hair from skin of patron by electrolysis. Uses electrodes to decompose cells holding hair, then removes hair from follicle using tweezers. BMS—MS

**Electromechanisms Design Drafter.**  Drafts designs of electromechanical equipment and confers with engineers and other drafters to interpret design concepts, determine nature and type of required detailed working drawings, and coordinate work with that of others. Compiles data, computes quantities, determines materials needed, and prepares cost estimate. MN

**Electromyographic Technician.**  Assists physicians in recording and analyzing bioelectric potentials that originate in muscle tissue, including the operation of various electronic devices, maintenance of electronic equipment, assisting with patient care, and record keeping. CM

**Electronic-Communications Technician.**  The electronics technician monitors frequencies for possible violations, conducts frequency measurements, tests equipment, analyzes applications for various licenses, and does other nonengineering technical work. CM—LMN

**Electronics Engineer.**  Works on research and development, production, and quality-control problems. The electronics engineer is highly specialized and may work in a specific area, such as the design and implementation of solid-state circuitry in radar, computers, or calculators. LMN

**Electronic-Parts Sales Representative.**  Sells television, radio, and other electronics parts to establishments such as appliance stores, dealers, and repair shops, or electronics- and aircraft-manufacturing firms. BM

**Electronic-Packaging Engineer.**  Performs design and development of the physical and mechanical aspects of electronic hardware for missile, spacecraft, aircraft, and ground-support equipment. The activities involve printed-circuit-board design, component selection, enclosive design, wiring, interconnects and connector design, interface compatibility, shielding, and consideration of thermal, vibration, shock, humidity, and altitude requirements. LM

**Electronic Technician.**  Helps engineers design and build experimental models, sets up and repairs electronic equipment for customers, and can do complex inspection and assembly work. CLM—CM

**Electronics Mechanic.**  Repairs electronic equipment, such as computers, industrial controls, radar systems, telemetering and missile-control systems, transmitters, antennas, and servomechanisms, following blueprints and manufacturers' specifications. Maintains records of repairs, calibrations, and tests. CM

**Electronics Photo Technician.**  Prints and develops film of circuit designs for use in fabricating printed circuit boards (PCB), using photographic equipment and knowledge of photographic processing. M

**Electro-Optics Physicist.**  Designs equipment for generating, propagating, detecting, and processing electromagnetic energy in the frequency band from infrared through ultraviolet. LMN

**Electroplater.**  Studies the job specifications which indicate the parts of the object to be plated, the type of plating metal to be applied, and the desired thickness of the plating, and then treats these parts in electrolytic and chemical baths to prevent corrosion. MN

**Electrotyper.**  Fabricates and finishes duplicate electrotype printing plates according to specifications, using hand tools, electroplating equipment, and metal casting, trimming, and forming machines. CM

**Elementary-School Teacher.**  Teaches elementary school pupils academic, social, and manipulative skills, in public or private educational system. Tries to develop in students good study and work habits and an appreciation for learning. LS—S

**Elevator Constructor.**  Assembles and installs electric and hydraulic freight and passenger elevators, escalators, and dumbwaiters, determining layout and electrical connections from blueprints. M

**Embalmer.**  Prepares bodies for interment in conformity with legal requirements. May arrange funeral details, such as type of casket or burial dress and place of interment. BL—BLM

**Emergency Medical Technician.**  Administers first-aid treatment to sick and injured persons and transports them to medical facility, working as member of emergency medical team. CL—LS—MNS

**Emergency Specialist.** Develops and implements hospital-wide procedures for dealing with in-house and community emergencies and disasters. LS

**Employee Relations Specialist.** Interviews workers to gather information on worker attitudes toward work environment and supervision received in order to facilitate resolution of employee relations problems that affect morale, motivation, and efficiency. BLS—BS

**Employee-Welfare Manager.** Directs welfare activities for employees and may assist in the solution of personal problems, such as recommending day nurseries for their children and counseling them on personality frictions or emotional maladjustments. BS

**Employer Relations Representative.** Establishes and maintains working relationships with local employers to promote use of public employment programs and services. BS

**Employment-Agency Manager.** Manages employment services and business operations of private employment agency. Directs hiring, training, and evaluation of employees. Analyzes placement reports to determine effectiveness of employment interviewers. Investigates and resolves customer complaints. BLS

**Employment Counselor.** Helps people who lack realistic career goals, adequate job training, or knowledge about the labor market. Assists the handicapped, older workers, and individuals displaced by automation and industry shifts, or who are unhappy with their present occupation; also serves welfare recipients, ex-prisoners, and the educationally and culturally deprived persons who turn to state or community agencies for advice. Interviews job seekers to learn employment-related facts about their interests, training, work experience, work attitudes, physical capacities, and personal traits. May arrange for aptitude and achievement tests and interest inventories, so that more objective advice may be given. BLS

**Employment Interviewer.** Interviews job applicants to select persons meeting employer qualifications. Searches files of job orders from employers and matches applicants' qualifications with job requirements and employer specifications. BCS

**Employment Supervisor.** Manages employment activities of establishment. Plans and directs activities of staff workers concerned with such functions as developing sources of qualified applicants, conducting screening interviews, administering tests, checking references and background, evaluating applicants' qualifications, and arranging for preliminary indoctrination and training for newly hired employees. Analyzes statistical data and other reports in order to identify and determine causes of personnel problems and to develop and present recommendations for improvement of establishment's employment policies, processes, and practices. BLS

**Endocrine Pharmacologist.** Studies the actions of certain drugs which are either hormones or hormone derivates, or drugs which do not possess intrinsic hormonal actions but which may modify the actions of normally secreted hormones. The field of endocrine pharmacology is of utmost importance, because hormones regulate metabolic processes, and some of the major unsolved problems in medicine deal with the nature and control of diseases of metabolic origin. L

**Endodontist.** Examines, diagnoses, and treats diseases of nerve, pulp, and other internal dental tissues affecting vitality of teeth. LMS

**Engineer.** Applies the theories and principles of science and mathematics to practical technical problems. An engineer's work is often the link between a scientific discovery and its useful application. Designs and develops consumer products. Determines the general way the device will work, designs and tests all components, and fits them together in an integrated plan. Evaluates the overall effectiveness of the new device, as well as its cost and reliability. In addition to design and development, many engineers work in testing, production, operation, or maintenance. Still others are in administration, management, and sales jobs where an engineering background is necessary. LMN

**Engineering Geologist.** Studies structure and composition of land to determine suitable sites for the construction of roads, airfields, tunnels, dams, and other structures. LMN

**Engineering Psychologist.** Examines, analyzes, and improves the relationship between persons and their immediate work space. Designs and constructs individual or group work areas that are conducive to efficient functioning in offices, laboratories, industrial plants, and space vehicles. BLS—LNS—LS

**Engineering Surveyor.** Measures construction sites, helps establish official land boundaries, assists in setting land evaluations, and collects information for maps and charts. CMN

**Engineering Technical Writer.** Puts scientific and technical information into language that can readily be understood by people who need to use it. Researches, writes, and edits technical materials and may also produce publications or audiovisual materials. LMN

**Engineering Technician.** Develops and tests machinery and equipment, applying knowledge of mechanical-engineering technology, under direction of engineering and scientific staff. LMN

**Entomologist.** Studies insects and their relation to plant and animal life. Identifies and classifies species of insects and allied forms, such as mites and spiders. Aids in control and elimination of agricultural, structural, and forest pests by developing new and improved pesticides and cultural and biological methods, including use of natural enemies of pests. LN

**Environmental Engineer.** Applies engineering principles to the control, elimination, and prevention of environmental hazards, such as air pollution, water pollution, solids pollution, and noise pollution. LMN

**Environmental-Engineering Technician.** Conducts tests and field investigations to obtain data for use by environmental, engineering, and scientific personnel in determining sources and methods of controlling pollutants in air, water, and soil, utilizing knowledge of agriculture, chemistry, meteorology, and engineering principles and applied technologies. LMN

**Environmental Health Specialist.** Enforces the health standards regarding food, water supply, sewage disposal, garbage disposal, and housing maintenance. The environmental health specialist improves unsafe methods of waste disposal and sanitary conditions; advises on difficult sanitation problems; or plans and administers environmental health programs. LMN

**Environmental Health Technician.** Assists in the survey of environmental hazards and performs technical duties, under professional supervision, in many areas of environmental health, such as pollution control, radiation protection, and sanitation protection. LMN

**Environmentalist.** Plans, develops, and implements standards and systems to improve the quality of air, water, food, shelter, and other environmental factors. Manages comprehensive environmental health programs, and promotes public awareness of the need to prevent and eliminate environmental health hazards. BLM

**Environmental Planner.** Plans and designs development of land areas for projects, such as parks and other recreational facilities, airports, highways and parkways, hospitals, schools, land subdivisions, and commercial, industrial, and residential sites. Compiles and analyzes data on such site conditions as geographic location; soil, vegetation, and rock features; drainage; and location of structures for preparation of environmental-impact report and development of landscaping plans. LMN

**Environmental Scientist.** Conducts research studies to develop theories or methods of abating or controlling sources of environmental pollutants, utilizing knowledge of principles and concepts of various scientific and engineering disciplines. LMN

**Epidemiologist.** Concerned with determining the distribution and causal factors of health problems, encompassing such areas as acute and chronic illness, communicable diseases, behavioral disorders, alcoholism, and drug abuse. CLN—CLS

**Escrow Officer.** Holds in escrow funds, legal papers, and other collateral posted by contracting parties to ensure fulfillment of contracts or trust agreements. B —BN

**Estate Appraiser.** Appraises property to determine value for purchase, sale, investment, mortgage, or loan purposes. Inspects and measures property for construction, condition, and functional design. Searches public records of sales, leases, assessments, and other transactions. Compiles data and estimates value and submits reports. BN

**Estimator.** Prepares cost estimates for product manufacture, construction projects, or services requested to aid management in bidding on, or determining price of, product or service. May conduct special studies to develop and establish standard hour and related-cost data or effect cost reductions. BN—N

**Executive Chef.** Coordinates activities and directs indoctrination and training of chefs, cooks, and other kitchen workers engaged in preparing and cooking foods in hotels or restaurants to ensure an efficient and profitable food service. B—BN

**Executive Secretary.** Keeps official corporation records and executes administrative policies determined by or in conjunction with other officials. Plans conferences. Directs recording of company stock issues and transfers and preparation and filing of corporate legal documents with government agencies to conform with statutes. BC—BCL—BCS

**Exercise Physiologist.** Works with clinicians in hospitals having rehabilitation programs to provide exercise, stress testing, and cardiovascular rehabilitation for patients. LMS

**Experimental Psychologist.** Plans, designs, conducts, and analyzes results of experiments to study problems in psychology. Studies behavior processes and works with human beings and lower animals, such as rats, monkeys, and pigeons. Prominent areas of experimental research include motivation, learning and retention, sensory and perceptual processes, and genetic and neurological factors in behavior. LNS—NS

**Exploration Geophysicist.** Engages in the search for oil and gas, minerals, ground water, or geothermal opportunities. Uses seismic prospecting techniques to locate oil and mineral deposits; induces electrical and electromagnetic energy in the earth to determine the distribution of ore bodies and rocks of different conductivities; and measures variations in temperature, radioactive emissions, or other physical properties. LMN

**Export Clerk.** Computes duties, tariffs, and weight, volume, and price conversions of merchandise exported to or imported from foreign countries. Examines documents, such as invoices, bills of lading, and shipping statements, to verify conversion of merchandise weights or volumes into system used by other country. BCN

**Export Manager.** Directs foreign sales and service outlets of an organization. Negotiates contracts with foreign sales and distribution centers to establish outlets. Directs clerical staff in expediting export correspondence, bid requests, and credit collections. Arranges shipping details, such as export licenses, customs declarations, and packing, shipping, and routing of product. Expedites import-export tariffs, licenses, and restrictions. BCN

**Extractive Metallurgist.** Originates, controls, and develops flotation, smelting, electrolytic, and other processes used in winning metals from their ores, for producing iron and steel, or for refining gold, silver, zinc, copper, and other metals. Studies ore reduction problems to determine most efficient methods of producing metals commercially. LN

**Farm-Equipment Dealer.** Must know the needs of farmers in the area and stock the latest equipment and machinery to meet those needs. Demonstrates and sells equipment, and provides mechanic services to repair the machinery that is sold. BM

**Farmer.** Raises both crops and livestock. Determines kinds and amounts of crops to be grown and livestock to be bred, according to market conditions, weather, and size and location of farm. Selects and purchases seed, fertilizer, farm machinery, livestock and feed. Hires and directs workers engaged in planting, cultivating, and harvesting crops. BM

**Farm-Management Adviser.** Instructs farmers and retail grain and feed-store customers in modern and scientific feed knowledge and farm-management techniques. Advises and assists farmers in securing services of veterinarian for treating larger animals. Assists farmers in setting up cost and production records to determine most economical method of farm operation. BS

**Farm Manager.** Schedules the plowing, fertilizing, planting, cultivation, and harvesting of fields, and the marketing of crops and livestock for absentee landowners and their tenants. B

**Farm Mechanic.** Maintains, repairs, and overhauls farm machinery, equipment, and vehicles, such as tractors, harvesters, pumps, tilling equipment, trucks, and other mechanized, electrically powered, or motor-driven equipment, on farms or in farm-equipment repair shops. M

**Fashion Coordinator.** Promotes new fashions and coordinates promotional activities to induce consumer acceptance. Studies fashion and trade journals, travels to garment centers, attends fashion shows, and visits manufacturers and merchandise markets to obtain information on fashion trends. Consults with buyer regarding type of fashions store will purchase and feature for season. BM

**Fashion Designer.** Creates new types and styles of apparel. In addition to creativity, designer must have practical knowledge of the apparel business so that new fashion ideas can be produced at competitive prices. BM

**Fashion-Design Teacher.** Instructs and demonstrates design courses in high schools, colleges, and technical schools specializing in art, community art centers, and evening adult art. BCM—BM—BMS—CMS

**Fashion Display Specialist.** Responsible for designing display windows and display units within department or clothing store. May have supervisory responsibilities as a coordinator for chain of stores. BM—LM

**Fashion Writer.** Writes fashion items for magazines and newspapers. Researches applicable information for historical periodicals, societies, and publishers. Writes fashion reviews for television news segments. CLM

**FBI Agent.** Investigates violations of federal laws in connection with bank robberies, kidnappings, white-collar crime, thefts of government property, organized crime, espionage, and sabotage. Conducts interviews, examines records, observes the activities of suspects, and participates in raids. CL

**Fiber Technologist.** Studies nature, origin, use, improvement, and processing methods of plant, animal, and synthetic fibers. Conducts experiments in blending fibers and develops improved manufacturing methods for converting fibers into cloth, felts, rugs, mattresses, and brushes. Conducts tests to determine tensile strength and stability in response to heat, light, and chemicals. LN

**Field Engineer.** Often called business-machine repairer or customer engineer. Makes regular visits for preventive maintenance to the offices and stores of customers in assigned area. M

**File Clerk.** Files correspondence, cards, invoices, receipts, and other records in alphabetical or numerical order, or according to subject matter, phonetic spelling, or other system. C

**Film Editor.** Edits motion-picture film, television videotape, and sound tracks. Evaluates and selects scenes in terms of dramatic and entertainment value and story continuity. Trims film segments to specified lengths and reassembles segments in sequence that present story with maximum effect. Reviews assembled film on screen and makes corrections. LM

**Film-Laboratory Supervisor.** Supervises and coordinates activities of workers engaged in developing photographic prints from negatives, copying and enlarging prints, and airbrushing and retouching prints. May assist in classification of pictures as confidential or restricted before their release from laboratory. BMN

**Film-Laboratory Technician.** Evaluates motion picture film to determine characteristics, such as sensitivity to light, density, and exposure time required for printing, using sensitometer, densitometer, and timer lights. Records test data and routes to motion picture film developer and motion picture film printer. BM—LMN

**Film Librarian.** Classifies, catalogs, and maintains library of motion picture films, photographic slides, video and audio tapes, or computer tapes and punch cards. Maintains records of items received, stored, issued, and returned. CL

**Film Producer.** Coordinates activities of personnel engaged in writing, directing, editing, and producing motion pictures. Reviews synopses and scripts and directs adaptation for screen. Determines treatment and scope of proposed productions and establishes departmental operating budgets. B

**Finance-Company Manager.** Manages branch or office of financial institution, such as bank, finance company, mortgage banking company, savings-and-loan association, or trust company. Directs and coordinates activities to implement institution's policies, procedures, and practices concerning granting or extending lines of credit, commercial loans, real estate loans, and consumer credit loans. BL—BLN

**Financial-Aid Counselor.** Interviews students applying for financial aid, such as loans, grants-in-aid, or scholarships, to determine eligibility for assistance in college or university. Determines amount of aid, considering such factors as funds available, extent of demand, and needs of student. BNS—CNS

**Financial Analyst.** Conducts statistical analyses of information affecting investment programs of public, industrial, and financial institutions. Interprets data concerning investments, their price, yield, stability, and future trends; constructs charts and graphs regarding investments; and summarizes data setting forth current and long-term trends in investment risks and measurable economic influences pertinent to status of investments. BLN

**Financial Planner.** Develops and implements financial plans for individuals, businesses, and organizations, using knowledge of tax and investment strategies, securities, insurance, pension plans, and real estate. Analyzes client's financial status, develops financial plan based on analysis, and discusses options with client. BLN

**Financial-Services Sales Agent.** Solicits applications for loans and new deposit accounts for bank or savings-and-loan association. Develops financing plan based on type of loan service required by customer. Reviews business trends and advises customers regarding quality or quantity of fluctuations. Contacts customers to solicit increased deposit balances or transfer of accounts from other banks, and to offer bank's services. BN

**Financial-Statement Clerk.** Requests financial information from bank loan applicants and prepares statements for use by lending officers. Reviews returned information for completeness. Prepares financial statements based on information received. C—CN

**Fingerprint Classifier.** Classifies fingerprints and compares fingerprints of unknown persons or suspects with fingerprint records to determine if prints were involved in previous crimes. May fingerprint prisoner; transfer residual fingerprints from objects such as weapons or drinking glasses; and keep files of criminals and suspects. C

**Fire Chief.** Directs training of personnel and administers laws and regulations affecting fire department. Supervises firefighters engaged in operation and maintenance of fire stations and equipment. Surveys buildings, grounds, and equipment to estimate needs of department and prepare departmental budget. BM

**Fire Inspector.** Inspects buildings and equipment to detect fire hazards and enforce local ordinances and state laws. Discusses condition with owner or manager and recommends safe methods of storing flammables or other hazardous materials. Issues summonses for fire hazards not corrected on subsequent inspection and enforces code when owner refuses to cooperate. BC—BCM

**Fire-Protection Engineer.** Advises and assists private and public organizations and military services for purposes of safeguarding life and property against fire, explosion, and related hazards. Designs or recommends materials or equipment, such as fire-detection equipment, alarm systems, and fire-extinguishing devices and systems, and advises on location, handling, installation, and maintenance. Conducts research and tests on fire retardants and fire safety of materials and devices, to determine fire causes and methods of fire prevention. BLM—LM

**Fire-Sprinkler Installer.** Lays out, fabricates, assembles, installs, and maintains piping and piping systems, fixtures, and equipment for sprinkler systems, on basis of knowledge of system operation and study of building plans or working drawings. M

**Fish-Hatchery Manager.** Determines, administers, and executes policies relating to administration, standards of hatchery operation, and maintenance of facilities. Confers with biologists and other fishery personnel to obtain data concerning fish habits. Oversees trapping and spawning of fish; incubating of eggs; rearing of fry; and movement of fish to lakes, ponds, and streams or commercial tanks. Prepares budget reports, and receives, accounts for, and dispenses funds. BC

**Fishery Engineer.** Operates and designs a wide range of gear, including pumps and engines, fishing tackle, and dockside facilities. M

**Fishery Scientist.** Studies biological, chemical, and physical factors that will, when coupled with fishing demands, affect the population dynamics of fin fish and shellfish. Suggests legal actions necessary to conserve overfished populations. L

**Fishery Technician.** Is familiar with fish population and environmental-survey techniques, tagging procedures, collecting methods, organ and tissue removal, and stomach analysis for food and feeding habits. Designs and constructs fishing gear and fishways, and aids in fish farming and hatchery production. CL

**Fishing-Boat Captain.** Commands fishing-vessel crew engaged in catching fish and other marine life. Plots courses on navigation charts and computes positions, using standard navigation aids, such as compass, radio fix, and navigation tables. Steers vessel and operates electronic equipment, such as radio, sonic depth finder, and radar. Purchases supplies and equipment for boats and contacts buyers to make arrangements for sale of catch. BM

**Floor-Covering Salesperson.** Displays and sells floor coverings, such as carpets, rugs, and linoleum. Explains composition, method of fabrication, and wearing qualities of various rugs and carpets. Estimates cost and amount of covering required, referring to customer's floor plans. BMN

**Floral Designer.** Designs and fashions live, cut, dried, and artificial floral and foliar arrangements for events such as holidays, anniversaries, weddings, balls, and funerals. Confers with client regarding price and type of arrangement desired. May decorate buildings, halls, churches, or other facilities where events are held. BM

**Floriculturist.** Deals with the science and practice of growing, harvesting, handling, design, use, and marketing of greenhouse and outdoor flowering plants. BL

**Flying Instructor.** Instructs student pilots in flight procedures and techniques. Accompanies students on training flights and demonstrates techniques for controlling aircraft. Explains operation of aircraft components and may give student proficiency test at termination of training. CMS—LMS

**Food-and-Beverage Manager.** Coordinates food-service activities of hotel or restaurant, or at social functions. Estimates food and beverage costs. Confers with food-preparation and other personnel to plan menus and related activities, such as dining room, bar, and banquet operations. Directs hiring and assignment of personnel. BN

**Food-and-Drug Inspector.** Inspects establishment where foods, drugs, cosmetics, and similar consumer items are manufactured, handled, stored, or sold, to enforce legal standards of sanitation, purity, and grading. Ascertains that required licenses and permits have been obtained and are displayed. Prepares reports on each establishment visited, including findings and recommendations for action. C

**Food Broker.** Sells bulk shipments of agricultural produce on commission basis to wholesalers or other buyers for growers or shippers. May call on wholesalers' customers, such as restaurants, hotels, and institutional food services, to promote sales and provide nutritional and other information about products. B

**Food Scientist.** Applies scientific and engineering principles in research, development, production technology, quality control, packaging, processing, and utilization of foods. May specialize in one phase of food technology, such as technical writing, teaching, consulting, or production inspection. May specialize in particular branch of food technology, such as cereal grains, meat and poultry, fats and oils, seafood, animal foods, beverages, flavors, sugars and starches, colors, preservatives, or nutritional additives. LN

**Football Coach.** Analyzes performance and instructs football players in game strategies and techniques to prepare them for athletic competition. Oversees daily practice of players to instruct them in areas of deficiency. Determines strategy during game, independently or in conference with other professional football coaches, based on factors such as weakness in opposing team. BLS—LS

**Foreign Correspondent.** Gathers newsworthy information in foreign countries to write articles for publication by newspapers, press services, and magazines. May interview people, review public records, attend events, and do research to describe, analyze, and interpret information. BL

**Foreign-Exchange Clerk.** Services foreign deposit accounts. Determines service charges for cashing or handling checks and posts computations onto customers' statements and account cards or deposit books. Sells drafts and certificates of deposit drawn on foreign banks. CN

**Foreign-Exchange Teller.** Buys and sells foreign currencies and drafts and sells traveler's checks, according to daily international exchange rates, working at counter in foreign-exchange office. Prepares sales slips and records transactions in daily log. Gives information to patrons about foreign currency regulations. CN—N

**Foreign-Student Adviser.** Assists foreign students in making academic, personal, social, and environmental adjustment to campus and community life. Develops and maintains case histories, noting language, educational, social, religious, or physical problems affecting students' adjustment. Interprets university regulations and requirements. Approves students' proposed budgets and requests release of funds from students' home governments to meet financial obligations. S

**Forensic Pathologist.** Studies nature, cause, and development of diseases, and structural and functional changes caused by them. Acts as consultant to other medical practitioners. Performs autopsies to determine nature and extent of disease, cause of death, and effects of treatment. May direct activities of pathology department. CLN

**Forensic Toxicologist.** Examines the medical and legal implications of the harmful effects of chemicals on people. CLN

**Forest Ecologist.** Conducts research on environmental factors affecting forests. Carries out studies to determine what conditions account for prevalence of different varieties of trees. Studies classification, life history, light and soil requirements, and resistance to disease and insects of different species. CL—CLN

**Forester.** Manages and develops forest lands and their resources for economic and recreational purposes. Plans and directs projects in forestation and reforestation. Maps forest areas, estimates standing timber and future growth, and manages timber sales. Directs suppression of forest fires and conducts fire-prevention programs. Plans campsites and recreation centers. Assists in planning and carrying out projects for control of floods, soil erosion, tree diseases, and insect pests in forests. BLM

**Forest-Nursery Supervisor.** Supervises and coordinates activities of workers engaged in planting, cultivating, and harvesting seedling forest trees and grading, bundling, baling, or otherwise packing trees for storage or shipment at forest nursery. BC

**Forest Ranger.** Patrols assigned area of forest to locate and report fires and hazardous conditions and to ensure compliance with fire regulations by travelers and campers. Serves as crew leader for larger fires. Participates in search for lost or injured persons and renders first aid. BL

**Forest Technician.** Compiles data pertaining to characteristics of forest tracts, under direction of forester; and leads workers in forest propagation, fire prevention and suppression, and facilities maintenance. Gathers basic forest data, such as topographical features, species and population of trees, wood units available for harvest, disease and insect damage, tree-seedling mortality, and conditions constituting fire danger. Gives instructions to visitors and enforces camping, vehicle use, fire building, and sanitation regulations. CL

**Forge-Shop Supervisor.** Supervises and coordinates activities of workers engaged in heating, forging, and inspecting metal workpieces and products. Inspects dies, machines, and work in process to detect malfunctions, and orders corrective action. BM

**Forms Analyst and Designer.** Examines and evaluates format and function of business forms. Confers with form users to gather recommendations for improvements, considering such characteristics as form necessity, completeness, design, text, and specifications as to size and color of paper, style of typeface, and number of copies. May design, draft, or prepare finished master copy for new or modified form. BCL—BCM

**Foundry Supervisor.** Supervises and coordinates activities of workers engaged in making cores and molds; in charging, operating, and tapping furnaces; in pouring molten metal into molds; and in chipping, grinding, and sandblasting castings. Examines materials and products at various stages of processing for conformance to specifications. BC—BCM

**Freight Clerk.** Verifies and keeps records on incoming and outgoing shipments and prepares items for shipment. Compares identifying information and counts, weighs, or measures items of incoming and outgoing shipments to verify against bills of lading, invoices, orders, or other records. Determines method of shipment, utilizing knowledge of shipping procedures, routes, and rates. C

**Freight-Traffic Consultant.** Advises industries, business firms, and individuals concerning methods of preparation of freight for shipment, rates to be applied, and mode of transportation to be used. Selects mode of transportation without regard to higher rates when speed is necessary. Files claims with insurance company for losses, damages, and overcharges on freight shipments. BC

**Front-Office Hotel Manager.** Coordinates front-office activities of hotel or motel and resolves problems arising from guests' complaints, reservation and room-assignment activities, and unusual requests and inquiries. Assigns duties and shifts to workers and observes performance to ensure adherence to hotel policies. B

**Fruit-and-Vegetable Field Servicer.** Advises growers when they have problems with equipment or chemicals. Gets feedback from the grower for improvements. Works closely with growers and college personnel when newly developed products or techniques are being field-tested. BL

**Fruit-and-Vegetable Grader.** Examines, sorts, and grades sample fruits and vegetables according to company or government specifications. Takes random samples from load, weighs sample and containers, and calculates net weight and tare of total load. CN

**Fruit-and-Vegetable Manager.** Coordinates all stages of production, from selection of varieties to delivery of the harvested crop to the packing shed, and its final shipment. Concerned with cost-account records, budgeting, and labor management, as well as cultural practices. On larger farms the management is often divided, with different individuals in charge of production, equipment and its maintenance, the packing shed, storage, and sales. B

**Fund Raiser.** Plans fund-raising programs for charities or other causes and solicits funds. Compiles and analyzes information about potential contributors to develop mailing or contact list and to plan selling approach. May organize volunteers and plan social functions to raise funds. BC

**Fund-Raising Director.** Directs and coordinates solicitation and disbursement of funds for community social welfare organizations. Establishes fund-raising goals according to financial need of agency. Initiates public relations program to promote community understanding and support for organization's objectives. Issues instructions to volunteer and paid workers regarding solicitations, public relations, and clerical duties. BCL

**Funeral Director.** Arranges and directs funeral services. Interviews family or other authorized person to arrange details, such as preparation of obituary notice, selection of urn or casket, determination of location and time of cremation or burial, selection of pallbearers, procurement of official for religious rites, and transportation of mourners. BS

**Furniture Designer.** Designs furniture for manufacture according to knowledge of design trends, offerings of competition, production costs, capability of production facilities, and characteristics of company's market. Sketches freehand design of article, then originates scale or full-size drawing. Prepares blueprints containing manufacturing specifications, kind of wood, and upholstery fabrics to be used in manufacturing article. BM

**Game Warden.** Patrols area to prevent game-law violations, investigates reports of damage to crops and property by wildlife, and compiles biological data. Collects and reports information on condition of wildlife in their habitat, availability of game food and cover, and suspected pollution of waterways. CL

**Garden-Center Buyer.** Responsible for locating

sources of and purchasing the kinds, quantity, and quality of plants and other items that will satisfy customer needs. The buyer must make necessary contacts with suppliers, and arrange delivery according to definite schedule. BCN—BN

**Garden-Center Landscape Designer.** Develops and prepares landscape designs for small homeowners according to specifications of the individual customer. BM

**Garden-Center Plant Doctor.** Is an information specialist who tries to solve customer's problems. In smaller garden centers the landscape designer and plant doctor may be the same individual. BL

**Garden-Center Manager.** Administrates and coordinates the entire marketing operation. Plans budgets, controls and evaluates each phase of the business, and makes needed operational changes. Supervises all activities in a small operation. B

**Gas-Dynamics Researcher.** Conducts theoretical thermodynamic analyses involving steady and nonsteady gas mixture flow. This involves preparation of computational methods of analysis of reaction engine processes using digital-computer programs. Conducts investigation in the general areas of combustion, detonation, shock dynamics, high temperatures, gaseous reactions, and magnetohydrodynamics. LN

**Gemologist.** Examines gemstones, such as jade, sapphires, and rubies, to evaluate their genuineness, quality and value. Grades stones for color, perfection, and quality of cut. May advise customers and others in use of gems to create attractive jewelry items. BCM

**Geneticist.** Studies inheritance and variation of characteristics in forms of life. Performs experiments to determine laws, mechanisms, and environmental factors in origin, transmission, and development of inherited traits. Analyzes determinants responsible for specific inherited traits. Devises methods for altering or producing new traits, making use of chemicals, heat, light, or other means. May perform human genetic counseling or medical genetics. LN

**Geodesist.** Studies size, shape, and gravitational field of earth. Employs surveying and geodetic instruments, such as transits, theodolites, and other engineering instruments, in setting up and improving network of triangulation over earth's surface, in order to provide fixed points for use in making maps. MN

**Geographer.** Studies nature and use of areas of earth's surface, relating and interpreting interactions of physical and cultural phenomena. Conducts research on physical and climatic aspects of area or region, making direct observation of landform, climates, soils, plants, and animals within area under study and incorporating available knowledge from related scientific fields, such as physics, geology, oceanography, meteorology, and biology. Studies human activities within given area, such as ethnic distribution, economic activity, and political organization. LN

**Geological Engineer.** Conducts a thorough geotechnical investigation to determine the detailed geological characteristics of a project site. Among the factors evaluated are bedrock lithologies and structure, fracture patterns, ground-water conditions, soil type and thickness, and topography. On the basis of this knowledge, project designs and specifications are prepared to gain maximum benefit from existing site conditions. LMN

**Geologist.** Research scientist who studies the physical aspects of the earth, including its origin, history, composition, and structure. Obtains physical data by drilling and by collecting and examining rocks and other samples. LMN

**Geo-Microbiologist.** Scientist concerned with methods to combat crop damage and increase crop yield. Works with organisms that fill an essential niche near the base of the food chain. CL—CLM—CLN

**Geomorphologist.** Studies the geologic process responsible for the creation of landforms, and is involved in the study of environmental problems. The growth of cities, the occupation of previously unused land areas, and the utilization of land in new ways require expert knowledge of surficial processes to ensure realistic planning and maximum safety from geological hazards, such as floods and landslides. Often works outdoors but some laboratory study is necessary, such as analysis of maps and air photographs, interpretation of data from remote-sensing techniques, and model studies involving stream tables, cold-temperature laboratories, or other equipment intended to simulate the natural environment. LMN

**Geophysicist.** Studies physical aspects of earth, including its atmosphere and hydrosphere. Investigates and measures seismic, gravitational, electrical, thermal, and magnetic forces affecting earth, utilizing principles of physics, mathematics, and chemistry. Compiles data to prepare navigational charts and maps, predict atmospheric conditions, prepare environmental reports, establish water supply and flood-control programs, and help locate petroleum deposits. LMN

**Geothermal Geologist.** Studies the distribution of heat within the earth, especially where anomalous heat can be discovered and exploited. Conducts various investigations, such as regional assessment for heat resources based on maps and reports; mapping, commonly in rugged terrain under harsh conditions, by foot, vehicle, or helicopter; spring-water sampling and analyzing; aiding or conducting geophysical surveys; and assessing the geothermal resource (heat). LN

**Geothermal-Power-Plant Supervisor.** Supervises and coordinates activities of workers engaged in installing, adjusting, repairing, and maintaining electrical and mechanical parts of hydroelectric turbines, generators, and auxiliary equipment. Trains workers in repair and maintenance procedures. BM—BMN

**Geriatric Nurse.** Is a registered nurse who specializes

in providing nursing care to older people. This includes assessing the needs of the elderly, and planning and implementing nursing care to meet these needs. CNS—LNS

**Geriatric Nurse Practitioner.** A registered nurse with special training who provides health services to older patients to maintain health, prevent illness, or deal with acute or chronic health problems. May perform physical examinations and diagnostic tests, develop and carry out treatment programs, or counsel patients about their health. CNS—LNS

**Geriatric Physical Therapist.** Specializes in the care of the elderly with disabilities such as arthritis, loss of limbs, or paralysis. May evaluate the extent of disability and plan a treatment program. Treatment may include exercise to improve muscle strength and coordination, or the application of hot and cold therapy, hydrotherapy, or electrical stimulus to relieve pain or to change the patient's condition. CMS—LMS

**Geriatric Psychologist.** Studies the process of aging and the problems of the aged. Provides counseling and therapy for older people who must cope with stress, depression, and loneliness resulting from the loss of spouse or friends, of job and income, of health and independence, and of social status and self-esteem. LS

**Geriatric Social Worker.** In a medical setting the geriatric social worker helps patients and their families handle problems related to physical or mental illness and disability. Works in the community, assisting residents in finding employment or housing and initiating community projects. Frequently provides the link between an older person and the complex array of services designed to provide help. CLS—LS

**Glass Decorator.** Etches or cuts artistic designs in glass articles, such as bowls, vases, and stemware, using acid solutions, sandblasting equipment, and design patterns. May etch design on inside, rather than outside, of article. May draw freehand designs on masked glassware. M

**Glass Inspector.** Visually inspects plate glass or glass products for defects, such as scratches, cracks, chips, holes, or bubbles. Rejects or classifies pieces for potential use, such as mirrors, glass pane, or furniture tops. C

**Glass Technologist.** Fabricates, modifies, and repairs experimental and laboratory glass products, using variety of machines and tools, and provides technical advice to scientific and engineering staff on function, properties, and proposed design of products. May design fixtures for use in production of prototype glass products and prepare sketches for machine-shop personnel; prepare cost estimates for prototype glass products; and requisition or recommend purchase of materials, tools, and equipment. MN

**Goldsmith.** Fabricates and repairs jewelry articles such as rings, brooches, pendants, bracelets, and lockets. Enlarges or reduces size of rings; repairs broken clasps, pins, rings, and other jewelry by soldering or replacing broken parts; and reshapes and restyles old jewelry, following designs or instructions. M

**Golf-Club Manager.** Manages golf club and directs activities of dining room and kitchen workers and crews that maintain club buildings, equipment, and golf course in good condition. Hires and discharges workers. Estimates quantities and costs of foodstuffs, beverages, and groundskeeping equipment to prepare operating budget. May assist in planning tournaments. BN

**Grain Broker.** Buys and sells grain on commission at customer's order through commodity exchange. Advises customer concerning probable price changes and factors that may affect them, such as crop carryover, normal grain production and consumption, foreign and domestic crop conditions, and price differentials between various grades of grain. B

**Grain Manager.** Manages grain elevator. Examines samples to determine extent of dirt, burrs, hulls, seeds, and other dockage. Extracts samples and forwards them to local grain exchange for analysis and certification of moisture and protein content. Calculates market value and bargains with sellers to obtain grain at favorable price. Reviews and approves grain settlements to ensure that payments are made according to weight, moisture, and protein content. BCN

**Grant Coordinator.** Develops and coordinates grant-funded programs for agencies, institutions, local government, schools, or police departments. Writes grant application according to format required and submits application to funding agency or foundation. BLN

**Graphic Designer.** Designs art and copy layouts for material to be presented in books, magazines, newspapers, television, and packaging. Studies illustrations and photographs to plan presentation of material, product, or service, using esthetic design concepts. LM

**Group-Insurance Sales Agent.** Explains group-insurance programs to promote sale of insurance to prospective clients, and establishes bookkeeping system for insurance plan. Explains types of insurance coverage, such as health, accident, life, or liability, and accounting documentation required by company. Plans and oversees incorporation of insurance program into company's bookkeeping system. Establishes client's method of payment. BN

**Group Leader** (social service). Leads informal group-work activities in hospital or community center, as directed by agency program staff. Interests participants in various activities, such as arts and crafts and dramatics. Demonstrates techniques for active sports, group dances, and games. Helps develop new skills and interests. BS

**Guidance Counselor.** Plans and supervises testing program in school system and devises and directs use of records, reports, and other material essential to program. Supervises school placement service. Counsels students on referral basis relative to educational and vocational objectives and personal and social problems. CLS—LS

**Gynecologist.** Diagnoses and treats diseases and disorders of female genital, urinary, and rectal organs. Uses physical and radiological examination findings, laboratory test results, and patient's statements as diagnostic aids. Discusses problems with patient, and prescribes medication, appropriate exercise, or hygienic regime, or performs surgery as needed to correct malfunctions or remove diseased organ. May care for patient throughout pregnancy and deliver babies. LMS—LS

**Hairpiece Stylist.** Specializes in dressing hair according to latest style, period, or character portrayal, following instructions of patron, makeup artist, or script. Studies facial features of patron or performing artist and arranges, shapes, and trims hair to achieve desired effect. BM—BMS

**Handicraft/Hobby-Shop Manager.** Manages hobby shops and coordinates activities of workers engaged in conducting classes in one or more crafts, such as woodworking, photography, and leather tooling. Plans and initiates promotional projects to publicize recreational facilities. BCM—BM

**Harbor Master.** Directs and coordinates activities of harbor police force to ensure enforcement of laws, regulations, and policies governing navigable waters and property under jurisdiction of municipality or port district. Establishes policies, defines responsibilities, and determines harbor operating procedures. BL

**Hardware Salesperson.** Sells hardware, electrical equipment, gardening tools and equipment, household hardware, paints, plumbing supplies, and woodworking equipment. Advises customer concerning quality and demonstrates uses of hardware, tools, and equipment. BM—BMN

**Head Nurse.** Directs nursing activities, assigns duties, and coordinates nursing service. Directs preparation and maintenance of patients' clinical records. Inspects rooms and wards for cleanliness and comfort. Accompanies physician on rounds, and keeps informed of special orders concerning patients. Orders or directs ordering of drugs, solutions, and equipment, and maintains records on narcotics. BCL—BCS—BLS

**Head Public Librarian.** Plans and administers program of library services. Analyzes, selects, and executes recommendations of personnel, such as department chiefs or branch supervisors. Coordinates activities of branch or departmental libraries. Analyzes and coordinates departmental budget estimates and controls expenditures to administer approved budget. BCL

**Health Administrator.** Coordinates the various functions and activities of a health organization. Makes decisions on such matters as the need for additional personnel and equipment, current and future space requirements, and the budget. Some health-service administrators oversee nursing, food services, and in-service training programs. BL

**Health-Care-Facilities Inspector.** Inspects health care facilities, such as hospitals, nursing homes, sheltered-care homes, maternity homes, and day care centers, to enforce public-health laws and to investigate complaints. Inspects physical facilities, equipment, accommodations, and operating procedures to ensure compliance with laws governing standards of sanitation, acceptability of facilities, record keeping, staff competence qualification, and ethical practices. C

**Health-Club Manager.** Supervises and coordinates activities of workers engaged in planning, selling, and instructing fitness plans for clients of health club. Demonstrates operation and explains purpose of equipment, such as treadmill exerciser and stationary bicycle, and instructs patrons in their use. B—BMS

**Health-Equipment Servicer.** Delivers, installs, demonstrates, and maintains rental medical equipment, such as respirator, oxygen equipment, wheelchairs, for use in private residences. M

**Health Officer.** Institutes programs of preventive health care. Gives immunizations, imposes quarantines, and establishes standards for hospitals, restaurants, and other areas of possible danger. BCL

**Health Physicist.** Protects the environment from potential radiation hazards. May engage in research, operational activities, education, or enforcement of governmental regulations. Assists engineers and scientists in designing facilities, and establishes new radiation-control programs for them; instructs radiation workers and the general public on the hazards associated with nuclear research and nuclear applications. LMN—LN

**Health-Science Librarian.** Specializes in health and medical information for use by medical researchers, health professionals, and students. In addition to general library responsibilities must have knowledge of books, journals, and reports that deal with medicine or allied health sciences. CL

**Health-Record Administrator.** Plans, develops, and administers medical-record systems for hospital, clinic, or health center to meet standards of accrediting and regulatory agencies. Collects and analyzes patient and institutional data. Develops and implements policies and procedures for documenting, storing, and retrieving information, and for processing medical-legal documents, insurance, and correspondence requests. BC

**Hearing-Aids Salesperson.** Sells hearing aids to customers in retail establishment. Tests customer's hearing, using audiometer, to determine need for hearing aid in cases where customer is not referred to store by physician. Demonstrates use of aid to customer and fits aid. May replace defective parts or make repairs to equipment. BMS—BS

**Heating and Air-Conditioning Drafter.** Performs duties of drafter but specializes in drawing plans for installation of heating, air-conditioning, and ventilating equipment. May calculate heat loss and heat gain for buildings for use in determining equipment specifications. May specialize in drawing plans for installation of refrigeration equipment. MN

**Heating-Plant Superintendent.** Supervises and coordinates workers engaged in producing and distributing steam and hot water in commercial or industrial establishments and in maintaining mechanical equipment, such as boilers, pipe systems, hot-water generators, hot-air furnaces, and air-cooling units. BM

**Helminthologist.** Studies characteristics, habits, and life cycles of parasitic worms, to determine manner in which they attack human beings and animals and effects produced. Investigates modes of transmission from host to host. Develops methods and agents to combat parasites. L

**Herpetologist.** Specializes in study of reptiles and amphibians, and investigates their embryonic development and their geographic distribution. May concentrate on only a very limited part of the organism—for example, the sperm or the vertebrae. May be employed as a museum curator, zoo curator, teacher, researcher, or environmental consultant for engineering firms and federal, state, or local environmental-protection agencies. L

**High-Energy Physicist.** Produces and studies strange new particles, such as baryons, mesons, neutrons, and electrons, that result when tremendous energies bombard targets. In this way a high-energy physicist studies the most fundamental constituents of matter and the forces between them. N

**High-School Principal.** Directs and coordinates educational, administrative, and counseling activities of secondary school. Confers with teaching personnel, pupils, and parents on matters pertaining to educational and behavioral problems. Establishes and maintains relationships with colleges, community organizations, and other schools to coordinate educational services. B—BS

**Highway Contractor.** Is a business manager who brings together the capital, equipment, manpower, and machinery to build a road to rigid specifications within a specified time limit. A contractor should know cost accounting, labor relations, and contract law in addition to having an engineering background. BLM—BLN

**Highway Engineer.** Plans, surveys, and designs highways. Performs qualitative tests of materials used in the construction of embankments, structures, and pavements. Employed, as a rule, by governmental agencies; however a very substantial amount of highway planning and design work is done by consulting engineering firms that often have governmental agencies as clients. LMN

**Highway Inspector.** Inspects and oversees construction of highways to ensure that procedures and materials comply with plans and specifications. Computes monthly estimates of work completed and approves payment for contractors. Prepares sketches of construction installations that deviate from original blueprints and reports such changes for incorporation on master blueprints. CM—CMN

**Histologist.** Studies human or animal tissue to provide data on body functions or cause and progress of disease. Devises and directs use of special stains and methods for isolating, identifying, and studying function, morphology, and pathology of obscure or difficult-to-identify cells, tissues, and connecting fibers. LN

**Historian.** Prepares a chronological record of events dealing with some phase of human activity, in terms of either individuals or social, ethnic, political, or geographic groupings. Consults sources of information, such as historical indexes and catalogs, archives, court records, diaries, news files, and miscellaneous published materials. Organizes and evaluates data on basis of authenticity and relative significance. CL

**Historic-Site Administrator.** Manages operation of historic structure or site. Oversees activities of building and grounds staff and other employees and assists in planning publicity. B

**Home Economist.** Improves products, services, and practices that affect the comfort and well-being of consumers in such fields as economics, housing, home management, home furnishings and equipment, food and nutrition, clothing and textiles, child development, and family relations. BS

**Home Extension Agent.** Develops, organizes, and conducts programs for individuals in rural communities to improve farm and family life. Lectures and demonstrates techniques in nutrition, clothing, home management, home furnishing, and child care. Advises families on budgeting and home remodeling; selects and trains club leaders to guide group discussions and demonstrations in sewing, food preparation, and home decoration. BCS—BS

**Home Health Technician.** Provides patient care, assistance, and instructions in household management and in-home medical care techniques to patients and families. Guides and encourages family to obtain optimal adjustment to illness or disability. LS

**Horticulturist.** Conducts experiments and investigations on problems of breeding, production, storage, processing, and transit of fruits, nuts, berries, vegetables, flowers, bushes, and trees. Experiments to develop new or improved varieties having higher yield, quality, nutritional value, resistance to disease, or adaptability to climates, soils, uses, or processes. L

**Hoisery Dye-Lab Technician.** Dyes knitted socks and cloth according to dye formulae and company specifications. Computes quantity of dyes required for machine of specified capacity. N

**Hospital Administrator.** Administers, directs, and develops hospital programs or services for scientific research, preventive medicine, medical and vocational rehabilitation, and community health and welfare promotion. Administers fiscal operations, such as budget planning, accounting, and establishing rates for hospital services. Directs hiring and training of personnel and coordinates activities of medical, nursing, and administrative staffs and services. BL

**Hospital Admitting Clerk.** Interviews incoming patient, records information required for admission, and assigns patient to room. Explains hospital regulations, such as visiting hours, payment of accounts, and schedule of charges. May arrange for special services, such as telephone or television set in patient's room and kosher or vegetarian diet. CS

**Hospital Central-Supply Supervisor.** Directs and supervises activities of personnel in hospital central supply room to furnish supplies and equipment. Instructs personnel in use of sterilizing equipment and water-distillation apparatus, setting up standardized treatment trays, and maintaining equipment. BC

**Hospital Engineer.** Supervises the maintenance of the hospital power plant and its mechanical, electrical, and electronic equipment. In addition serves as a resource person and adviser to the hospital administrator and others in planning the renovation and expansion of existing facilities or the design of new ones. BM—BMN

**Hospital Food-Service Administrator.** Responsible for the preparation of all meals in the hospital setting. Works with dietitian to organize and prepare regular meals and special dietary services for patients and employees. BC

**Hospital Insurance Clerk.** Verifies hospitalization-insurance coverage, computes patients' benefits, and compiles itemized bills. Contacts companies with unpaid insurance claims to obtain settlement of claim. Prepares forms outlining hospital expenses for governmental, welfare, and other agencies paying bill of specified patient. C

**Hospital Personnel Director.** Recruits, screens, and places new employees. May be responsible for recommending employees for promotion, transfer, or dismissal; manages employee services; administers vacation policies, insurance plans, and pension plans; organizes on-the-job and in-service training programs, refresher courses for all levels of hospital personnel; develops employee recreational activities. BN

**Hospital Pharmacist.** Functions as a drug consultant to the physician. Provides drug information, checks dosage, determines contraindications, prepares injected medicine for use in a sterile environment, and engages in clinical research. Other duties include ordering, distributing, and storing drugs, as well as the maintenance of a current drug-information library for hospital personnel. CLN

**Hospital Pharmacist Administrator.** Involved in all aspects of health care administration, focusing on insurance programs, third-party payment plans, management, patient monitoring and compliance, and the social implications of pharmacy practice. BLN

**Hospital Purchasing Director.** Administers and directs the purchase of supplies, materials, and equipment necessary for the efficient functioning of all hospital departments. May be involved in buying everything from computers for the accounting department to surgical instruments for the operating room, from a drug station for the hospital pharmacy to trays for food service, from thermometers for the nurses' stations to equipment for the laboratory. BN

**Hotel Bell Captain.** Determines work schedules and keeps time records of bellmen. Instructs workers regarding requests from guests concerning hotel facilities, local merchants, and attractions. Furnishes information, makes reservations, and obtains tickets for guests to social and recreational events or for travel. BC

**Hotel Manager.** Establishes standards for personnel administration and performance, service to patrons, room rates, advertising, publicity, credit, food selection and service, and type of patronage to be solicited. Plans dining room, bar, and banquet operations. Allocates funds, authorizes expenditures, and assists in planning budgets for departments. B

**Hotel Night Auditor.** Verifies and balances entries and records of financial transactions reported by various hotel departments during the day. CN

**House Builder.** Builds and repairs houses, barns, commercial buildings, and garages, according to rough sketches or verbal orders, performing the duties of several building-trades craftspersons. Might not be an expert in any one trade. May prepare own building plans and sublet portions of work to specialist. BM—BMN

**Human Resource Adviser.** Assists personnel in identifying, evaluating, and resolving human relations and work-performance problems within establishment in order to facilitate communication and improve employee human relations skills and work performance. BLS

**Hydraulic Engineer.** Designs and directs construction of power and other hydraulic-engineering projects for control and use of water. Computes and estimates rates of water flow. Specifies type and size of equipment used in transporting water and converting water power into electricity. MN

**Hydraulic Repairer.** Maintains and repairs hydraulic systems of machinery and equipment, such as robots, applying knowledge of hydraulics and mechanics. M

**Hydrographic Survey Technician.** Assists with data acquisition, processing, and analysis of hydrographic data to determine trends in movement and utilization of water. Work ranges from surveying and engineering in tidal and coastal areas to geomagnetic and hydrospace seismological observations. Responsible for operating standard surveying and measuring instruments and navigational equipment. MN

**Hydroponics-Nursery Manager.** Determines type and

quantity of horticultural plants to be grown under controlled conditions in hothouse or greenhouse or under natural weather conditions in field. Directs and coordinates activities of workers engaged in planting seeds; raising and feeding plants; controlling plant growth and diseases; and transplanting, potting, or cutting plants for marketing. BCL—BL

**Hypnotherapist.**    Consults with client to determine nature of problem. Prepares client to enter hypnotic state by using individualized methods and techniques of hypnosis based on interpretation of test results and analysis of client's problem. May train client in self-hypnosis conditioning. LS

**Ichthyologist.**    A biologist who studies fish. May concentrate on the structure, development, heredity, environmental relationships, behavior, or life processes of fishes. L

**Illuminating Engineer.**    Plans construction and coordinates operation of facilities for transmitting power from distribution points to consumers. Lays out substations and overhead and underground lines in urban and rural areas. Plans layout of pole lines and underground cable. MN

**Immigration Lawyer.**    A specialized attorney working with foreign governments, consulates, and embassies regarding residency requirements, employment procedures, naturalization, and requirements for immigration. BL—BLS

**Import-Export Agent.**    Supervises workers engaged in receiving and shipping freight, documentation, waybilling, assessing charges, and collecting fees for shipments. Negotiates with domestic customers to resolve problems and arrive at mutual agreements, and with foreign shipping interests to contract for reciprocal freight-handling agreements. BC

**Industrial-Arts Teacher.**    Lectures, illustrates, or demonstrates to teach proper use of shop tools and machines, safety practices, and theory as applied to industrial arts. May specialize in woodworking or metalworking, electricity, graphic arts, or mechanical drawing. BMS—MNS—MS

**Industrial-Cafeteria Manager.**    Supervises workers engaged in preparing and serving balanced meals to employees of industrial plant. Plans daily menus, purchases and keeps adequate supplies of food, and oversees storage and issuance of supplies. B—BCM—BN

**Industrial Designer.**    Originates and develops ideas to design the form of manufactured products. Consults with engineering, marketing, production, and sales representatives to establish design concepts. Usually specializes in specific product or type of product, including, but not limited to, hardware, motor vehicle exteriors and interiors, scientific instruments, industrial equipment, luggage, jewelry, housewares, toys, or novelties. LM

**Industrial Economist.**    Directs the economic-research activity of a company, and provides senior management with economic and market forecasts, along with analyses of other pertinent environmental information, as inputs for corporate strategy decisions. The results of an industrial economist's work are relied upon in short- and long-range financial, profit, and market planning, including the evaluation of proposals to expand into new markets. BLN

**Industrial Editor.**    Confers with executives, department heads, and editorial staff to formulate policy, coordinate department activities, establish production schedules, solve publication problems, and discuss plans and organizational changes. Writes or assigns staff members or free-lance writers to write articles, reports, editorials, reviews, and other material. Organizes material, reviews, and evaluates work of staff members, and makes recommendations and changes. BCL—BL

**Industrial Engineer.**    Plans utilization of production facilities and personnel to improve efficiency of operations in industrial establishment. Establishes work-measurement programs and makes sample observations of work to develop standards of manpower utilization. Analyzes utilization of manpower and machines in units and develops work-simplification programs. BLM—BLN—LMN

**Industrial-Engineering Technician.**    Studies and records time, motion, methods, and speed involved in performance of maintenance, production, clerical, and other worker operations to establish standard production rate and to improve efficiency. Prepares charts, graphs, and diagrams to illustrate work flow, routing, floor layouts, material handling, and machine utilization. BLM—BLN—LMN

**Industrial-Equipment Sales Representative.**    Sells industrial machinery, such as metalworking, woodworking, food-processing, and plastic-fabricating machines, utilizing knowledge of manufacture, operation, and uses of machinery. Computes cost of installing machinery and anticipated savings in production costs. Reviews existing plant machinery layout and draws diagrams of proposed machinery layout to effect more efficient space utilization. BM

**Industrial Health Physicist.**    Frequently works at nuclear-reactor sites administering both the plant chemistry and radiation-safety programs. Reviews radiological health-monitoring data for permanent-site employees, area surveys, radiation records, and internal and external dosimetry information; studies laboratory results to ensure operation of the nuclear units within prescribed limits; and consults with engineers in the design of other company nuclear facilities. BMN—LMN—LN

**Industrial Hygienist.**    Conducts health program in industrial plant or governmental organization to recognize, eliminate, and control occupational health hazards and diseases. Investigates adequacy of ventilation, exhaust equipment, lighting, which may affect employee health, comfort, or efficiency. Collaborates with industrial health engineer and occupational physician to institute control and remedial measures for hazardous conditions and equipment. LMS

**Industrial Microbiologist.** Studies growth, structure, and development of bacteria and other microorganisms in beverages, cosmetics, dairy products, pharmaceuticals, and chemical solvents. Makes chemical analyses of substances produced by bacteria and is responsible for following government regulations regarding allowable number of microorganisms in the final product. CLN

**Industrial Occupational Analyst.** Researches occupations and analyzes and integrates data to develop and devise concepts of worker relationships, modify and maintain occupational-classification system, and provide business, industry, and government with technical occupational information necessary for utilization of work force. Prepares results of research for publication in form of books, brochures, charts, films, and manuals. CL

**Industrial Pharmacologist.** Studies effects of drugs, gases, dusts, and other materials on tissue and physiological processes of animals and human beings. Standardizes drug dosages or methods of immunizing against industrial diseases; investigates preventive methods and remedies for diseases, such as silicosis and lead, mercury, and ammonia poisoning; and analyzes food preservatives and colorings, vermin poisons, and other materials to determine toxic or nontoxic properties. CLN

**Industrial Organizational Psychologist.** Develops and applies psychological techniques to personnel administration, management, and marketing problems. Develops interview techniques, rating scales, and psychological tests to assess skills, abilities, aptitudes, and interests as aids in selection, placement, and promotion. Conducts research studies of organizational structure, communication systems, group interactions, and motivational systems, and recommends changes to improve efficiency and effectiveness of individuals, organizational units, and organizations. BLS

**Industrial Sociologist.** Specializes in research on group relationships and processes in an industrial organization. BLS

**Industrial X-Ray Operator.** Radiographs metal, plastics, and concrete for flaws, cracks, or presence of foreign materials. Marks defects appearing on film and assists in analyzing findings. M

**Information Clerk.** Provides information and answers inquiries of persons coming into establishment regarding activities conducted at establishment, and location of departments, offices, and employees within organization. C

**Information Consultant.** Advises management on development, marketing strategy, and business expansion through technology information systems. BL

**Information Manager.** Manages information and

record systems, oversees information storage and retrieval, provides information and consults on information problems within an organization. BCL—BL

**Information Marketing Manager.** Disseminates information on products and services available in the information industry. B

**Information-Processing Engineer.** Analyzes data-processing requirements to determine appropriate electronic data-processing system for projects or workloads, and plans layout of new-system installation or modification of existing system. Uses knowledge of electronics and data-processing principles and equipment. CLM—LM

**Information Scientist.** Designs information system to provide management or clients with specific data from computer storage, utilizing knowledge of electronic-data-processing principles, mathematics, and computer capabilities. May specialize in specific field of information science, such as scientific or engineering research, or in specific discipline, such as business, medicine, education, aerospace, or library science. LMN

**Information-System Programmer.** Develops computer programs for input and retrieval of physical-science, engineering, or medical information, text analysis, and language, law, military, or library-science data. Writes programs for classification indexing, input, storage, and retrieval of data and facts, display devices, and interfacing with other systems equipment. LN

**Inhalation Therapist.** Administers respiratory-therapy care and life support to patients with deficiencies and abnormalities of cardiopulmonary system, under supervision of physician and by prescription. Inspects and tests respiratory-therapy equipment to ensure proper operating condition. MNS—MS

**Instructional Technologist.** Plans and produces audio, visual, and audiovisual material for communication, information, training, and learning purposes. May develop manuals, texts, workbooks, or related materials for use in conjunction with production materials. LM

**Insurance Agent.** Contacts new prospects to sell insurance and explain features and merits of policies offered. Suggests additions or changes that should be made in the client's existing insurance program. B

**Insurance Analyst.** Conducts statistical analyses of information affecting investment programs of public, industrial, and financial institutions. Interprets data concerning investment prices, yield, stability, and future trends. Constructs charts and graphs regarding investments. Summarizes data setting forth current long-term trends in investment risks and measurable economic influences pertinent to status of investments. LN

**Insurance Claims Examiner.** Reviews and investigates details of the claims to make sure that the adjusters, who do most of the investigation work, have followed proper procedures. Verifies and approves payments, maintains records, and prepares reports to be submitted to the data-processing department. C

**Insurance Clerk.** Compiles records of insurance policies covering risks to property and equipment of industrial organization; files records of insurance transactions; and keeps calendar of premiums due and expiration dates of policies. Compiles statistical data for reports to insurance company and departments in organization. CN

**Insurance Sales Representative.** Counsels the customers as to what type of insurance is needed, and how much should be bought. Makes sure that the customer is adequately protected against catastrophe at a price that he or she can afford, and that the customer fully understands the types of losses covered in the policy. B

**Insurance Sales Underwriter.** Decides if insurance company will select a risk after analyzing information on insurance applications, reports of safety engineers, and actuarial studies (reports that describe the probability of loss). May specialize by the type of risk insured, such as fire, auto, marine, or worker's compensation, though the trend today is toward "package" underwriting, in which various types of risks are insured under a single policy. BL—BNS

**Intelligence Research Specialist.** Confers with military leaders and supporting personnel to determine dimensions of problem and discuss proposals for solution. Develops plans for predicting cost and probable success of each alternative, according to research techniques and mathematics or computer formulations. Evaluates results of research and prepares recommendations. CL—L—LN

**Interior Designer.** Plans, designs, and furnishes interior environments of residential, commercial, and industrial buildings. Confers with client to determine architectural preferences, purpose and function of environment, budget, type of construction, and equipment to be installed. Subcontracts fabrication, installation, and arrangement of carpeting, fixtures, accessories, draperies, paint and wall coverings, artwork, and furniture. BM

**Internal Affairs Investigator.** Investigates complaints filed against police officers by citizens. Conducts investigations to establish facts supporting complainant or accused, writes report of findings, and testifies at hearings as requested. CLS

**Internal Auditor.** Conducts independent protective and constructive audits for managements to review effectiveness of controls, financial records, and operations. Analyzes data obtained for evidence of deficiencies in controls, duplication of effort, extravagance, fraud, or lack of compliance with management's established policies or procedures. BLN—LN

**Internal Revenue Agent.** Conducts independent field audits and investigations of federal income-tax returns to verify or amend tax liabilities. Analyzes accounting books and records to determine appropriateness of accounting methods employed and compliance with statutory provisions. Investigates documents, financial transactions, operation methods, industry practices, and such legal instruments as vouchers, leases, contracts, and wills, to develop information regarding inclusiveness of accounting records and tax returns. CLN

**International Banker.** Maintains bank's balances on deposit in foreign banks to ensure foreign-exchange position, and determines prices at which such exchange shall be purchased and sold, based on demand, supply, and stability of currency. Establishes local rates based upon money-market quotations or customer's financial standing. BN

**International Freight Forwarder.** Advises business firms concerning methods of preparation of freight for international shipment, rates to be applied, and method of transportation to be used. BC

**International Lawyer.** Conducts lawsuits, draws up legal documents, forms contracts, mediates disputes, and counsels on tariff laws for clients with overseas branches or with extensive foreign trade. Negotiates terms of trade agreements with executives of foreign corporations. BL

**Internist.** Diagnoses and treats diseases and injuries of human internal organ systems. Examines patient for symptoms of organic or congenital disorders and determines nature and extent of injury or disorder, using diagnostic aids, such as X-ray machine, blood tests, electrocardiography. Prescribes medication and recommends dietary and activity program as indicated by diagnosis. LNS—LS

**Invertebrate Paleontologist.** Is concerned with collecting, preparing, and studying fossils without backbones. Uses fossils as devices for recognizing divisions of the geologic calendar; as the only direct evidences of evolution through time, by morphologic change in response to external factors; in reconstructing ancient environments and ancient geography. L

**Irrigation Engineer.** Plans, designs, and oversees construction of irrigation projects for transporting and distributing water to agricultural lands. LM—LMN

**Jeweler.** May design, make, repair, or sell jewelry. Many jewelers combine all these different aspects of the business. Works with precious stones, synthetics, silver, gold, platinum, or other metals. B—BM

**Job Analyst.** Collects, analyzes, and prepares occupational information to facilitate personnel, administration, and management functions of organization. Utilizes developed occupational data to evaluate or improve methods and techniques for recruiting, selecting, promoting, evaluating, and training workers. BL

**Job Development Specialist.** Promotes and develops employment and on-the-job training opportunities for disadvantaged applicants. Assists employers in revising standards that exclude certain applicants and informs business and the public about training programs through various media. BL

**Journal Clerk.** Records business transactions in journals, and transfers entries from one accounting record to another. Records information, such as date, address, identification number, disposition of correspondence, purchase orders, invoices, or checks. C

**Judge.** Arbitrates disputes; advises counsel, jury, litigants, or court personnel; and administers judicial system. Reads or listens to allegations made by plaintiff in civil suits to determine their sufficiency. Examines evidence in criminal cases to determine if evidence will support charge. Sentences defendant in criminal cases, on conviction by jury, according to statutes. LS

**Keypunch Operator.** Operates alphabetic and numeric keypunch machine, similar in operation to electric typewriter, to transcribe statistical data from source material onto punch cards, to be used for subsequent processing by automatic or electronic data-processing equipment. C

**Kindergarten Teacher.** Teaches elementary, natural, and social science, personal hygiene, music, art, and literature to children from four to six years old, to promote their physical, mental, and social development. Observes children to detect signs of ill health or emotional disturbance, and to evaluate progress. S

**Laboratory-Animal Technician.** Provides animal care. Gives injections, takes samples of various body fluids or tissues, observes reactions of animals to different tests, makes chemical analyses, and takes physiological recordings. Works under the direction of veterinarians, physiologists, or microbiologists. C—CS

**Laboratory Assistant.** Performs duties according to type of research in which supervising scientist is engaged. Prepares samples for analysis or examination and performs routine laboratory tests. CLM—CLN—CMN

**Laboratory Test Mechanic.** Sets up and operates equipment to test metal aircraft structural, hydraulic, and pneumatic parts, assemblies, and mechanisms, according to standard procedures, to discover faults of design and fabrication. CLM—M

**Labor-Relations Consultant.** Manages labor-relations program. Analyzes text of collective-bargaining agreement and develops interpretation of intent, spirit, and terms of contract, to counsel management or labor in development and application of labor relations, policies, and practices. BLS

**Labor-Union Business Agent.** Manages business affairs of labor unions. Promotes local membership, places union members on jobs, arranges local meetings, and maintains relations between union and employers and press representatives. Visits work sites to ensure that management and employees adhere to union contract specifications. BL

**Landscape Architect.** Gives professional advice on land-planning problems; selects suitable sites; makes preliminary studies, sketches, models, and reports; prepares working drawings, cost estimates, and specifications for the taking of contractors' bids; super-vises construction; and approves the quality of materials and work. BLM—BMN

**Land Surveyor.** Plans, organizes, and directs work of one or more survey parties engaged in surveying to determine precise location and measurements of points, elevations, lines, areas, and contours for construction, mapmaking, land division, titles, mining, or other purposes. CMN

**Laser-Beam-Color-Scanner Operator.** Sets up and operates computer-controlled laser-beam color scanner to enlarge and screen film separations used in preparation of lithographic printing plates. M

**Laser Technician.** Constructs and tests prototype laser devices, applying theory and principles of laser engineering and electronic circuits. Sets up precision electronic and optical instruments to test device, utilizing specified electrical or optical inputs. LMN

**Law-Enforcement Director.** Administers, plans, and organizes program for units of local and state agencies concerned with law enforcement, criminal justice, corrections, juvenile delinquency, and rehabilitation. Promotes community acceptance of crime and delinquency programs through news and other media. BL

**Lawyer.** Conducts criminal and civil lawsuits, draws up legal documents, advises clients as to legal rights, and practices other phases of law. Gathers evidence in divorce, civil, criminal, and other cases to formulate defense or to initiate legal action. Represents client in court. May act as trustee, guardian, or executor. BLS—LS

**Legal Assistant.** Researches law, investigates facts, and prepares documents to assist lawyer. Appraises and inventories real and personal property for estate planning. Delivers or directs delivery of subpoenas to witnesses and parties to action. BC—BCS—C—CL—CLS

**Legal Secretary.** Prepares legal papers and correspondence of a legal nature, such as summonses, complaints, motions, and subpoenas. May review law journals and other legal publications to identify court decisions pertinent to pending cases and submit articles to company officials. BCS—C

**Legal Stenographer.** Takes dictation of correspondence, reports, and other matter, and transcribes from shorthand, stenotype, or recording equipment. Performs variety of clerical duties. C

**Legislative Assistant.** Assists legislator in preparation of proposed legislation. Conducts research into subject at hand and develops preliminary draft of bill. Analyzes pending legislation and suggests action to be taken to legislator. Assists in campaign activities and drafts speeches for legislator. L

**Legislative Reporter.** Employed in state and federal legislatures. Uses stenotype to record the speeches and debates of the legislators. May handle hearings conducted by various committees. C

**Lens Grinder.** Sets up and operates grinding and polishing machines to make lenses, optical flats, and other precision elements for optical instruments and ophthalmic goods, such as telescopes, microscopes, aerial cameras, military optical systems, and eyeglasses, or for use as standards. M

**Lens Prescription Clerk.** Selects lens blanks for production of eyeglasses, according to prescription specifications; determines lens power and other specifications; reorders to keep proper inventory. CMN

**Letter Carrier.** Sorts mail for delivery and delivers mail to residences and business establishments along route. Completes delivery of specified types of mail. C

**Librarian.** Maintains library collections of books, serial publications, documents, and audiovisual and other materials, and assists groups and individuals in locating and obtaining materials. May select, order, catalog, and classify materials. BCL—CL

**Library Technical Assistant.** Provides information service, such as answering questions regarding card catalogs, and assists public in use of bibliographic tools. Directs activities of workers in maintenance of stacks, card-preparation activities in catalog department, and reserve-desk operation of circulation department. C

**Life-Insurance Sales Agent.** Provides individuals and businesses with protection against risk of future losses and against financial pressure. Identifies prospective policyholders, analyzes their life- and health-insurance needs, and recommends solutions that fit their budgets. B

**Limnologist.** Studies plants and animals living in water, and environmental conditions affecting them. Investigates salinity, temperature, acidity, light, oxygen content, and other physical conditions of water to determine their relationship to aquatic life. LN

**Literary Agent.** Markets clients' manuscripts to editors, publishers, and other buyers. Contacts prospective purchaser of material, basing selection upon knowledge of market and specific content of manuscript. Negotiates contract between publisher and client. B—BL

**Lithographer.** Responsible for a variety of printing activities ranging from photographing copy and pictures to making the final printing plates. May specialize as a camera operator, artist, stripper, or platemaker. M

**Livestock Rancher.** Selects and breeds animals according to knowledge of animals, genealogy, characteristics, and qualities desired in offspring. Brands, tattoos, notches ears, and attaches tags to identify animals. Operates farm machinery to plant, cultivate, and harvest feed crops. Arranges for sale of animals and products. May hire and supervise workers; exercise and train horses; and groom and exhibit animals at livestock shows. B

**Livestock-Workers Supervisor.** Supervises workers who feed, weigh, medically treat, and transfer livestock. Observes livestock handling and issues movement and health-treatment instructions to direct livestock processing and transfer. Checks condition of stockyard structures and equipment. B

**Loan Interviewer.** Interviews applicants applying for loans to elicit information, prepares loan-request papers, and obtains relevant documents. Verifies credit ratings, projected earnings, and net worth. CNS

**Loan Officer.** Examines, evaluates, authorizes, or recommends approval of customer applications for lines of credit, commercial loans, real-estate loans, consumer-credit loans, or credit-card accounts. May supervise loan personnel; handle foreclosure proceedings; analyze potential loan markets to develop prospects for loans; and buy and sell contracts, loans, or real estate. BL—BLN

**Lobbyist.** Contacts and confers with members of legislature and other holders of public office to persuade them to support legislation favorable to client's interests. Prepares news releases and informational pamphlets and conducts news conferences in order to state client's views and to inform public of features of proposed legislation considered desirable or undesirable. May contact regulatory agencies and testify at public hearings to enlist support for client's interests. B

**Logging Contractor.** Directs and coordinates activities of workers engaged in logging operations. Plans, schedules, and coordinates logging operations in accordance with production requirements and in compliance with safety laws and regulations. Prepares production and personnel time records for management. BC

**Logistics Engineer.** Plans, directs, and coordinates program designed to provide customers with logistics technology that ensures effective and economical support for manufacturing or servicing of products, systems, or equipment. Analyzes contractual commitments, customer specifications, design changes, and other data to plan and develop logistics-program activities. BL—L

**Mail Clerk.** Sorts incoming mail for distribution and dispatches outgoing mail. Readdresses undeliverable mail bearing incomplete or incorrect address. Examines outgoing mail for appearance, and seals and stamps envelopes by hand or machine. May weigh mail to determine that postage is correct. C

**Mail-Room Supervisor.** Supervises and coordinates activities of clerks who open, sort, and route mail and prepare outgoing material for mailing. Reads letters and determines department or official for whom mail is intended and informs mail clerk of routing. BC

**Maintenance-Data Analyst.** Prepares schedules for preventive maintenance of equipment to ensure uninterrupted operation. Reviews maintenance schedules, calculates work-hours required, prepares inspection tests and repairs. CLM

**Mammalian Physiologist.** Deals with the functions of organ systems of mammals, their problems, and their bearing on human and veterinary medicine. L

**Management Analyst.** Analyzes business or operation procedures to devise most efficient methods of accomplishing work. Plans study of work problems and procedures, such as organizational change, communications, information flow, integrated production methods, inventory control, or cost analysis. Analyzes data gathered and prepares recommendations. BL

**Manifest Clerk.** Compiles and types transportation billing documents listing details of freight shipped by carrier. Computes and compares figures and totals on documents with statement of accounts submitted by accounting department to verify accuracy of documents. CN

**Manual-Arts Therapist.** Instructs patients in prescribed manual-arts activities to prevent anatomical and physiological deconditioning, and to assist in maintaining, improving, or developing work skills. Collaborates with other members of rehabilitation team in planning and organizing work activities consonant with patients' capabilities and disabilities. Prepares reports evaluating patients' progress and ability to meet physical and mental demands of employment. MS—S

**Manufacturing Engineer.** Directs and coordinates manufacturing processes in industrial plant. Determines space requirements for various functions and plans or improves production methods including layout, production flow, tooling and production equipment, material, fabrication, assembly methods, and manpower requirements. Reports to management on manufacturing capacities, production schedules, and problems. BMN—MN

**Manugrapher.** Traces and paints advertising material on poster paper, using projector, brushes, and drawing instruments. M

**Map Editor.** Verifies accuracy and completeness of topographical maps from aerial photographs and specifications. Views photographs and old maps and records and examines corresponding area of map to verify correct identification of specified topographical features and accuracy of contour lines. CM

**Marine Biologist.** Studies the plant and animal species living in the oceanic environment. Searches for new foods and drugs from the ocean, studies effects of pollution, and tries to find better ways of raising crops in experimental underwater farms. L

**Marine Ecologist.** Studies the mutual relationships among marine organisms and their environment. Examines effects on these organisms of environmental influences such as rainfall, temperature, season, and state of tide. L

**Marine Economist.** Studies and analyzes economic factors involved in marine-related products, such as distribution, and use of goods and services. Techniques of financing projects and marketing products are examined, and improvements are suggested. Organizational structures of marine-related business concerns are outlined, and governmental regulations and requirements are studied. BLN

**Marine Engineer.** Designs and oversees installation and repair of marine power plants, propulsion systems, heating and ventilating systems, and other mechanical and electrical equipment in ships, docks, and marine facilities. May specialize in design of equipment, heat exchangers, fire-control and communication systems, electric power systems, or steam-driven reciprocating engines. LM—LMN—MN

**Marine Geologist.** Explores and maps the ocean floor. Analyzes rocks from the depths of the ocean while searching for minerals, petroleum, and rare metals under the sea. LM—LMN

**Marine Machinist.** Installs ship machinery, such as propelling machinery, auxiliary motors, pumps, ventilating equipment, and steering gear, working from blueprints and using hand tools. Tests and inspects installed machinery and equipment during dock and sea trials. May set up and operate machine shop to fabricate replacement parts. M

**Marine Meteorologist.** Studies atmospheric conditions, such as temperature, winds, and currents, with emphasis upon the interaction of the atmosphere with the ocean. Utilizing this knowledge, the marine meteorologist hopes to make accurate weather forecasts. L

**Marine Surveyor.** Surveys marine vessels and watercraft, such as ships, boats, tankers, and dredges, to ascertain condition of hull, machinery, equipment, and equipage, to determine repairs required for vessel to meet requirements for insuring. LMN

**Market-Research Analyst.** Researches market conditions in local, regional, or national area to determine potential sales of product or service. Establishes research methodology and designs format for data gathering, such as surveys, opinion polls, or questionnaires. Gathers data on competitors and analyzes prices, sales, and methods of marketing and distribution. Collects data on customer preferences and buying habits. BCL—BL

**Masseur/Masseuse.** Massages customers using hands or vibrating equipment. Administers steam or dry heat, ultraviolet or infrared irradiation, or water treatments on request or instructions of physician for hygienic or remedial purposes. BM

**Materials Engineer** Plans and implements laboratory operations to develop material and fabrication procedures to fulfill product-cost and performance standards. Reviews product-failure data and interprets laboratory tests to establish or rule out material and/or process causes. LMN

**Materials Scientist.** Conducts programs for studying structures and properties of various materials, such as metals, alloys, ceramics, semiconductors, and polymers to obtain research data. LMN

**Mathematical Statistician.** Develops and tests experimental designs, sampling techniques, and analytical methods, and prepares reports on applicability, efficiency, and accuracy of statistical methods used by physical and social scientists, including applied statisticians, in obtaining and evaluating data. LN—N

**Mathematical Technician.** Applies mathematical for-

...s, principles, and methodology to technological problems in relation to specific industrial and research objectives. Reduces information to mathematical terms, flow charts, graphs, or other media, and processes data through punching or sorting machines or other data-processing equipment. CMN—MN—N

**Mathematics Teacher.** Studies, organizes, and teaches mathematical principles and procedures to students in an effective and meaningful manner. Evaluates student achievement and progress. LNS—NS

**Mechanical-Design Engineer.** Designs mechanical or electromechanical products or systems, such as instruments, controls, engines, machines, and mechanical, thermal, hydraulic, or heat-transfer systems. LM—LMN

**Mechanical Engineer.** Directs and coordinates construction and installation activities to ensure conformance of products and systems with engineering design and customer specifications. May evaluate and recommend design modifications to eliminate malfunctions or changes in machine system function. LMN

**Mechanical Inspector.** Inspects and tests completed instruments and their subassemblies. Verifies dimensions of parts and location of holes, grooves, and other points according to blueprints, using such measuring devices as calipers, micrometers, and dial indicators. CMN—CN

**Media Clerk.** Keeps record of client's advertising schedules for advertising agency. Records media used, such as newspapers and magazines, and expenses incurred. Determines cost of advertising space in various media in other areas, considering, for comparison, such factors as size and population of city, space rates, and kind and frequency of publication. C—CN

**Media Director.** Plans and administers media programs in advertising department of corporation. Confers wtih representatives of advertising agencies, product managers, and advertising staff in order to establish media goals, objectives, and strategies within budget limitations. BLM

**Medical Assistant.** Prepares treatment room for examination and treatment of patient. Prepares inventory of supplies to determine items to be replenished. Interviews patients and checks pulse, temperature, blood pressure, weight, and height. May operate equipment, give injections or treatments, and assist in laboratory. May perform secretarial tasks. CLS—CS

**Medical Chemistry Technologist.** Performs qualitative and quantitative chemical analyses of body fluids and exudates to provide information used in diagnosing and treating diseases. LN

**Medical Illustrator.** Makes sketches and constructs tri-dimensional models to illustrate surgical and medical research procedures, anatomical and pathological specimens, and unusual clinical disorders. Develops drawings, diagrams, and models illustrating medical findings for use in publications, exhibits, consultations, research, and teaching activities. LM

**Medical Librarian.** May work in the acquisitions department within the medical library, examining and ordering new medical books, journals, and audiovisual materials for the collections. May work as a cataloguer, assigning headings that capture the subject matter of the new books; and keeps abreast of additions and changes in the vocabulary of medicine. CL

**Medical-Office Receptionist.** Receives callers, determines nature of business, and directs callers to destination. May receive patients in physician's office and perform variety of clerical duties. C—CS

**Medical Parasitologist.** Studies characteristics, habits, and life cycles of animal parasites to determine manner in which they attack human beings and effects produced. Investigates modes of transmission from host to host. Develops methods and agents to combat parasites. CL—CLN

**Medical Photographer.** Photographs medical phenomena to provide illustrations for scientific publications, records, and research and teaching activities. Makes still and motion picture reproductions of patients and anatomical structures. May design special equipment and processing formulas, and specialize in a particular technique, such as cinematography, color photography, or photomicrography. CM

**Medical Physicist.** Applies knowledge and methodology of science of physics to all aspects of medicine. Plans, directs, conducts, and participates in supporting programs to ensure effective and safe use of radiation and radionuclides in human beings by physician specialist. Directs and participates in investigations of biophysical techniques associated with any branch of medicine. LMN

**Medical-Records Administrator.** Plans, develops, and administers medical-record systems for hospital, clinic, health center, or similar facility, to meet standards of accrediting and regulatory agencies. Develops in-service educational materials and conducts instructional programs for health-care personnel. BCL

**Medical-Records Clerk.** Compiles, verifies, and files medical records of patients and compiles statistics for use in reports and surveys. Records diagnoses and treatments, including operations performed, for use in completing hospital-insurance billing forms. C

**Medical Secretary.** Performs secretarial duties utilizing knowledge of medical terminology and hospital, clinic, or laboratory procedures. Takes dictation. Compiles and records medical charts, reports, and correspondence. May prepare and send patients' bills and record appointments. BCS—C—CLS—CS

**Medical Social Worker.** Aids patients and their families with personal and environmental difficulties that predispose them to illness or interfere with their obtaining maximum benefits from medical care. Works in close collaboration with medical doctor and other members of health team to further their understanding of significant social and emotional factors underlying patient's health problem. Utilizes such resources as family and community agencies to assist patient in resuming life in community or learning to live within patient's disability. CLS—LS—S

**Medical Technologist.** Performs complicated chemical, microscopic, and bacteriological tests to provide data for use in treatment and diagnosis of disease. The medical technologist examines body fluids microscopically; makes cultures of body-fluid or tissue samples to determine the presence of bacteria, parasites, or other microorganisms; and analyzes the samples for chemical content or reaction. May type and cross-match blood samples; research and develop laboratory techniques; teach; or perform administrative duties. CLN

**Medical Voucher Clerk.** Examines vouchers forwarded to insurance carrier by doctors who have made medical examinations of insurance applicants, and approves vouchers for payment based on standard rates. CN

**Membership Solicitor.** Solicits membership for club or trade association. Visits or contacts prospective members to explain benefits and costs of membership and to describe organization and objectives of club or association. May collect dues and payments for publications from members. B

**Memorial Designer.** Designs and builds plaster models of monuments, statues, and memorials. Interviews customer to obtain information regarding size, style, and motif of memorial. BM

**Mental-Health Technician.** Works directly with mental patients, families, and communities, under the supervision of a physician or psychiatrist. Interviews individuals and families for background and history data; involved in individual and group counseling, community surveys, activity therapy, and teaching social-living skills to patients. Also serves as a referral and information person to help people find the services they need. CLS—CS—LS

**Metallographer.** Conducts microscopic, macroscopic, and other tests on samples of metals and alloys for purposes of metallurgical control over products or use in developing new or improved grades and types of metals and alloys or production methods. Interprets findings and prepares drawings, charts, and graphs for inclusion in reports. LMN

**Metallurgical Analyst.** Analyzes data obtained from investigation of physical and chemical properties of metals to select method, standards, and procedures of examination and testing and conducts tests. Writes report indicating deviations from specifications and recommends corrective measures for approval. LN

**Metallurgical Engineer.** Designs rolling mills, heat-treatment facilities, and metalworking plants. Uses knowledge of metals for the selection, melting, and control of alloys used in casting; is familiar with the various grades of metals and how sound alloys can be produced; understands metal properties, such as strength and hardness, and uses this information to evaluate metal results and to recommend procedures of melting, alloying, and pouring of molten metal to achieve desired properties. LMN

**Metallurgical-Engineering Technician.** Performs a wide variety of functions, such as testing the mechanical properties of materials; chemical and spectrographic analysis of materials; development of manufacturing process; examining and photographing the microstructure of materials by use of optical and electron microscopes; X-ray analysis; and calculations and report writing. LMN

**Meteorological-Equipment Repairer.** Installs, maintains, and repairs electronic, mercurial, aneroid, and other types of weather-station equipment. Tests meteorological instruments for compliance with printed specifications and schematic diagrams. MN

**Meteorological Technician.** Observes and records weather conditions for use in forecasting. May collect upper-air data on temperature, humidity, and winds, using weather balloon and radiosonde equipment. May conduct pilot briefings. CMN

**Meteorologist.** Analyzes and interprets meteorological data gathered by surface and upper-air stations, satellites, and radar to prepare reports and forecasts. Prepares special forecasts and briefings for those involved in air and sea transportation, agriculture, fire prevention, and air-pollution control. CL

**Meter Inspector.** Tests accuracy of gas-flow meters, using testing apparatus. Reads instruments to obtain data, such as specific gravity and temperature of gas, and clocks number of seconds required for specified volume of gas to pass through meter. Adjusts meters to correct inaccurate readings. CM

**Meter Installer.** Installs residential-type gas meters and regulators in buildings. Inspects appliances to detect gas leaks, using portable testing device, and notifies customer of needed repair. M

**Metrologist.** Develops and evaluates calibration systems that measure length, mass, time, temperature, electric current, luminous intensity, or derived units of physical or chemical measure. Directs engineering, quality, and laboratory personnel in design, manufacture, evaluation, and calibration of measurement standards, instruments, and test systems. LMN

**Microbiologist.** Studies growth, structure, development, and general characteristics of bacteria and other microorganisms. Isolates and makes cultures of significant bacteria or other microorganisms in prescribed or standard inhibitory media, controlling such factors as moisture, aeration, temperature, and nutrition. Identifies microorganisms by microscopic examination of physiological, morphological, and cultural characteristics. CL—L

**Microfilm Technologist.** Uses a wide range of sophisticated equipment to miniaturize or reproduce documents and other records. MN

**Micrographics-Services Supervisor.** Supervises workers engaged in making microfilm or microfiche copies of records. Keeps file indicating priority, date due, and status of job. Examines material in process and suggests improved methods of reproduction. BC—BCM

**Microwave Engineer.** Sets up, tests, and operates microwave transmitter to broadcast programs originating at points distant from studio in absence of telephone-wire system. MN

**Mineralogist.** Identifies and classifies the crystalline compounds that exist at the earth's surface, within the earth's interior, in lunar materials, and in meteorites. Uses this information to help interpret the sequence of geological events that led to the formation of mineral deposits, and uses modern instruments to determine the composition and properties of exceedingly small particles. CLM

**Mineral-Processing Engineer.** Directs the processes that separate minerals from worthless material so that they may be put to practical use throughout the various utilizing industries. Decides which processing method is to be used. Crushing, grinding, and treatment with chemicals, heat, water, and electrolysis are some of the means employed. LM—LMN

**Mine Superintendent.** Plans and coordinates activities of personnel engaged in mining coal, ore, or rock at one or more underground or surface mines, pits, or quarries. Studies survey data and confers with engineering, maintenance, and supervisory personnel to plan development of mine. Tours mine to detect and resolve safety, personnel, and production problems. BM

**Mining Engineer.** Determines locations and plans effective and economical extraction of coal, metallic ores, nonmetallic minerals, and building materials, such as stone or gravel. Conducts or collaborates in geological exploration to determine location, size, accessibility, and estimated value of deposit. LMN

**Mobile-Canteen Operator.** Serves sandwiches, salads, beverages, desserts, candies, and tobacco to employees in industrial establishment. B

**Mobile-Crane Operator.** Operates gasoline- or diesel-powered crane mounted on specially constructed truck chassis to lift and move materials and objects. Drives truck to work site and directs activities of hoisting laborer in placing blocks and outriggers to prevent capsizing when crane is lifting heavy loads. M

**Modeling Instructor.** Instructs individuals and groups in techniques and methods of self-improvement, utilizing principles of modeling, such as visual poise, wardrobe coordination, and cosmetic application. BS—S

**Model Maker.** Builds and models scale models, using clay, metal, wood, fiberglass, and other substances, depending on industry for which model is constructed, such as ship and boat building or automobile manufacturing. MN

**Molded-Parts Inspector.** Inspects molded storage-battery parts, such as grids, straps, vent plugs, washers, and gaskets, for conformance to specifications. Measures parts to determine dimensional accuracy, using gauges such as micrometers and vernier scales. CN

**Molecular Pharmacologist.** Studies the biochemical and biophysical characteristics of interactions between drug molecules and those of the cell. Seeks precise mathematical, physical, and chemical expressions of such interactions. N

**Mortgage-Accounting Clerk.** Keeps records of mortgage loans. Records data such as loan number, selling price, and taxes of mortgaged property. Computes interest and principal payments on loans, using calculating machines. Prepares applications for insurance on property and for extensions on delinquent loans. CN

**Motion-Picture Projectionist.** Sets up and operates motion-picture projection and sound-reproducing equipment to produce coordinated effects on screen. M

**Museum Ceramics Restorer.** Cleans, preserves, restores, and repairs objects made of glass, porcelain, china, fired clay, and other ceramic materials. M

**Museum-Exhibit Designer.** Designs display for period in art history. Basic knowledge of graphic design, type, lettering, and color drafting and model-building and carpentry skills are necessary. Also an understanding of architectural design is helpful, particularly in determining how to move people through the display. M

**Music Librarian.** Classifies and files musical recordings, sheet music, original arrangements, and scores for individual instruments. Selects music for subject matter of program or for specific visual or spoken action. CL

**Music Mixer.** Operates console to regulate volume level and quality of sound during filming of motion pictures, recording sessions, or television and radio productions. May copy and edit recordings. M

**Music Therapist.** Plans, organizes, and directs music activities and learning experiences as part of care and treatment of patients to influence behavioral changes leading to enhanced experience and comprehension of self and environment. Studies and analyzes patient's reactions to various experiences and prepares reports describing symptoms indicative of progress or regression. LS—S

**Mutuel Department Manager.** Coordinates activities of workers engaged in selling parimutuel tickets and calculating amount of money to be paid to patrons holding winning tickets at racetrack. Adjusts customer complaints. B—BN

**Mycologist.** Studies mechanism of life processes of edible, poisonous, and parasitic fungi to discover those which are useful to medicine, agriculture, and industry for development of drugs, medicines, molds, and yeasts. May specialize in research and development in such fields as antibiotics or fabric deterioration. LN

**Naprapathist.** Applies pressure and movement to bring motion and release of tension into abnormally tensed and rigid ligaments and muscles of the human body. LMS

**Natural-Gas Utilization Manager.** Negotiates contracts with representatives of oil producers, refiners, and pipeline carriers for purchase, sale, or delivery of natural gas. Coordinates work of sales, production, and shipping departments to implement procurance of products in accordance with refinery needs. B

**Naturopathic Physician.** Diagnoses, treats, and cares for patients using system of practice that bases treatment of physiological functions and abnormal conditions on natural laws governing human body. Utilizes physiological, psychological, and mechanical methods, such as food and herb therapy, psychotherapy, electrotherapy, natural medicines, and natural foods. LNS—LS

**Naval Architect.** Designs and oversees construction and repair of marine craft and floating structures. Studies design proposals and specifications to establish basic characteristics of craft, such as size, weight, speed, propulsion, armament, cargo, displacement, draft, crew and passenger complements, and fresh- or saltwater service. LMN

**Nematologist.** Studies nematodes (roundworms) that are plant-parasitic, transmit diseases, attack insects, or attack soil, freshwater, or marine plants. Identifies and classifies nematodes and studies structure, behavior, biology, ecology, physiology, nutrition, culture, and distribution. Investigates and develops pest management and control measures, such as chemical, hot-water and steam treatments, soil fumigation, biological crop rotations, and cultural practices. CL—L

**Neurologist.** Diagnoses and treats organic diseases and disorders of nervous system. Studies results of chemical, microscopic, biological, and bacteriological analyses of patient's blood and cerebrospinal fluid to determine nature and extent of disease or disorder. Studies results of electroencephalograms or X-rays to detect abnormalities in brain-wave patterns. LS

**Neuropharmacologist.** Studies drugs that modify the functions of the nervous system, including the brain, spinal cord, and nerve fibers that communicate with all parts of the body. May probe the neurochemical disorders underlying specific disease states to find new ways to use drugs in the treatment of disease, as well as studying drugs already in use to determine more precisely the neurophysiological or neurobiochemical changes they produce. LN—LNS

**Neurosurgeon.** Performs surgery on nervous system to correct deformities, repair injuries, prevent diseases, and improve patients' function. LM—LMS

**News Analyst.** Analyzes current news items on the basis of personal knowledge of and experience with subject matter. Gathers information and develops subject perspective through research, interviews, experience, and attendance at political conventions, news meetings, sports events, and social functions. When working in broadcast medium, may either record or present live commentary. CL

**News Assistant.** Compiles, dispenses, and files news stories and related copy to assist editorial personnel in broadcasting newsroom. Telephones government agencies and sports facilities and monitors other stations to obtain weather, traffic, and sports information; reaches people involved in news events to obtain further information or to arrange for on-air or background interviews by news-broadcasting personnel. CL

**Newspaper Art Director.** Responsible for making newspapers look more attractive. Involved in news makeup; appearance of the ads; the use of color anywhere in the newspaper; and responsibility for the quality of printing. BM

**Newspaper Columnist.** Analyzes news and writes column or commentary. Gathers information and analyzes and interprets it to formulate and outline story idea. Selects material most pertinent to presentation and organizes it into acceptable media form and format. CL

**Newspaper Editor.** Formulates editorial policy and directs operation of newspaper. Confers with editorial-policy committee and heads of production, advertising, and circulation departments to develop editorial and operating procedures and negotiate decisions affecting publication. Writes lead editorials or notifies editorial-department head of position to be taken on specific public issues. BL

**Newspaper Editorial Writer.** Writes comments on topics of reader interest to stimulate or mold public opinion, in accordance with viewpoints and policies of publication. May specialize in one or more fields, such as international affairs, fiscal matters, or national or local politics. BL—LS

**News Photographer.** Photographs newsworthy events, locations, people, or other illustrative or educational material for use in publications or telecasts. Submits negatives and pictures to editorial personnel. Often specializes in one phase of photography, such as news, sports, or special features, or as free-lance photographer. CM—M

**News Reporter.** Collects and analyzes information about newsworthy events to write news stories. Gathers and verifies factual information regarding story through interview, observation, and research. Organizes material, determines slant or emphasis, and writes story according to prescribed editorial style and format standards. CLS

**Noise Technologist.** Supports new business and current production programs in noise technology, including the development of acoustic linings, jet sound suppressors, cabin noise insulation, and structural tuning/damping. Estimates community, ramp, and interior noise. Assesses impact of existing and proposed noise regulations. MN

**Notereader.** Operates typewriter to transcribe stenotyped notes of court proceedings following standard formats. C

**Nuclear Engineer.** Conducts research into problems of nuclear-energy systems; designs and develops nuclear equipment; and monitors testing, operation, and maintenance of nuclear reactors. Studies nuclear fuel cycle to define most economical uses of nuclear material and safest means of waste-products disposal. LMN

**Nuclear-Fuels Research Engineer.** Studies behavior of various fuels and fuel configurations in differentiated reactor environments to determine safest and most efficient usage of nuclear fuels. LN

**Nuclear Medical Technologist.** Prepares, administers, and measures radioactive isotopes in therapeutic, diagnostic, and tracer studies, utilizing a variety of radioisotope equipment. Concerned with safety and is responsible for disposal of radioactive waste, safe storage of radioactive waste, and the inventory and control of radiopharmaceuticals. CLN

**Nuclear Physicist.** Probes the complex world inside the atomic nucleus. Conducts research into phases of physical phenomena, develops theories and laws on basis of observation and experiments, and devises methods to apply laws and theories of physics to industry, medicine, and other fields. Describes and expresses most observations and conclusions in mathematical terms. LN—N

**Nurse Aide.** Assists in care of hospital patients. Transports patients to treatment units, or assists them to walk. Takes and records temperature, pulse, and respiration rates as directed. May clean, sterilize, store, prepare, and issue dressing packs and treatment trays. CS—S

**Nurse Anesthetist.** Administers intravenous, spinal, and other anesthetics to render persons insensible to pain during surgical operations and other medical and dental procedures. Observes patient's reaction during anesthesia, periodically counting pulse and respiration, taking blood pressure, and noting skin color and dilation of pupils. LMN

**Nurse Clinician.** A registered nurse with special training who provides health services to patients to maintain health, prevent illness, or deal with acute or chronic health problems. May perform physical examination and diagnostic tests, develop and carry out treatment programs, or counsel patients about their health. May work in specialized areas, such as geriatrics, family care, or pediatrics. LS

**Nurse-Midwife.** Provides medical care and treatment to obstetrical patients under supervision of obstetrician; delivers babies; and instructs patients in prenatal and postnatal health practices. May conduct classes for groups of patients and families to provide information concerning pregnancy, childbirth, and family orientation. LS

**Nursing-Home Dietitian.** Creates and maintains standards of food production and service within the nursing home. Responsible for regular and special dietary menu planning. Instructs the patients regarding their diets. BCL

**Nursing-Home Food-Service Supervisor.** Plans, coordinates, and supervises the preparation of meals. Directs food-service employees in making meals not only nutritious but colorful and appealing. Must pay close attention to proper portion control and careful purchasing. BMS

**Nursing-Home Recreational Therapist.** In charge of leisure activities within a nursing home. Schedules and supervises holiday celebrations according to residents' preferences. Often works with community groups to provide varied and interesting programs. S

**Nursing-Home Social-Work Supervisor.** Is concerned with the psychological and social needs of residents. Encourages them to accept their aging or chronic illnesses. Also works with their families, helping them understand and deal with the problems related to the mental or physical disability. BS—S

**Nutritionist.** Counsels individuals and groups on sound nutrition practices to maintain and improve health. Work covers such areas as special diets, meal planning and preparation, and food budgeting and purchasing. May work in community health and be responsible for the nutrition components of preventive health and medical-care services. May also work as a consultant to hospitals or commercial enterprises, including food processors and equipment manufacturers. BNS—CNS—NS

**Occupational-Safety-and-Health Inspector.** Inspects work environment, machinery, and equipment in establishments and other work sites for conformance with governmental standards according to procedure or in response to complaint or accident. Writes new safety-order proposals designed to protect workers from hazards not previously covered. CM—CMS

**Occupational Therapist.** Plans, organizes, and conducts occupational-therapy program to facilitate rehabilitation of mentally, physically, or emotionally handicapped. Selects constructive activities suited to individual's physical capacity, intelligence level, and interest to upgrade patient to maximum independence, prepare patient for return to employment, assist in restoration of function, and aid in adjustment to disability. BLS—LS—S

**Ocean Engineer.** Develops, constructs, and refines instruments needed for oceanographic work and study. The propagation of sound through the sea is of special concern to the ocean engineer who studies how temporal and spatial variations in temperature, density, and other factors influence its path. Involved in projects to adapt navigation channels for deep tankers and cargo vessels; assesses the feasibility of all forms of coastal construction; and gives advice on ways to stem shoreline erosion. May also specialize in ocean mining, fisheries engineering, offshore petroleum engineering, ship hydrodynamics, and materials and corrosion. LMN—MN

**Oceanographer.** Uses the principles and techniques of

natural sciences, mathematics, and engineering to study oceans—their movements, physical properties, and plant and animal life. Researches on land or aboard research cruises to develop practical methods for forecasting weather, developing fisheries, mining ocean resources, and improving national defense. Uses computer or plots maps to test theories about the ocean. May study undersea mountain ranges and valleys, oceanic interactions with the atmosphere, and layers of sediment on or beneath the ocean floor. LMN—LN

**Oceanographic Technician.** Assists oceanographers in a variety of chemical and physical tests and analyses, such as tide and current studies, water analysis for dissolved gases and minerals, and wave studies; keeps inventory of laboratory stock; calibrates and operates measuring and surveying instruments used in oceanographic data acquisition, keeps records, plots graphs and profiles, and reduces processed oceanographic-station data to a standard format. LMN—MN

**Office Clerk.** Writes or types bills, statements, receipts, checks, or other documents, copying information from one record to another. Proofreads records or forms. Sorts and files records. Addresses, stuffs, and stamps envelopes and sorts mail. Answers telephone, conveys messages, and runs errands. C

**Office-Machines Sales Representative.** Sells office machines, such as typewriters and adding, calculating, and duplicating machines. May instruct employees or purchasers in use of machine, make machine adjustments, and sell office supplies. B—BM

**Office Manager.** Analyzes and organizes office operations and procedures, such as typing, bookkeeping, preparation of payrolls, flow of correspondence, filing, and requisition of supplies. Evaluates office production, revises procedures, or devises new forms to improve efficiency of work flow. Prepares employee ratings and coordinates activities of various workers within department. B—BC

**Office Nurse.** Cares for and treats patients in office, as directed by physician. May administer injections and medications; dress wounds and incisions; assist with emergency and minor surgery; clean and sterilize instruments and equipment; conduct laboratory tests; record and develop electrocardiographs and X-rays. CLS—LS

**Offset-Duplicating-Machine Operator.** Operates offset duplicating machine to reproduce charts, schedules, bulletins, and related matter according to oral instructions or specifications on job order. CM

**Oil-Field Pipeline Supervisor.** Supervises and coordinates activities of workers engaged in digging, operating pipe-laying machines, and installing of pipe, pumps, valves, and meters to construct and maintain pipelines. BM

**Oil-Well Services Supervisor.** Supervises and coordinates activities of workers engaged in operating pumping and bleeding equipment to cement, acidize, and fracture oil and gas wells. Confers with drilling and production superintendent to determine well conditions, pipe sizes, and characteristics of oil- or gas-bearing rock formations to be treated. Evaluates job performance of workers. BM

**Open-Pit-Mining Engineer.** Deals with the extraction of ore-bearing rock from its location in the earth and its subsequent transportation to a preparation point. May be responsible for planning new mines, laying out the system, and specifying power, haulage, drainage, and other requirements. Responsible for seeing that the surveying is done; maps are properly prepared and kept up to date; and modifications in the mine are made as needed. LM

**Operations Research Analyst.** Conducts analyses of management and operational problems and formulates mathematical or simulation models of problem. Analyzes problem in terms of management information and conceptualizes and defines problem. Studies information and selects plan from competitive proposals that afford maximum probability of profit or effectiveness in relation to cost or risk. BLN

**Ophthalmic-Lens Inspector.** Inspects precision optical and ophthalmic lenses to ensure that specified standards have been met, using precision measuring instruments. Examines lenses for defects; verifies lens dimensions; and compares lens with sample to verify specific colors. CM

**Ophthalmologist.** Diagnoses and treats diseases and injuries of eyes. Examines patient for symptoms indicative of organic or congenital ocular disorders, and determines nature and extent of injury or disorder. Performs various tests to determine vision loss; prescribes and administers medications; and performs surgery if indicated. Directs remedial activities to aid in regaining vision or to utilize remaining sight. LMS

**Optical-Effects-Camera Operator.** Sets up and operates optical printers and related equipment to produce fades, dissolves, superimpositions, and other optical effects often required in today's motion pictures. LM

**Optical Engineer.** Designs optical systems with characteristics to fit within specified physical limits of precision optical instruments, such as cameras, lens systems, telescopes, and viewing and display devices. Determines specifications for operations and makes adjustments to calibrate and obtain specified operational performance. Designs inspection instruments to test optical system for defects. LMN—MN

**Optical Physicist.** Studies and researches light, how to produce it, and how to control it. Engages in research to discover efficient ways of using laser beams and turning sunlight efficiently into electricity. LMN

**Optician.** Sets up and operates machines to grind eyeglass lenses to prescription specifications and assembles lenses in frames. Inspects mounted lenses for conformance to specifications. Examines broken lenses to identify original lens prescription, using power-determining and optical-centering instruments. M—MN

**Optometric Assistant.**    Measure patient's vision, helps patient with eye exercises, and performs clerical office duties. CMS

**Optometrist.**    Examines eyes to determine visual efficiency and performance, diseases, or other abnormalities by means of instrumentation and observation, and prescribes corrective procedures. Conserves, improves, and corrects vision through use of lenses, prisms, vision therapy, visual training, and control of visual environment. MNS—MS

**Oral Pathologist.**    Examines and diagnoses tumors and lesions of mouth. Examines specimens from mouth to determine pathological conditions using microscope and other laboratory equipment and applying knowledge of dentistry. CLN—LN

**Oral Surgeon.**    Performs surgery on mouth and jaws. Executes difficult and multiple extractions of teeth. Removes tumors and other abnormal growths. Prepares mouth for insertion of dental prostheses. Corrects abnormal jaw relations, and sets fractures of jaws. LMS—M—MS

**Order Clerk.**    Processes orders for material or merchandise received by mail or telephone or personally from customer. Informs customer of unit prices, shipping date, anticipated delays, and any additional information needed by customer. Records and files copy of orders received according to expected delivery date. C

**Order-Department Supervisor.**    Coordinates activities of personnel of order-writing department. Directs establishment and maintenance of customer order records, such as discount classifications, cost basis, special routing, and transportation information. Supervises workers writing master orders used by production, shipping, invoicing, advertising, cost, and estimating departments. B—BCN

**Order Detailer.**    Compiles specifications from customer's order to provide detailed worksheets for use in plant as guides in assembly or manufacture of products. Computes data for worksheet, such as quantity of materials, production rate, completion date, and method to be used. CMN—CN

**Orientation and Mobility Instructor.**    Teaches the visually handicapped person how to use a sighted person as a guide; how to use a cane to travel in both familiar and unfamiliar surroundings; and how to use arms and hands for protection in moving about in familiar indoor settings. MS—S

**Ornithologist.**    Studies origin, interrelationships, classification, life histories, habits, life processes, diseases, relation to environment, growth and development, genetics, and distribution of birds. Studies birds in natural habitat and collects, dissects, and examines specimens. L

**Orthodontic Technician.**    Constructs and repairs appliances for straightening teeth according to orthodontist's prescription. Shapes, grinds, polishes, carves, and assembles metal and plastic appliances, such as retainer, tooth bands, and positioners. Tests appliances for conformance to specifications. M

**Orthodontist.**    Prevents, diagnoses, and corrects deviations from normal that occur in growth, development, and position of teeth and other dental/facial structures. Designs intra- and extraoral appliances to alter position and relationship of teeth and jaws to produce and maintain normal function. M—MS

**Orthopedic Surgeon.**    Deals with bones of the human skeleton, including all problems related to the treatment of muscles, tendons, joints, fractures, and dislocations. May treat patients without surgery, using appliances such as casts and braces, supplemented by special exercises as remedies. LMS—M—MS

**Orthoptist.**    Aids person with correctable focusing defects to develop and use binocular vision. Measures visual acuity, focusing ability, and motor movement of eyes. Develops visual skills, near-visual discrimination, and depth perception, using developmental glasses and prisms. M—MNS—MS

**Orthotist.**    Provides care to patients with disabling conditions of limbs and spine by fitting and preparing devices known as orthoses. Formulates design of orthosis; performs fitting and makes adjustments to ensure fit, function, cosmesis, and quality of work. M—MS

**Osteopathic Physician.**    Diagnoses, prescribes for, and treats diseases of human body, relying upon medical and surgical modalities and, when deemed beneficial, manipulative therapy of biomechanics. Examines patient and corrects disorders of musculoskeletal system. May practice any of known medical and surgical specialties. CMS—LMS

**Otolaryngologist.**    Diagnoses and treats diseases of ear, nose, and throat. Determines nature and extent of disorder, and prescribes and administers medications or surgery. Performs tests to determine extent of loss of hearing or speech due to disease or injury to ear, larynx, and related areas. LMS—MNS

**Package Designer.**    Designs containers for products, such as food, beverages, toiletries, cigarettes, and medicines. Confers with representatives of other departments to determine type of product market and market requirements. Renders design and fabricates model in paper, wood, glass, plastic, or metal, and makes necessary changes in product before manufacture. M

**Paleontologist.**    Studies fossilized remains of plants and animals found in geological formations to trace evolution and development of past life and identify geological formations. Prepares reports on findings for further scientific study, or as aid to location of natural resources, such as petroleum-bearing formations. May organize scientific expeditions and supervise removal of fossils from soil deposits and rock formations. L

**Paraoptometric.**    Functions as technical aide to optometrist. Performs preliminary eye tests. Determines the power of lenses in old and new prescriptions; assists the patient in frame selection; instructs patient on the proper wear and care of contact lenses; and works with individual who has perceptual difficulties. May work with patients who require lenses and special therapeutic devices after cataract surgery. BMS—MNS—MS

**Parasitologist.** Studies characteristics, habits, and life cycles of animal parasites, such as protozoans, tapeworms, flukes, and other parasitic organisms, to determine manner in which they attack human beings and animals and effects produced. Develops methods and agents to combat parasites. L

**Parcel-Post Clerk.** Wraps, inspects, weighs, and affixes postage to parcel-post packages and records C.O.D. and insurance information. May compute cost of merchandise, shipping fees, and other charges, and bill customer. C

**Parking Analyst.** Develops plans for construction and use of revenue-producing vehicle parking facilities. Plans and conducts comprehensive field surveys to locate sites for new facilities. LM

**Park Ranger.** Enforces laws, regulations, and policies in state or national park. Provides information pertaining to park use, safety requirements, and points of interest. Directs traffic, investigates accidents, and patrols area to prevent fires, vandalism, and theft. Directs or participates in first aid and rescue activities. May supervise workers engaged in construction and maintenance of park facilities. BL

**Park Superintendent.** Coordinates activities of park rangers and others engaged in development, protection, and utilization of national, state, or regional park. Prepares estimates of costs to plan, provide, or improve fish and wildlife protection, recreation, and visitor safety. B

**Parole Officer.** Engages in activities related to release of juvenile or adult offenders from correctional institutions. Establishes relationship with offender and studies offender's social history prior to and during institutionalization. Helps parolee secure necessary education or employment and refers parolee to social resources of community that can aid in rehabilitation. LS—S

**Parts-Order and Stock Clerk.** Purchases, stores, and issues spare parts for motor vehicles or industrial equipment. Keeps records of parts received and issued, and periodically inventories parts in storeroom. C

**Passenger-Service Representative.** Renders variety of personal services to airline passengers requiring other than normal service, such as company officials, distinguished persons, foreign-speaking passengers, invalids, and unaccompanied children. BCS—BS

**Passport-Application Examiner.** Approves applications for passports and related privileges and services. Answers questions of individuals concerning applications procedures. C

**Patent Attorney.** Specializes in patent law. Advises clients, such as inventors, investors, and manufacturers, concerning patentability of inventions, infringement of patents, validity of patents, and similar matters. Prepares applications for patents. Prosecutes or defends clients in patent-infringement litigations. May specialize in protecting American trademarks and copyrights in foreign countries. BCL—BL—BLM—CLM

**Pathologist.** Studies nature, cause, and development of diseases, and structural and functional changes caused by them. Makes diagnosis from body tissues, fluids, secretions, and other specimens of presence and stage of disease, using laboratory procedures. Performs autopsies to determine nature and extent of disease, cause of death, and effects of treatment. CL—L

**Patients' Librarian.** Directs library program for residents and staff of hospital or correctional institution. Prepares operational budgets, reviews requests, and selects books according to mental state, educational background, and special needs of residents. CNS—CS

**Pawnbroker.** Estimates pawn or pledge value of such articles as jewelry, cameras, and musical instruments, and lends money to customer. Weighs gold or silver articles or employs acid tests to determine karat content and purity to verify value of articles. Computes interest when pledges are redeemed or extended. Sells unredeemed pledged items. B—BC

**Payroll Clerk.** Computes and records earnings from time sheets, then subtracts deductions, such as income-tax withholdings, Social Security payments, union dues, insurance, credit-union payments, and bond purchases. Enters net wages on earnings-record card, check, check stub, and payroll sheet. CN

**PBX Operator.** Operates switchboard to relay incoming, outgoing, and interoffice calls. May operate system of bells to call individuals to the phone. May perform clerical duties, such as typing, proofreading, and sorting mail. C

**Pediatrician.** Plans and carries out medical-care program for children from birth through adolescence. Other fields of interest and responsibilities span such areas as infectious diseases, newborn care, environmental hazards, nutrition, accident prevention, drugs, cardiology, and pediatric pharmacology. LNS—LS

**Penologist.** Specializes in research on punishment for crime and control and prevention of crime, management of penal institutions, and rehabilitation of criminal offenders. BLS—LS

**Performance Analyst.** Predicts flight vehicle performance and variations affected by aerodynamic configuration, propulsion system, and mode of operation. Calculates lift and drag characteristics for the appropriate flight regime (speed, altitude, and atmosphere) and range of vehicle attitudes. Interprets and applies given propulsion and weight data. Determines the relative effects of major design parameters and their optimum relationship to each other to guide the design improvement of existing or projected vehicle designs. Calculates the specific performance characteristics of designated vehicles from the point of take-off or launch, through acceleration, cruise, reentry or deceleration, and landing. LN

**Periodontist.** Treats inflammatory and destructive diseases of tissue near teeth. Cleans and polishes teeth, eliminates irritating margins of fillings, and corrects occlusions. LMS—MNS

**Personal Manager.** Manages affairs of performers in negotiating with officials of unions, motion picture or television studios, theatrical productions, or entertainment center in regard to favorable contracts and fees. Advises client concerning contracts, wardrobe, and effective presentation of act. Manages business details of tours and engagements, and makes disbursements for road expenses. BC—BCS—BS

**Personnel Administrator.** Advises management concerning the maximum utilization of the talents of individual employees. Interviews and hires new employees, evaluates their progress and potential, trains them for greater efficiency, explains and enforces management policies and procedures, arbitrates differences, plans wage and salary schedules, supervises benefit programs, and ensures compliance with labor laws. B—BN—BNS

**Personnel Scheduler.** Compiles weekly personnel-assignment schedules for production department in manufacturing plant. Studies production schedules to determine personnel requirements. CNS

**Pesticide-Control Inspector.** Inspects operations of distributors and commercial applicators of pesticides to determine compliance with government regulations on handling, sale, and use of pesticides. CL

**Petroleum Engineer.** Applies the basic sciences of chemistry, geology, and physics to the development, recovery, and field processing of petroleum. Evaluates probable well production rate during natural or simulated-flow production phases. Provides technical consultation during drilling operations to resolve problems such as bore directional change or invasion of subsurface water in well bore. LMN—MN

**Petroleum-Engineering Professor.** Conducts college or university courses for prospective petroleum engineers. Prepares and delivers lectures, assigns outside readings, and compiles and evaluates examinations. Materials center around technical and cost factors to plan methods of recovering maximum oil and gas. MNS

**Petroleum Geologist.** Explores and charts stratigraphic arrangement and structure of earth to locate gas and oil deposits. Studies well logs, analyzes cores and cuttings from well drillings, and interprets data obtained by electrical or radioactive well logging. LMN—MN

**Petroleum Inspector.** Inspects consignments of crude or refined petroleum to certify conformance with contract specifications. Measures amounts, calibrates tanks, and examines for discoloration or water. CMN

**Petroleum Researcher.** Researches petroleum reservoirs to determine what engineering techniques should be used to secure maximum economic recovery of the petroleum. Also, some research is aimed toward the development of improved methods for assisted oil recovery. LMN

**Petrologist.** Investigates composition, structure, and history of rock masses forming earth's crust. Applies findings to such fields of investigation as causes of formations, breaking down and weathering, chemical composition and forms of deposition of sedimentary rocks, methods of eruption, and origin and causes of physical changes. LM

**Pharmaceutical Detailer.** Sells ethical drugs and other pharmaceutical products to physicians, dentists, hospitals, and retail and wholesale drug establishments. Discusses dosage, use, and effect of new drugs and medicinal preparations. B

**Pharmacist.** Specialist in the science of drugs—their composition, chemical and physical properties, manufacture, and uses in the normal body as well as in the person who is ill. Familiar with tests for purity and strength. CLN—LN

**Pharmacologist.** Studies effects of drugs, gases, dusts, and other materials on tissues and physiological processes, noting effects on circulation, respiration, digestion, or other vital processes. Standardizes drug dosages or methods of immunizing against industrial diseases. CLN—LN

**Photogrammetrist.** Analyzes data and prepares original maps, charts, and drawings from aerial photographs, and surveys and applies standard mathematical formulas and photogrammetric techniques to identify, scale, and orient geodetic points, elevations, and other planimetric or topographic features and cartographic detail. LMN—MN

**Photographic Engineer.** Designs and constructs special-purpose photographic equipment and materials for use in scientific or industrial applications, utilizing knowledge of various engineering disciplines, chemistry, and photographic equipment and techniques. May have specialty in high-speed photography, radiography, graphic arts, or aerial and space photography. MN

**Photographic-Equipment Technician.** Assembles, repairs, and tests cameras and photographic equipment according to specifications. Measures camera shutter speed and adjusts mechanism. Verifies accuracy of light meters, measures speed of movie cameras, and repairs lenses that need focusing. CMN

**Photography Teacher.** Conducts courses in photography. Prepares and delivers lectures, stimulates class discussion, and demonstrates functions of photographic equipment. Provides laboratory experience and evaluates students' work. MNS

**Photojournalist.** Photographs newsworthy events, locations, people, or other illustrative or educational material for use in publications or telecasts. Usually specializes in one phase of photography, such as news, sports, or special features, or as free-lance photographer. LM

**Photolithographer.** Sets up and operates camera to photograph illustrations and printed material and produces film or glass negatives or positives used in the preparation of lithographic printing plates. M

**Physiatrist.** Specializes in clinical and diagnostic use of physical agents and exercises to provide physiotherapy for physical, mental, and occupational rehabilitation of patients. Instructs physical therapist and other personnel in nature and duration of treatment, and prescribes exercises designed to develop functions of specific anatomical parts or specific muscle groups. MS

**Physical Anthropologist.** Studies meanings and causes of human physical differences and interrelated effects of culture, heredity, and environment on human form. Studies human fossils and their meanings in terms of long-range human evolution. Studies growth patterns, sexual differences, and aging phenomena of human groups, current and past. L

**Physical Chemist.** Studies the physical characteristics of and investigates the reactions of atoms and molecules, to seek quantitative explanations stated in precise mathematical terms. LN—N

**Physical-Education Instructor.** Teaches individual and team sports to students, utilizing knowledge of sports techniques and physical capabilities of students. Teaches advanced calisthenics, gymnastics, or corrective exercises, determining type and level of difficulty of exercises, corrections needed, and appropriate movements. S

**Physical Metallurgist.** Investigates and conducts experiments concerned with physical characteristics, properties, and processing of metals to develop new alloys, applications, and methods of commercially fabricating products from metals. Consults with engineers and officials to develop methods of manufacturing alloys at minimum cost. LN

**Physical Therapist.** Plans and administers medically prescribed physical-therapy treatment programs for patients to restore function, relieve pain, and prevent disability following disease, injury, or loss of body part. Works at hospital, rehabilitation center, nursing home, or home health agency, or in private practice. Reviews and evaluates physician's referral and patient's medical records to determine physical-therapy treatment required. Instructs patient in physical-therapy procedures to be continued at home. CMS—LMS

**Physical-Therapy Aide.** Uses therapy equipment to help patient strengthen muscles. Aide performs some clerical duties and attends to the upkeep of mechanical equipment. CMS

**Physician.** Attends to variety of medical cases in general practice: examines patients; orders or executes various tests, analyses, and X-rays to provide information on patient's condition; analyzes reports and findings of tests and of examination, and diagnoses condition; administers or prescribes treatment and drugs; provides prenatal care to pregnant women, delivers babies, and provides postnatal care to mother and infant; and reports births, deaths, and outbreak of contagious diseases to proper authorities. LNS—LS

**Physicist.** Most physicists specialize in one branch or more of the science; elementary-particle physics; nuclear physics; atomic, electron, and molecular physics; physics of condensed matter; optics, acoustics, and plasma physics; and the physics of fluids. Growing numbers of physicists are specializing in fields combining physics and a related science, such as astrophysics, biophysics, chemical physics, and geophysics. LMN—LN

**Physiologist.** Conducts research on cellular structure and organ-system functions of plants and animals. Studies growth, respiration, circulation, excretion, movement, reproduction, and other functions of plants and animals under normal and abnormal conditions. Performs experiments to determine effects of internal and external environmental factors on life processes and functions, and studies glands and their relationship to bodily functions. L

**Planimeter Operator.** Traces boundary lines of land plots on aerial photographs to determine acreage, using planimeter. Records figures. CMN

**Plant Breeder.** Plans and carries out breeding studies to develop and improve varieties of crops. Improves specific characteristics, such as yield, size, quality, maturity, and resistance to frost, drought, disease, and insect pests, utilizing principles of genetics and knowledge of plant growth. CMN

**Plant Pathologist.** Conducts research in nature, cause, and control of plant diseases and decay of plant products. Studies and compares healthy and diseased plants to determine symptoms of diseased condition. Isolates disease-causing agent, studies habits and life cycle, and devises methods of destroying or controlling agent. L

**Plant Physiologist.** Performs research on physiological processes in plants, including photosynthesis, respiration, mineral-element nutrition, water relations, absorption, and translocation; effects of light, temperature, and moisture; effects of chemicals on plant growth; effects and nature of plant growth regulators; physical properties and chemical composition and their relation to soil and atmospheric environment; maturity, ripening, storage life, and quality of plants. L

**Plasma Physicist.** Conducts theoretical and experimental research relating plasma diagnostic techniques to combustion studies. This work is directed toward establishing the feasibility of producing desirable modifications of combustion phenomena and flame properties utilizing the principles of plasma physics. Conducts basic theoretical and experimental studies on the properties and behavior of inhomogeneous plasmas, such as the excitation of plasma oscillations by means of electron beams, measurement of plasma oscillation damping caused by various mechanisms, diffusion of both gaseous and electron-hole plasmas across magnetic fields, and diagnostic research on radio propagation in plasmas. LMN

**Plastics Engineer.** Deals with taking apart raw materials, such as coal tar, coal, petroleum, wood, natural gas, and salt, and rearranging their molecules to make synthetic materials. May engage in pure research, design, development, technical service, marketing, consulting, or teaching. LMN

**Plastic Surgeon.** Specializes in skin grafts and bone transplants to restore or repair damaged, lost, or deformed parts of face and body. LMS

**Playroom Attendant.** Entertains children in nursery of department store, country club, or similar establishment as service to patrons. Reads aloud, organizes games, and gives elementary lessons in arts and crafts. CMS—CS

**Plumber.** Assembles, installs, and repairs pipes, fittings, and fixtures of heating, water, and drainage systems, according to specifications and plumbing codes. Studies building plans and working drawings to determine work required and sequence of installations. M

**Podiatrist.** Diagnoses foot ailments, diseases, and congenital or acquired deformities. Treats diseases and deformities of foot by mechanical, electrical, and surgical methods. Prescribes drugs. Does not perform foot amputations. Refers patients to other physician when symptoms observed in feet and legs indicate systemic disorders, such as arthritis, heart disease, diabetes, or kidney trouble. LS

**Police-Academy Instructor.** Instructs probationary and experienced police officers in such phases of police work as police science, police ethics, investigative methods and techniques, government, law, community relations, marksmanship, self-defense, and care of firearms. LS

**Police Chief.** Directs and coordinates activities of police department. Coordinates and administers daily police activities through subordinates. Directs activities of personnel engaged in preparing budget proposals, maintaining police records, and recruiting men. May assist one or more subordinates in investigation or apprehension of offenders. B

**Police Inspector.** Inspects police stations and examines personnel and case records to ensure that police personnel conform to prescribed standards of appearance, conduct, and efficiency. Prepares reports concerning discipline, efficiency, and condition of force within division. May serve as police liaison on civic boards engaged in improving community living. CS

**Police Officer.** Patrols assigned beat on foot, using mo-

torcycle or patrol car, or on horseback to control traffic, prevent crime or disturbance of peace, and arrest violators. Reports hazards; renders first aid at accidents and investigates causes and results of accident; inspects public establishments requiring licenses to ensure compliance with rules and regulations; warns or arrests persons violating animal ordinances; and issues tickets to traffic violators. LS

**Policy-Loan Calculator.** Compiles and computes loan or surrender value of life insurance policy and calculates repayments using interest tables. CN—N

**Political-Science Professor.** Teaches political behavior of specialized groups, individuals, and political systems. Analyzes political history while teaching students to interpret the results. May be a consultant to business groups or lobbies. BLS

**Political Scientist.** Studies phenomena of political behavior, such as origin, development, operation, and interrelationships of political institutions. Conducts research utilizing information available on governmental institutions, public law and administration, political party systems, and international law. Analyzes and interprets results of studies, and prepares reports detailing findings, recommendations, or conclusions. BL—L

**Pollution-Control Engineer.** Plans and conducts engineering studies to analyze and evaluate pollution problems, methods of pollution control, and methods of testing pollution sources to determine physiochemical nature and concentration of contaminants. Performs engineering calculations to determine pollution emissions from various industrial sources and to evaluate effectiveness of pollution-control equipment. BMN—LMN

**Polygraph Examiner.** Interrogates and screens individuals to detect deception or to verify truthfulness, using polygraph techniques which measure and record bodily changes. Interprets, diagnoses, and evaluates emotional and nonemotional reactions to questions recorded on graph. May appear in court as witness on matters relating to polygraph examinations. CLS—LS

**Postal Clerk.** Sells postage stamps, postal cards, and stamped envelopes; issues money orders; registers and insures mail and computes mailing costs of letters and parcels; examines mail for correct postage and cancels mail; weighs parcels and letters and computes mailing cost based on weight and destination. C

**Postmaster.** Organizes and supervises workers engaged in postal activities such as processing incoming and outgoing mail; issuing and cashing money orders; selling stamps, bonds, and certificates; and collecting box rents, to ensure efficient service to patrons. Confers with suppliers to obtain bids for proposed purchases; requisitions supplies; and disburses funds as specified by law. BC

**Poultry Scientist.** Conducts research in breeding,

feeding, and management of poultry. Examines selection and breeding practices to increase efficiency of production and improve quality of poultry products. Studies effects of management practices and processing methods on quality of eggs and other poultry products. LN

**Poultry Veterinarian.** Advises individual poultry raisers on poultry problems. Gathers information on care, condition, performance, and action of birds from owner. Inspects flocks, pens, and housing. Diagnoses disease and prescribes treatment. Culls undesirable birds from flock. Suggests feed changes to increase egg production or growth of fowl. LN

**Preparole-Counseling Aide.** Provides individual and group guidance to inmates of correctional facility who are eligible for parole and assists in developing vocational and educational plans in preparing inmates for reentry into community life. BS—S

**Preservationist.** Restores and preserves archaeological specimens. Records treatment of each artifact. Cleans and repairs ancient pottery, weapons, and tools as a whole or fragmented remains. CLM

**Printed Circuit Designer.** Designs and drafts layout for printed circuit boards (PCBs) according to engineering specifications, using knowledge of electronics, drafting, and standard design requirements. M

**Prisoner-Classification Interviewer.** Interviews new prison inmates to obtain social and criminal histories to aid in classification and assignment of prisoners to appropriate work and other activities. Gathers data, such as work history; school, criminal, and military records; family background; habits; religious beliefs; and prisoner's version of crime committed. Analyzes prisoner's social attitudes, mental capacity, character, and physical capabilities and prepares admission summary based on data obtained. CLS

**Probate Lawyer.** Specializes in settlement and planning of estates. Drafts wills, deeds of trusts, and similar documents to carry out estate planning of clients. Probates wills and represents and advises executors and administrators of estates. BLN—BNS—CNS—LNS

**Proctologist.** Diagnoses and treats disorders of the lower digestive tract. LMS

**Procurement Clerk.** Compiles information and records to prepare purchase orders for procurement of material. Consults catalogs and interviews suppliers to obtain prices and specifications. Compiles records of items purchased or transferred between departments; prices; deliveries; and inventories. May compare prices, specifications, and delivery dates and award contract to bidders or place orders with suppliers. BC—BCN

**Produce-Department Manager.** Supervises and coordinates activities of workers in retail store. Assigns duties to workers and schedules work hours and vacations. Evaluates worker performance and recommends retention, transfer, or dismissal. Orders

merchandise, supplies, and equipment. May plan department layout or merchandise or advertising display; listen to customer complaints; and examine returned merchandise. B

**Production-Control Supervisor.** Supervises and coordinates activities of those who expedite flow of materials, parts, assemblies, and processes within or between departments of industrial plant. Schedules sequences of operations and work flow. BCM

**Production Clerks' Supervisor.** Supervises and coordinates activities of production clerks engaged in keeping records and preparing statistical statements on production of manufactured goods and use of raw materials. BCN

**Production Engineer.** Plans and coordinates production procedures in an industrial plant. Directs production departments; introduces more efficient production-line methods; and initiates and directs other procedures to increase company output. LM

**Production-Planning Supervisor.** Plans and prepares production schedules for manufacture of industrial or commercial products. Analyzes production specifications and plant-capacity data and performs mathematical calculations to determine manufacturing processes, tools, and manpower requirements. Plans sequence of fabrication, assembly, installation, and other manufacturing operations. CLN—CN

**Professor of Educational Statistics.** Conducts college or university course in educational statistics. May also teach related courses in tests and measurements. Stimulates class discussion, assigns problems, grades students' performance. May conduct research. LNS—NS

**Project Engineer.** Directs, plans, and formulates engineering program and organizes project staff. Assigns project personnel to specific phases or aspect of project, such as technical studies, product design, preparation of specifications and technical plans, and product testing. Evaluates and approves design changes, specifications, and drawing releases. BMN

**Promotion Designer.** Works for a specific company and designs the material necessary to sell the company's services or products, with the exception of consumer advertising. The output may include brochures, slide presentations, catalogs, posters, and direct mail pieces. BM

**Proof-Machine-Operator Supervisor.** Supervises and coordinates activities of workers engaged in operating machines to sort, record, and prove records of bank transactions. Trains new workers to operate machines. BCM

**Proofreader.** Reads typescript (original copy) or proof of type setup to detect and mark for correction any grammatical, typographical, or compositional errors. May measure dimensions, spacing, and positioning of page elements (copy and illustrations) to verify conformance to specification. C—CN

**Prosthetics Technician.** Fabricates, fits, maintains,

and repairs artificial limbs, plastic cosmetic appliances, and other prosthetic devices, according to prescription specifications and under guidance of prosthetist. Tests prostheses for freedom of movement, alignment of parts, and biomechanical stability. M

**Prosthetist.** Provides care to patients with partial or total absence of limb by planning fabrication of, writing specifications for, and fitting devices known as prostheses under guidance of and in consultation with physician. Evaluates prosthesis on patient and makes adjustments to ensure fit, function, comfort, and workmanship. Instructs patient in prosthesis use. LMS

**Protozoologist.** Studies characteristics, habits, and life cycle of one-celled, free-living, and parasitic organisms to determine manner in which they attack human beings and animals and effects produced. L

**Provider.** Compiles detailed work sheets from customer's order for use in textile plant. Computes data for work sheet such as quantity of materials to be used, mixing of printing colors, cloth printing process, production rates, and completion date. CMN

**Psychiatric-Hospital Cook.** Prepares meals for patients and employees of psychiatric hospital and oversees patients assigned to kitchen for work therapy. Performs usual cooking procedures and encourages, praises, diverts, or corrects patient-worker as necessary to guide patient during work therapy. BMS

**Psychiatric-Hospital Groundskeeper.** Maintains the grounds of psychiatric hospital. Cuts lawns, trims flower beds, prunes shrubs and trees, rakes and burns leaves, etc. Demonstrates work methods to orient patient-worker. Observes, encourages, praises, diverts, or corrects patient-worker to monitor and guide patient during work therapy. BMS

**Psychiatric Nurse.** Works under the supervision of a psychiatrist in the treatment of mental patients. Provides therapy and clinical nursing care, counsels and provides assistance in the planning of treatment, and carries out the administrative and technical aspects of nursing. LNS—LS

**Psychiatric Social Worker.** Provides psychiatric social work assistance to mentally or emotionally disturbed patients and to their families, collaborating with psychiatric and allied team in diagnosis and treatment plan. Investigates case situations and presents information to other members of health team on patient's family and and social background pertinent to diagnosis and treatment. CLS—LS—S

**Psychiatrist.** Studies, diagnoses, and treats mental, emotional, and behavioral disorders. Organizes data concerning patient's family, personal (medical and mental) history, and onset of symptoms obtained from patient, relatives, and other sources. Orders laboratory and other special diagnostic tests and evaluates data obtained. Treats or directs treatment of patient utilizing a variety of psychotherapeutic methods and medications. LNS—LS

**Public Finance Specialist.** Applies principles of accounting to analyze past and present financial operations and estimates future revenues and expenditures to prepare budget. May assist communities to develop budget and efficient use of funds. BN

**Public-Health Dentist.** Determines changes, trends, and discrepancies in community dental-care pattern. Conducts field trials on new dental equipment, methods, or procedures. Instructs community, school, and other groups on dental hygiene. BMS—MNS

**Public-Health Educator.** Plans, organizes, and directs health-education programs for group and community needs. Develops and maintains cooperation among public, civic, professional, and voluntary agencies. Prepares and disseminates educational and informational materials. Promotes health discussions in schools, industry, and community agencies. BS

**Public-Relations Representative.** Plans, directs, and conducts public-relations program designed to create and maintain a public informed of employer's programs, accomplishments, or point of view. Prepares and distributes fact sheets, news releases, photographs, scripts, motion pictures, or tape recordings to media representatives. May specialize in researching data, creating ideas, writing copy, laying out artwork, contacting media representatives, or representing client before general public. B

**Public-Utility Sales Representative.** Solicits prospective and existing commercial and residential clients to promote economical use of utilities. Quotes rates and installation charges and estimates operating costs. BMN

**Pulp and Paper Tester.** Tests samples of each batch of pulp and run of paper, using standard testing equipment and chemical analyses, to control quality and uniformity of products. Records test data and prepares report for machine operators. L—LN

**Purchasing Agent.** Purchases raw materials or other unprocessed goods for processing, or machinery, equipment, tools, parts, produce, and other supplies or services necessary for operation of organization. Estimates values according to knowledge of market prices. Reviews bid proposals from vendors and enters into contracts within budget. BCN—BN

**Purchasing Analyst.** Compiles and analyzes statistical data to determine feasibility of buying products and to establish price objectives for contract transactions. Keeps informed on price trends and manufacturing processes. Obtains data for cost analysis; confers with vendors; and analyzes vendor's operations to determine factors that affect prices. LN

**Purchasing Manager.** Directs and coordinates activities of personnel engaged in purchasing and distributing raw materials, equipment, machinery, and supplies. Analyzes market and delivery conditions to determine present and future material availability. BLN

**Quality-Control Coordinator.** Coordinates activities of workers engaged in testing and evaluating product in order to control quality of manufacture and to ensure compliance with any legal standards. BC—BCM—BCN

**Quality-Control Engineer.**  Plans and directs activities concerned with development, application, and maintenance of quality standards for processing materials into partially finished material or product. Develops and initiates methods and procedures for inspection, testing, and evaluation. LN

**Quality-Control Technician.**  Tests and inspects products at various stages of production process and compiles and evaluates statistical data to determine and maintain quality and reliability of products. Selects products for tests at specified stages in production process, and tests for such criteria as dimensions, performance, and mechanical, electrical, or chemical characteristics. LN

**Quantitative Psychologist.**  Administers, scores, and interprets intelligence, aptitude, achievement, and other psychological tests. Times and records results. Interprets test results in light of standard norms, and limitations of test in terms of validity and reliability. NS

**Radiation Therapist.**  A physician who specializes in the use of radiation for the treatment of disease. Uses radiation therapy, radiologic physics, treatment planning, implantation of radiation sources, and radiation safety. The therapist is aware of the effect of ionizing radiations on cells and tissues, their quantitative assessment, and the mechanisms by which they occur and may be modified or enhanced. LMS

**Radiobiologist.**  Studies the effects of radiation on living material, including both plants and animals. Studies are performed at all levels of molecular damage, alterations of subcellular levels, cell death or altered function, and harmful effects on intact tissues or organs. LN

**Radiologic Technologist.**  May specialize in X-ray technology, which is primarily concerned with the diagnosis of disease and injury; radiation-therapy technology, used in the treatment of disease; of nuclear-medicine technology, employed in the diagnosis and treatment of disease by the use of radioactive substances. LM—LMS

**Railroad Station Agent.**  Supervises and coordinates activities of workers engaged in selling tickets and checking baggage at railroad station. Answers inquiries from patrons concerning schedules. Requisitions supplies; and verifies records of daily ticket sales and cash receipts. BC

**Range Manager.**  Conducts research in range problems to provide sustained production of forage, livestock, and wildlife. Plans and directs construction and maintenance of range improvements, such as fencing, corrals, reservoirs for stock watering, and structures for soil-erosion control; develops methods for controlling poisonous plants and for protecting range from fire and rodent damage; and develops improved practices for range reseeding. L

**Rate-and-Cost Analyst.**  Supervises and coordinates statistical clerks engaged in compiling power-generation and transmission data, preparing charts and graphs, and making statistical computation for utility district. Analyzes and interprets trends to assist in planning budgets and construction expenditures. LN

**Rate Supervisor.**  Supervises traffic-rate clerks engaged in determining and quoting rates applicable to shipments of merchandise, products, and equipment. Using existing rates and routes, tries to effect reduction in transportation costs and prepares reports of estimated savings. BCN

**Real-Estate Agent.**  Is generally an independent sales worker who contracts services with a licensed broker. Shows and sells real estate, handles rental properties, and obtains "listings" (owner agreements to place properties for sale with the firm). Represents property owners in selling or renting their properties. B—BCN

**Real-Estate Appraiser.**  Appraises property to determine value for purchase, sale, investment, mortgage, or loan purposes. Interviews persons familiar with property; inspects property for construction condition and functional design; computes depreciation and reproduction costs; considers location; and searches public records of sales, leases, and assessments. BMN—BN—N

**Reception Clerk.**  Interviews applicants for employment and processes application forms. Refers qualified applicants to employing official. May inform applicant of acceptance or rejection for employment. May compile personnel records. BCS

**Receptionist.**  Receives callers at establishment, determines nature of problem or business, and directs them to their destinations. C—CS

**Record Clerk.**  Compiles data and computes statistics for use in statistical studies from source materials, such as production and sales records, quality-control and test records, personnel records, time sheets, survey sheets, and questionnaires. Assembles, classifies, and computes statistical data according to formulas. CN

**Recording Engineer.**  Operates disk or tape recording machine to record music, dialogue, or sound effects of phonograph recording sessions, radio broadcasts, television shows, training courses, or conferences, or to transfer transcribed material to sound-recording medium. M

**Records-Management Analyst.**  Examines and evaluates records-management systems to develop new or improve existing methods for efficient handling, protecting, and disposing of business records and information. Drafts office and storage area layout to plot location of equipment and to compute space available. CLM

**Recreation Facility Manager.**  Manages recreation facilities, such as tennis courts, golf courses, or arcade. Coordinates activities of workers engaged in providing services. B

**Recreation Leader.**  Conducts recreation activities with groups in such facilities as settlement house, institution for children or aged, hospital, armed services, and penal institution. Organizes, promotes, and develops interest in arts and crafts, sports, games, music, dramatics, social recreation, camping, and hobbies. S

**Recreational Therapist.** Plans, organizes, and directs medically approved recreation program for patients in hospitals and other institutions. Content of program is regulated in accordance with patients' capabilities, needs, and interests. Prepares reports for patient's physician or treatment team, describing patient's reactions and symptoms indicative of progress or regression. LS—S

**Referral Aide.** Receives callers and responds to complaints. Questions callers to ascertain nature of complaints, then routes to proper department. Contacts complainant to verify data and follows up on results of referral. CLS—CS

**Reliability Engineer.** Analyzes preliminary engineering-design concepts of major product, such as aircraft, naval vessel, or electronic communication or control system, to recommend design or test methods for attaining customer-specified operational reliability. LM

**Religious-Activities Director.** Directs activities of denominational group to meet religious needs of students. Advises groups in promoting interfaith understanding. Provides counseling and guidance relative to marital, health, financial, and religious problems. BLS—CLS—CS

**Research Mathematician.** Conducts research in such branches of mathematics as algebra, geometry, number theory, logic, and topology, and studies and tests hypotheses and alternative theories. Acts as adviser or consultant to research personnel concerning mathematical methods and applications. LN

**Reservation Clerk.** Obtains travel and hotel accommodations for guests and employees of industrial concern. Prepares passenger travel booklet containing tickets, copy of itinerary, written lodging confirmations, pertinent credit cards, and travel suggestions. Keeps current directory of hotels, motels, and timetables, and answers inquiries concerning routes, fares, and accommodations. C

**Reservoir Engineer.** Responsible for developing the strategy to be used in predicting oil and gas reserves. Estimates the amount of oil and gas contained in the reservoir based on existing engineering and geologic data. Predicts the amount of oil and gas that can be recovered, the number and spacing of wells required, and the rates at which these wells will produce. LN

**Residence Counselor.** Provides individual and group guidance services to dormitory students relative to problems of scholastic, educational, and personal-social nature. Supervises dormitory activities; investigates reports of misconduct and attempts to resolve or eliminate cause of conflict. May interview all dormitory students to determine need for counseling. S

**Respiratory Therapist.** Renders treatment, under physician's orders, to patients with lung disorders such as asthma, emphysema, pneumonia, and bronchitis. May work in pulmonary laboratory to help evaluate various cardiopulmonary diseases, and assist the physician in determining the type and extent of the patient's disease, as well as how well the therapy prescribed is working. LMS—MS

**Respiratory-Therapy Aide.** Assists personnel in therapy department of hospital, performing such tasks as cleaning, disinfecting, and sterilizing equipment and supplies used. Assists in administration of gas or aerosol therapy to patients. MS

**Retail-Store Art Director.** Designs the store's posters and signs and interiors. May plan the ads that a store places with various publications. BM

**Retirement Officer.** Provides information and advice concerning provisions and regulations of retirement program for employees. Explains retirement annuity system to personnel officers and covered employee groups. BLS—BNS—BS—NS

**Right-of-Way Agent.** Negotiates with property owners and public officials to secure purchase or lease of land and right-of-way for utility lines, pipelines, and other construction projects. May examine public records to determine ownership and property rights. May be required to know property law. BL

**Roulette Dealer.** Conducts gambling at roulette table. Ensures that wagers are placed before winning number is determined, announces winning number, and computes payable odds. Pays winning bets and collects losing bets. CN

**Safety Engineer.** Develops and implements safety program to prevent or correct unsafe environmental working conditions, utilizing knowledge of industrial processes, mechanics, chemistry, psychology, and industrial health and safety laws. Designs, builds, and directs installation of guards on machinery, belts, and conveyors. Inspects premises for fire hazards and adequacy of fire protection. LM

**Safety Inspector.** Inspects machinery, equipment, and working conditions to ensure compliance with occupational safety and health regulations. Tests working areas for noise, toxic materials, and other hazards. Investigates accidents to ascertain causes for use in recommending preventive safety measures and developing safety program. BCM—CM

**Sales Manager.** Manages sales activities of establishment. Directs staffing, training, and performance evaluations to determine and control sales program. Assigns territories to sales personnel. Reviews market analyses to determine customer needs, volume potential, price schedules, and discounts rates, and develops sales campaign. B

**Sanitation Officer.** Enforces sanitation regulations and laws concerned with food processing and serving, collection and disposal of solid wastes, sewage treatment, noise, ventilation, etc. May conduct training program in environmental health practices. CMS

**Schedule Planning Manager.** Negotiates with governmental regulatory body for changes in airline company's flight schedule. Considers factors such as current and projected traffic load, routes of competitors, and profitability of route operations. BN

**School Media Specialist.** Assesses needs of students and faculty for information, and develops programs to stimulate students' interest in reading and use of resources. Selects and organizes books, films, tapes, records, and other materials and equipment. CLS

**School Nurse.** Plans policies, standards, and objectives of school health program, in cooperation with medical authority and administrative school personnel. Participates in medical examinations and reviews findings to evaluate health status of pupils and progress of program. Instructs classes in child care, first aid, and home nursing, and establishes nursing policies to meet emergencies. LS

**School Secretary.** Performs secretarial duties in school. Receives and deposits funds for lunches, school supplies, and student activities. May procure assignments and texts for absent students for delivery to homes. C—CS

**School Social Worker.** Aids children having difficulty adapting to school life. Consults with parents, teachers, and other school personnel to determine causes of problems and effect solutions. Recommends treatment to effect remedy. Serves as liaison between school and community resources, such as family-service agencies, child-guidance clinics, protective services, doctors, and ministers. CLS—LS

**School Superintendent.** Directs and coordinates activities concerned with administration of school system. Administers program for selection of school sites and construction of buildings; directs preparation and presentation of school budget and determines amount required to finance educational program; supervises examining, appointing, training, and promotion of teaching personnel. B

**Secondary-School Teacher.** Teaches one or more subjects to students in secondary schools using various teaching methods. Prepares teaching outline for course of study, assigns lessons, and corrects homework papers. Administers tests to evaluate pupils' progress. BCS—BS—S

**Secretary.** Schedules appointments, gives information to callers, takes dictation, and otherwise relieves officials of clerical work and minor administrative and business details. Reads and routes incoming mail. Composes and types routine correspondence; files correspondence and other records; oversees clerical workers; and records minutes of staff meetings. BC—C

**Secretary to Town Health Services.** Carries out minor administrative and general secretarial office duties in municipal office of health services. CMS

**Securities-Brokerage Manager.** Directs and coordinates brokerage activities concerned with buying or selling commodities, contracts, or securities and mutual funds. Establishes internal control procedures to control margin accounts, short sales, and options and

to reduce office errors and client complaints. Conducts staff meetings of personnel to discuss changes in policy or redirection of sales emphasis. B

**Security Consultant.** Plans, directs, and oversees implementation of comprehensive security systems for protection of individuals, homes, and businesses. Investigates various crimes against client. BLS

**Seed Analyst.** Tests seed for germination, purity, and weed content. Plants definite number of seeds in box of pure soil and counts number of plants that grow to calculate percentage of germination. Inspects seed with magnifying glass or microscope for chaff, bits of wood, and weed content. L

**Seismologist.** Determines the place and time that earthquakes occur each year. For earthquakes, instrumentally recorded work is done in analysis centers, built around large computers housed in university or government laboratories. LMN

**Services Clerk.** Compiles reports and calculates tariff assessments for services rendered vessels using harbor facilities. BCN—CN

**Set Designer.** Designs and creates stage sets for theatrical productions. Confers with director regarding interpretation and set requirements. Conducts research to determine appropriate architectural and furnishing styles. Renders sketches and models of ideas, estimates costs, and presents drawings for approval. Must have a knowledge of drawing, plan drafting, painting, model building, carpentry, and lighting. M

**Shipping-and-Receiving Clerk.** Verifies and keeps records on incoming and outgoing shipments and prepares items for shipment. Determines best method for shipment. Examines incoming shipments, records storage, and corresponds with shipper to rectify damages. BCN—CN

**Shopping Investigator.** Shops in commercial, retail, and service establishments to test integrity of sales and service personnel, and evaluates sales techniques and services rendered to customers. Observes employees during sales transactions to detect irregularities in listing prices or handling cash. BCL

**Silviculturist.** Manages tree nurseries and thins forests to encourage natural growth of sprouts or seedings of desired varieties. Conducts research in such problems of forest propagation and culture as tree growth rate, effects of thinning on forest yield, duration of seed viability, and effects of fire and animal grazing on growth, seed production, and germination of different species. BL—BLN

**Skating-Rink Manager.** Manages ice- or roller-skating rink and coordinates activities of workers engaged in selling admission tickets, issuing skates to patrons, and enforcing skating rules and regulations. Plans and initiates promotional projects to advertise establishment. B

**Social Director.** Creates friendly atmosphere for guests in hotels and resorts or for passengers aboard ship. Greets new arrivals, acquaints them with recreational facilities, encourages them to participate in activities. Arranges details of planned activities and may assist management in resolving guests' complaints. BCS—CS

**Social-Group Worker.** Develops program content and organizes and leads activities planned to enhance social development of individual members and accomplishment of group goals. Interviews and plans group composition in relation to personal and social compatibility of members. CLS—LS—S

**Social Psychologist.** Investigates psychological aspects of human interrelationships to gain understanding of individual and group thought, feeling, and behavior. Evaluates individual and group behavior, developing such techniques as rating scales and sampling methods to collect and measure data. Conducts surveys and polls to measure and analyze attitudes and opinions as basis for predicting economic, political, and other behavior. LNS—LS

**Social-Services Director.** Directs agency providing services in social-welfare field to individuals, groups, or community. Works with board of directors and committees to establish policies and programs and administers such programs. May direct or coordinate fund-raising, public relations, and fact-finding or research activities. B

**Sociologist.** Studies the behavior and interaction of groups; traces their origin and growth; and analyzes the influence of group activities on individual members. These groups include families, tribes, communities, and governments, along with a variety of social, religious, political, business, and other organizations. May be involved in research, writing, or administration at a university; may supervise or consult with the operation of social-service agencies. LS

**Soil Scientist.** Studies soil characteristics and maps soil types, and investigates responses of soils to known management practices to determine use capabilities of soils and effects of alternative practices on soil productivity. L

**Solid-State Physicist.** Conducts research into phases of physical phenomena. Studies crystals of metals, insulators, and semiconductors. Develops theories and laws on basis of observation and experiments and devises methods to apply laws and theories of physics to industry, medicine, and other fields. Performs experiments with various types of equipment to observe structure and properties of matter, transformation and propagation of energy, relationships between matter and energy, and other physical phenomena. N

**Space Physicist.** Studies the region between the planets, such as nuclear particles, atoms and molecules, dust and meteorites, various kinds of radiation, and nearly perfect vacuums. The findings are used in designing protection systems for astronauts as well as establishing satellites for weather forecasting and for long-range relay of television programs and telephone calls. N

**Special-Education Director.** Formulates special-education programs and policies for public shools, public

agencies, and state institutions, relating to education and training of mentally and physically handicapped children. Organizes and conducts conferences to interpret policies and programs and train and prepare teachers, instructors, and other personnel. Administers federally funded contracts and ensures that goals are met. BS

**Spectographer.** Conducts spectrographic examinations of metal and mineral samples using various measuring instruments. Computes percentage composition of samples by comparing intensity ratio with standard charts. N

**Speech Pathologist.** Specializes in diagnosis and treatment of speech and language problems to restore communicative efficiency to individuals with communication problems. Provides counseling and guidance to speech- and language-handicapped individuals, May direct scientific projects investigating biosocial phenomena associated with voice, speech, and language. LS

**Sporting-Goods Salesperson.** Sells sporting goods and athletic equipment. Explains care of equipment, regulations of games, and fish and game laws. Informs customers of areas for hunting, fishing, or skiing, and cost of such outings. B

**Sports Marketer.** Creates and implements marketing relationships between athletes and product sponsors, including commercials and endorsements. B

**Stationary Engineer.** Operates and maintains stationary engines and mechanical equipment, such as steam engines, air compressors, generators, motors, turbines, and steam boilers to provide utilities such as light, heat, or power for buildings and industrial processes. M

**Statistical Clerk.** Compiles data and computes statistics for use in statistical studies. Assembles and classifies statistics, then computes. CLN—N

**Statistician.** Conducts research into mathematical theories and proofs that form basis of science of statistics and develops statistical methodology. Examines theories, such as probablity and inference, to discover mathematical bases for new or improved methods of obtaining and evaluating numerical data. N

**Stenotype Operator.** Takes dictation of correspondence, reports, and other matter on machine that writes contractions or symbols for full words on paper roll. Operates typewriter to transcribe notes. C

**Stockbroker.** Buys and sells stocks and bonds for individuals and organizations as representative of stock-brokerage firm, applying knowledge of securities, market conditions, government regulations, and financial circumstances of customers. Transmits buy or sell orders to trading division in accordance with customer's wishes. Develops portfolio of selected investments for customers. B—BN

**Stockroom Supervisor.** Supervises and coordinates activities of workers concerned with ordering, receiving, storing, inventorying, issuing, and shipping materials, supplies, tools, equipment, and parts, in stockroom, warehouse, or yard. Studies records and recommends remedial actions for reported nonusable, slow-moving, and excess stock. BC

**Storage-Battery Inspector.** Inspects and tests storage batteries in process of manufacture or before shipment to verify conformity with mechanical, chemical, and electrical specifications. Examines for defects, tests specific gravity of acids, and records inspection results. CMN

**Stratigrapher.** Studies relative position and order of succession of deposits containing or separating archaeological fossil or plant material. Studies relation of life of past ages, evolutionary changes as recorded by fossil animals and plants, and successive changes in distribution of land and sea as interpreted from character and fossil content of sedimentary rocks. L

**Summer-Camp Director.** Directs activities of recreation or youth work camp. Plans programs of recreational and educational activities; hires and supervises camp staff; arranges for required licenses, certificates, and insurance coverage to meet health, safety, and welfare standards for campers and for camp operation. Keeps records regarding finances, personnel actions, enrollments, and program activities related to camp business operations and budget allotments. BCS

**Surgeon.** Performs surgery to correct deformities, repair injuries, prevent diseases, and improve function in patients. Examines patient to verify necessity of operation, estimate possible risk to patient, and determine best operational procedure. LMS

**Surgical-Appliance Salesperson.** Fits and sells surgical appliances, such as abdominal supports, braces, cervical collars, and artificial limbs, using knowledge of anatomy, orthopedics, orthotics, and prosthetics. Writes specifications for and orders custom-made appliances. BLM

**Surgical Technologist.** Works in the operating room performing a variety of tasks as a member of the surgical team. Is responsible for the cleanliness, safety, and efficiency of the operating room. Prepares materials for use at the operating table and assists in the use of these materials. May concentrate in a specialized area of operating-room surgery. LM

**Survey Worker.** Interviews people and compiles statistical information on public issues or consumer buying habits. Asks questions following specified questionnaire and classifies and sorts responses by specified criteria. CN

**Systems Analyst.** Analyzes business procedures and problems to refine data and convert them to programmable form for electronic data-processing. Specifies in detail logical and/or mathematical operations to be performed by various equipment units and/or comprehensive computer programs and operations to be performed by systems personnel. LN

**Tabulating-Machine Operator.** Operates machine that processes from tabulating cards into printed records. Observes machine for malfunctions; routes processed cards to next work station; and may tend machine that

performs individual functions such as sorting, interpreting, and collating. MN

**Tax Accountant.** Prepares tax returns of individual, business establishment, or other organization. Examines accounts and records and computes tax returns; advises management regarding effects of business, internal programs and activities and other transactions upon taxes and represents principal before various governmental taxing bodies. May devise and install tax record systems. BCN—BLN

**Tax Attorney.** Advises individuals, businesses, and other organizations concerning income, estate, gift, excise, property, and other federal, state, local, and foreign taxes. Prepares opinions on tax liability resulting from prospective and past transactions. Represents clients in tax litigation. BLN—BNS—CNS—NS

**Tax-Attorney Secretary.** Performs secretarial duties utilizing knowledge of accounting and legal terminology. Prepares legal papers; reviews tax journals and other publications to identify recent court decisions. Gives information to callers and relieves officials of minor clerical work or giving of minor advice. CNS

**Tax Auditor.** Audits financial records to determine tax liability. Reviews information gathered from taxpayer to verify net worth or reported financial status and identify potential tax issues. Analyzes issues to determine nature and direction of investigation required. Develops and evaluates evidence of taxpayer finances to determine tax liability. BCN—CN

**Tax-Fraud Investigative Aid.** Establishes files, documents, and correspondence relating to tax cases. Researches taxpayer's records and internal-management regulations. CNS—NS

**Taxpayer Service Representative.** Assists taxpayers by answering questions regarding tax matters. Provides information for individuals to aid in solving tax problems and determining federal tax obligations. BNS—CNS—NS

**Tax Preparer.** Prepares income tax returns for individuals and small businesses. Reviews financial records, income statements, and documentation of expenditures to determine forms needed. BCN—CN

**Teacher Aide.** Assists teaching staff. Plans, prepares, and develops various teaching aids and presents subject matter to students, using methods such as lecture, discussion, and supervised role playing. Prepares, gives, and grades examinations. CS

**Teacher of the Hearing-Impaired.** Teaches school subjects to aurally handicapped students, using various methods such as lipreading, finger spelling, cued speech, and sign language. Instructs deaf and hard-of-hearing students in communications skills; plans curriculum and prepares lessons; encourages students to participate in verbal learning experiences to ensure their comprehension of subject matter and to develop their social skills and ability to communicate. LS

**Teacher of the Visually Handicapped.** Teaches school subjects to visually handicapped, using Braille system. Transcribes lessons into Braille for blind students or into boldface type for partially sighted. Promotes other sensory learning experiences to ensure comprehension of subject matter. CMS

**Technical-Course Sales Representative.** Contacts prospects, explains courses and benefits, quotes fees, and advises prospective students on course selection on the basis of their vocational objectives. Frequently is graduate of program. BMS—BNS

**Technical Illustrator.** Lays out and draws illustrations for reproduction in reference works, brochures, and technical manuals dealing with assembly, installation, operation, maintenance, and repair of machines, tools, and equipment. Prepares drawings from blueprints, designs, mock-ups, and photoprints. May draw cartoons and caricatures to illustrate operation, maintenance, and safety manuals and posters. LM—M

**Technical Training Coordinator.** Coordinates activities of instructors engaged in training employees or customers of industrial or commercial establishment. BCL

**Technical Writer.** Develops, writes, and edits material for reports, manuals, briefs, instruction books, catalogs, and related technical and administrative publications concerned with work methods and procedures. CLM—LM

**Television Director.** Interprets script, conducts rehearsals, and directs and integrates all audio and video elements of television program. Informs technicians of scenery, light, props, and other equipment desired. Approves scenery, costumes, choreography, and music. Issues instructions to technicians during telecast to keep them informed of effects desired. BM —BMS

**Television Producer.** Plans and coordinates various aspects of television programs. Interviews and selects screenwriters and casts principals. Obtains costumes, props, music, and other equipment and personnel to complete production. Gives instructions to staff to schedule and conduct rehearsals; reviews production to ensure that objectives are attained; and reviews budget and expenditures for programs. B

**Test Fixture Designer.** Plots and draws schematics for test fixture heads used in testing printed circuit boards for electrical shorts and breaks. M

**Textile Stylist.** Originates designs for fabrication of cloth, specifying weave pattern, color, and gauge of thread, to create new fabrics according to functional requirements and fashion preferences of consumers. BMN

**Theatrical Special-Effects Technician.** Fabricates, installs, and activates equipment to produce special effects such as rain, snow, explosions, and other mechanical and electrical effects required by theatrical productions. Reads scripts to determine type of special effects required. LM

**Theater-Arts Teacher.** Teaches acting principles and techniques. Conducts readings to evaluate student's talent. Adapts course of study and training methods to meet student's need and ability. Rehearses and drills students to ensure that they master parts. Assigns nonperforming students to backstage production tasks, such as constructing, painting, and moving scenery, and operating stage lights and sound equipment. BS—S

**Theater Stage Manager.** Prepares rehearsal call sheets. Lays out acting areas, using tape and following floor plan. Oversees distribution of equipment and may supervise special effects. BCM

**Ticket Broker.** Purchases entertainment tickets in blocks at box office prices, usually before attraction opens. Prices tickets for profitable resale and sells tickets to public in accordance with legal regulations. BCN

**Tire Technician.** Tests experimental and sample production tires to determine strength, wearability, and causes of failure. Operates test equipment, analyzes results, and records information on graphs for comparisons. CLM

**Title Searcher.** Searches public and private records to compile list of legal instruments pertaining to property titles, such as mortgages, deeds, and assessments, for insurance, real estate, or tax purposes. C

**Tool-and-Die Maker.** Analyzes specifications, sets up and operates machine tools and fits and assembles parts to make and repair metalworking dies, cutting tools, gauges, and machinists' hand tools, applying knowledge of tool and die designs and construction, shop mathematics, metal properties, machining, and assembly procedures. LM—LMN—MN

**Tool Designer.** Designs broaches, milling-machine cutters, drills, and other cutting tools, and related jigs, dies, and fixtures for production or experimental use in metalworking machines. Studies specifications and confers with engineering and shop personnel to resolve design problems. Applies algebraic and geometric formulas and standard tool-engineering data to develop tool configuration. LMN

**Topographic Surveyor.** Calculates latitude, longitude, angles, areas, and other information for mapmaking from field notes secured by engineering survey party, using reference tables and calculating machine or computer. MN

**Tourist-Information Assistant.** Provides travel information to tourists at state information center. Answers questions concerning resorts, historical sights, and other tourist attractions. Helps tourist follow map and gives proper directions. CMS—CS

**Toxicologist.** Examines the interaction between chemicals and biologic mechanisms. Investigates the harmful effects of chemicals encountered either incidentally out of the atmosphere, by contact, or by introduction as food additives; explores the harmful effects of chemicals that are intentionally administered to ecosystems for the purpose of achieving a specific reaction; and examines the medical and legal implications of the harmful effects of chemicals on people. LNS

**Traffic Manager.** Directs and coordinates traffic activities of organization. Determines most efficient and economical routing and mode of transportation, using rate and tariff manuals and motor-freight and railroad guidebooks. Directs scheduling of shipments and notifies concerned departments or customers of arrival dates. CN

**Traffic-Rate Clerk.** Compiles and computes rates, fares, and other charges for transportation services according to rate tables and tariff regulations. CN—N

**Travel Agent.** Plans itineraries and arranges accommodations and other travel services for customers of travel agency. Considers destination, mode of transportation, travel dates, financial limitations, and accommodations required. BC

**Travel-Information-Center Supervisor.** Supervises the workers engaged in greeting and welcoming motorists at state highway information center. Provides maps, brochures, and directions to points of interest. BCS

**Trust-Evaluation Clerk.** Determines value of customer trust-account assets and charges fees to accounts for services. Computes unit value of assets to set fee. Compiles bond-price data, trust investment-fund reports, and analysis of customers' financial status. BCN

**Ultrasound Technologist.** Operates ultrasound diagnostic equipment to produce two-dimensional ultrasonic patterns and positive pictures of internal organs, for use by professional personnel in diagnosis of disease, study of malfunction of organs, and prenatal examination of fetus and placenta. LMS—MNS

**Urban Sociologist.** Specializes in research on origin, growth, structure, and demographic characteristics of cities and social patterns and distinctive social problems that result from urban environments. LNS

**Urologist.** Diagnoses and treats diseases and disorders of genitourinary organs and tract. Performs surgery as indicated. Prescribes and administers urinary antiseptics to combat infections. LMS

**Vector Control Assistant.** Assists public health staff in activities concerned with identification, prevention, and control of disease-carrying insects and rodents. L

**Veterinarian.** Diagnoses and treats diseases and disorders of animals. Advises on care and breeding of animals. May restrict practice to dogs, cats, and other pets, or to single species, such as cattle, horses, or poultry. May engage in research and development, consultation, administration, teaching, technical writing, and sale or production of commercial products. L—LS

**Veterinary Bacteriologist.** Studies biology, ecology, etiology, and immunology of bacteria and other microorganisms causing diseases in animals. Investigates efficiency of vaccines, antigens, antibiotics, and other materials in prevention, diagnosis, and control of animal diseases. CL—L

**Veterinary-Hospital Attendant.** Cleans and disinfects animal cages, and sterilizes laboratory equipment and surgical instruments. Examines animals for signs of illness; records such information as genealogy, diet, weight, medications, food intake, and license number. Anesthetizes, inoculates, bathes, clips, and grooms animals. C

**Veterinary-Laboratory Technician.** Prepares vaccines, biologicals, and serums for prevention of animal diseases and tests vaccines for sterility and virus inactivity. May administer vaccines to animals. CNS

**Video Operator.** Controls video console to regulate transmission of television scenes. Previews program to be used next to determine that signal is functioning and that program will be ready at required time. MN

**Vocational Rehabilitation Consultant.** Develops and coordinates implementation of vocational rehabilitation programs. Monitors program operations and recommends additional measures to ensure programs meet defined needs. BLS

**Voice Pathologist.** Diagnoses and treats voice disorders, such as those associated with professional use of the voice. LS

**Volume Computer.** Tends machine, equipped with pen attachments and meter charts, that computes volume of gas flowing through meter. Records computations in log. CMN

**Wage-and-Salary Administrator.** Directs development and application of techniques of job analysis, job description, evaluation grading, and pricing in order to determine and record job factors and to determine and convert relative job worth into monetary values to be administered according to pay-scale guidelines and policy. BL—BLN

**Wardrobe Supervisor.** Attends to costumes of members of cast. Refits and redesigns costumes to fill needs and desires of individual cast members. Supervises others who aid cast in quick costume changes. BMS

**Warehouse Manager.** Directs warehousing activities for commercial or industrial establishment. Establishes operational procedures for incoming and outgoing shipments, handling and disposition of materials, and keeping warehouse inventory current. BC

**Water-Pollution Technician.** Determines the extent of pollution in bays, estuaries, and the oceans; involved in research concerning control and abatement of industrial and other pollutants. Assists life scientists in conducting ecological studies in waters suspected of being polluted. LN

**Water-Treatment-Plant Operator.** Controls treatment-plant machines and equipment to purify and clarify water for human consumption and for industrial use. Records data, such as residual content of chemicals, water turbidity, and water pressure. CM—CMN

**Weapons-Instrument Mechanic.** Repairs, tests, and calibrates optical-mechanical instruments, such as range finders and gun directors, according to specifications. Fabricates replacement parts, adjusts readings on instruments to calibrate properly, and measures dial graduations to verify accuracy. CMN

**Wedding Consultant.**  Advises prospective brides in all phases of wedding planning, such as etiquette, attire of wedding party, and selection of trousseau. May compile and maintain gift register; attend rehearsals and wedding ceremony to give advice on etiquette; and accompany bride when shopping in store. BS

**Weighing-and-Measuring-Instruments Salesperson.**  Sells scales, dynamometers, and other measuring devices, utilizing knowledge of capabilities and limitations of measuring instruments, engineering specifications, and catalogs. BN

**Weight Engineer.**  Calculates weight data of structural assemblies, components, and loads of ships, planes, space vehicles, and missiles. Studies weight factors involved in new designs or modifications. May prepare cargo and loading sequences to maintain balance of vehicle within specified load limits. LMN—MN

**Welfare Director.**  Directs administration of public welfare program in conformity with policies of welfare board to plan activities and expenditures. Coordinates activities of staff engaged in investigating and counseling welfare claimants and in processing welfare claims. B—BLS

**Wharfinger.**  Compiles reports such as dockage, demurrage, wharfage, and storage, to ensure that shipping companies are assessed specified harbor fees. Compares information on statement, records, and reports with ship's manifest to determine that weight, measurement, and classification of commodities are in accordance with tariff. C

**Wholesaler.**  Manages establishment engaged in purchasing, wholesaling, and distributing merchandise and supplies to retailers, industrial and commercial consumers, or professional personnel. B

**Wildlife-Control Agent.**  Controls animal population in geographical district and investigates crop- and property-damage claims caused by wildlife. Recommends changes in hunting and trapping regulations and seasons, and relocation of animals in overpopulated areas. CL

**Wood Technologist.**  Conducts research to determine composition, properties, behavior, utilization, development, treatments, and processing methods of wood and wood products. Develops and improves methods of seasoning, preservation, and treating wood with substances to increase resistance to wear, fire, fungi, and insects. LN

**Word-Processing Specialist.**  Processes written communications for business. Takes dictation by means of dictating and transcribing equipment. Frequently uses automatic typewriter. C

**Yacht Designer.**  Designs original plans and remodeling plans for yachts, powerboats, cruisers, and sailing boats. Uses stock designs for those who cannot afford custom designs. Inspects and evaluates boats for prospective buyers, insurance companies, and money-lending institutions. BM

**Youth Correctional-Education Supervisor.**  Directs and coordinates educational, administrative, and counseling activities of educational programs in juvenile halls, prison farms, halfway houses, and programs that serve youth offenders. Establishes and maintains relationships with wardens, state departments of Education and Corrections. BMS

**Zoologist.**  Studies origin, interrelationships, classification, life histories, habits, life processes, diseases, relation to environment, growth and development, genetics, and distribution of animals. Studies animals in natural habitat and collects specimens for laboratory study. L—LN

## BUSINESS

| | | | | |
|---|---|---|---|---|
| 1. a b c d | 13. a b c d | 25. a b c d | 37. a b c d | 49. a b c d |
| 2. a b c d | 14. a b c d | 26. a b c d | 38. a b c d | 50. a b c d |
| 3. a b c d | 15. a b c d | 27. a b c d | 39. a b c d | 51. a b c d |
| 4. a b c d | 16. a b c d | 28. a b c d | 40. a b c d | 52. a b c d |
| 5. a b c d | 17. a b c d | 29. a b c d | 41. a b c d | 53. a b c d |
| 6. a b c d | 18. a b c d | 30. a b c d | 42. a b c d | 54. a b c d |
| 7. a b c d | 19. a b c d | 31. a b c d | 43. a b c d | 55. a b c d |
| 8. a b c d | 20. a b c d | 32. a b c d | 44. a b c d | 56. a b c d |
| 9. a b c d | 21. a b c d | 33. a b c d | 45. a b c d | 57. a b c d |
| 10. a b c d | 22. a b c d | 34. a b c d | 46. a b c d | 58. a b c d |
| 11. a b c d | 23. a b c d | 35. a b c d | 47. a b c d | |
| 12. a b c d | 24. a b c d | 36. a b c d | 48. a b c d | |

## CLERICAL

| | | | | |
|---|---|---|---|---|
| 1. a b c d | 17. a b c d | 33. a b c d | 49. a b c d | 65. a b c d |
| 2. a b c d | 18. a b c d | 34. a b c d | 50. a b c d | 66. a b c d |
| 3. a b c d | 19. a b c d | 35. a b c d | 51. a b c d | 67. a b c d |
| 4. a b c d | 20. a b c d | 36. a b c d | 52. a b c d | 68. a b c d |
| 5. a b c d | 21. a b c d | 37. a b c d | 53. a b c d | 69. a b c d |
| 6. a b c d | 22. a b c d | 38. a b c d | 54. a b c d | 70. a b c d |
| 7. a b c d | 23. a b c d | 39. a b c d | 55. a b c d | 71. a b c d |
| 8. a b c d | 24. a b c d | 40. a b c d | 56. a b c d | 72. a b c d |
| 9. a b c d | 25. a b c d | 41. a b c d | 57. a b c d | 73. a b c d |
| 10. a b c d | 26. a b c d | 42. a b c d | 58. a b c d | 74. a b c d |
| 11. a b c d | 27. a b c d | 43. a b c d | 59. a b c d | 75. a b c d |
| 12. a b c d | 28. a b c d | 44. a b c d | 60. a b c d | 76. a b c d |
| 13. a b c d | 29. a b c d | 45. a b c d | 61. a b c d | 77. a b c d |
| 14. a b c d | 30. a b c d | 46. a b c d | 62. a b c d | 78. a b c d |
| 15. a b c d | 31. a b c d | 47. a b c d | 63. a b c d | |
| 16. a b c d | 32. a b c d | 48. a b c d | 64. a b c d | |

## LOGIC

| | | | | |
|---|---|---|---|---|
| 1. a b c d | 12. a b c d | 23. a b c d | 34. a b c d | 45. a b c d |
| 2. a b c d | 13. a b c d | 24. a b c d | 35. a b c d | 46. a b c d |
| 3. a b c d | 14. a b c d | 25. a b c d | 36. a b c d | 47. a b c d |
| 4. a b c d | 15. a b c d | 26. a b c d | 37. a b c d | 48. a b c d |
| 5. a b c d | 16. a b c d | 27. a b c d | 38. a b c d | 49. a b c d |
| 6. a b c d | 17. a b c d | 28. a b c d | 39. a b c d | 50. a b c d |
| 7. a b c d | 18. a b c d | 29. a b c d | 40. a b c d | 51. a b c d |
| 8. a b c d | 19. a b c d | 30. a b c d | 41. a b c d | 52. a b c d |
| 9. a b c d | 20. a b c d | 31. a b c d | 42. a b c d | 53. a b c d |
| 10. a b c d | 21. a b c d | 32. a b c d | 43. a b c d | 54. a b c d |
| 11. a b c d | 22. a b c d | 33. a b c d | 44. a b c d | |

## MECHANICAL

| | | | | |
|---|---|---|---|---|
| 1. a b c d | 10. a b c d | 19. a b c d | 28. a b c d | 37. a b c d |
| 2. a b c d | 11. a b c d | 20. a b c d | 29. a b c d | 38. a b c d |
| 3. a b c d | 12. a b c d | 21. a b c d | 30. a b c d | 39. a b c d |
| 4. a b c d | 13. a b c d | 22. a b c d | 31. a b c d | 40. a b c d |
| 5. a b c d | 14. a b c d | 23. a b c d | 32. a b c d | 41. a b c d |
| 6. a b c d | 15. a b c d | 24. a b c d | 33. a b c d | 42. a b c d |
| 7. a b c d | 16. a b c d | 25. a b c d | 34. a b c d | 43. a b c d |
| 8. a b c d | 17. a b c d | 26. a b c d | 35. a b c d | |
| 9. a b c d | 18. a b c d | 27. a b c d | 36. a b c d | |

## NUMERICAL

| | | | | |
|---|---|---|---|---|
| 1. a b c d | 11. a b c d | 21. a b c d | 31. a b c d | 41. a b c d |
| 2. a b c d | 12. a b c d | 22. a b c d | 32. a b c d | 42. a b c d |
| 3. a b c d | 13. a b c d | 23. a b c d | 33. a b c d | 43. a b c d |
| 4. a b c d | 14. a b c d | 24. a b c d | 34. a b c d | 44. a b c d |
| 5. a b c d | 15. a b c d | 25. a b c d | 35. a b c d | 45. a b c d |
| 6. a b c d | 16. a b c d | 26. a b c d | 36. a b c d | 46. a b c d |
| 7. a b c d | 17. a b c d | 27. a b c d | 37. a b c d | 47. a b c d |
| 8. a b c d | 18. a b c d | 28. a b c d | 38. a b c d | |
| 9. a b c d | 19. a b c d | 29. a b c d | 39. a b c d | |
| 10. a b c d | 20. a b c d | 30. a b c d | 40. a b c d | |

## SOCIAL

| | | | | |
|---|---|---|---|---|
| 1. a b c d | 12. a b c d | 23. a b c d | 34. a b c d | 45. a b c d |
| 2. a b c d | 13. a b c d | 24. a b c d | 35. a b c d | 46. a b c d |
| 3. a b c d | 14. a b c d | 25. a b c d | 36. a b c d | 47. a b c d |
| 4. a b c d | 15. a b c d | 26. a b c d | 37. a b c d | 48. a b c d |
| 5. a b c d | 16. a b c d | 27. a b c d | 38. a b c d | 49. a b c d |
| 6. a b c d | 17. a b c d | 28. a b c d | 39. a b c d | 50. a b c d |
| 7. a b c d | 18. a b c d | 29. a b c d | 40. a b c d | 51. a b c d |
| 8. a b c d | 19. a b c d | 30. a b c d | 41. a b c d | 52. a b c d |
| 9. a b c d | 20. a b c d | 31. a b c d | 42. a b c d | 53. a b c d |
| 10. a b c d | 21. a b c d | 32. a b c d | 43. a b c d | 54. a b c d |
| 11. a b c d | 22. a b c d | 33. a b c d | 44. a b c d | 55. a b c d |

# Acknowledgments

*Warm thanks to:*

Our clients: school headmasters, deans, and guidance counselors; employment agency managers; directors of women's centers; and especially the participants in our testing sessions throughout the years. Without you this book would never have been started.

Fred Hills, Senior Editor at Simon and Schuster, for his enthusiasm and expert editorial guidance through various stages of our manuscript.

Our literary agent, Julian Bach, for his encouragement, good advice, and friendship.

The U.S. Department of Labor, Bureau of Labor Statistics, for providing the *Dictionary of Occupational Titles and Occupational Outlook Handbook;* and to the hundreds of professional societies, trade associations, unions, industrial organizations, and colleges that have generously given us valuable career information for the Directory of careers.

# About the Authors

*Barry Gale* holds degrees in education, counseling, and psychological testing and has worked most of his adult life as a career counselor. A noted lecturer, he is President of Career Aptitude Testing, Ltd., and conducts seminars for educational institutions, corporations, and state governmental agencies, teaching positive solutions to workplace problems. *Linda Gale* is Executive Director of Career Aptitude Testing, Ltd., and coauthor of four career books.